PRINCIPLED SPYING

'If spying is the world's second oldest profession, or perhaps the oldest, ethical issues it raises are almost as old. But as this wonderful conversation between an eminent practitioner and a senior scholar displays, those have been reshaped by the long transition from royal sovereigns to popular sovereignty, and sharpened more recently by the focus on terrorism and the rise of big data. The former both makes "war" continuous and puts enormous pressure on warning. That pressure then stresses ethics in familiar collection, like interrogation, but also requires searching through big data sets, including information about innocent citizens for tips about would-be terrorists. Omand and Phythian creatively apply the principles of just war to intelligence, and make a strong argument for a new "social compact," one that benefits from the paradox of Edward Snowden's revelations, which were very damaging but also sparked a real conversation about privacy and other ethical issues inherent in intelligence in this era that is neither peace nor war.'

Gregory Treverton, former chair of the
US National Intelligence Council

'*Principled Spying* is a must read for all involved in the intelligence profession as well as for those who are interested in understanding how intelligence agencies can and should operate ethically in the 21st century. David Omand and Mark Phythian provide a comprehensive review and stimulating discussion of the role and responsibilities of intelligence professionals and how the ethical foundations of liberal democracies can be preserved and even strengthened by "principled spying." A most compelling narrative!'

John Brennan, Former Director, CIA

'Most people agree that a safe society means that intelligence gathering is necessary but too few agree on its limits in a free society. This valuable book, a debate between two informed and experienced experts, provides perceptive insights to help both the public and the policy makers come to the right decisions.'

George Robertson, Secretary General, NATO 1999-2003,
UK Secretary of State for Defence 1997-99

'A provocative work by an intelligence mandarin and senior scholar, both committed to ethical discourse and principles.'

Rhodri Jeffreys-Jones, author of *We Know All about You:
The Story of Surveillance in Britain and America*

PRINCIPLED SPYING

THE ETHICS OF SECRET INTELLIGENCE

DAVID OMAND AND
MARK PHYTHIAN

OXFORD
UNIVERSITY PRESS

OXFORD

UNIVERSITY PRESS

Great Clarendon Street, Oxford, OX2 6DP,
United Kingdom

Oxford University Press is a department of the University of Oxford.
It furthers the University's objective of excellence in research, scholarship,
and education by publishing worldwide. Oxford is a registered trade mark of
Oxford University Press in the UK and in certain other countries

© David Omand and Mark Phythian 2018

The moral rights of the author have been asserted

First Edition published in 2018

Impression: 1

British Library Cataloguing in Publication Data

Data available

ISBN 978-0-19-878559-0

Printed in Great Britain by
Clays Ltd, Elcograf S.p.A

CONTENTS

PREFACE

We came together some years ago as a former practitioner in the fields of intelligence, security, and defense and a professor of political science to discuss amicably in academic seminars the part that secret intelligence has played in Western society over the years and the strange fascination that it continues to exert over the public through books, films, and television. The question of how far a state should authorize its agents to go in seeking and using secret intelligence is one of the big unresolved issues of public policy for democracies in the early twenty-first century and sits at the heart of broader debates concerning the relationship between the citizen and the state. Publics need—and want—protection from the very serious threats posed by domestic and international Islamist terrorism and from serious criminality. They also want to be safe in using cyberspace and to have active foreign and aid policies to help resolve outstanding international problems. Secret intelligence is widely accepted as essential to these tasks and as a legitimate function of the nation-state, yet the historical record shows it also can pose significant ethical risks.

Public confidence in US and UK intelligence was rocked by the failures to assess correctly the intelligence on weapons of mass destruction in the run-up to the 2003 Iraq War, and the range of inquiries that followed posed acute ethical questions concerning the intelligence-customer relationship, political pressure, and truth telling. Coming on the heels of the Iraq War intelligence debacle was the exposure of the methods the United States used after the September 11, 2001, terrorist attacks (9/11) to capture and coercively interrogate terrorist suspects and its continued use of secret intelligence to target drone strikes to kill terrorist suspects. Not only has intelligence as a governmental activity come to have a greater global salience than ever before but also questions of ethics—what it is right to do and when and how boundaries should be drawn—are now seen as being central to intelligence activity.

Together we wrote up our discussions and published them in an article early in 2013 in the *International Journal of Intelligence and Counterintelligence*.[1] No sooner had we gone to print than controversy once again swept the media with the publication from mid-2013 onward of top secret US National Security Agency (NSA) and UK Government Communications Headquarters materials leaked by NSA contractor Edward Snowden. That material opened up a fresh public controversy over the subject of intelligence and ethics including many previously highly classified activities such as the mining of bulk personal data and computer interference. The US administration first commissioned a detailed review of its communications and intelligence technologies, and sought advice from the Privacy and Civil Liberties Oversight Board. Then President Barack Obama issued a new presidential policy directive to the US intelligence community tightening the rules for bulk and other digital intelligence gathering to enhance public confidence in privacy and civil liberties protection. The British government and Parliament in parallel embarked on the long and controversial journey that ended with a complete rewrite of terrorism investigation legislation and drafted the new Investigatory Powers Act 2016. Many of the academic and public events we have attended over the last few years to discuss the draft legislation and the ethical relationship between our rights to both privacy and security have been highly polarized and have left both of us, from our different vantage points, feeling dissatisfied with the quality of analysis being brought to bear.

As a first step, in light of the Snowden revelations, both of us contributed to a roundtable discussion on their implications in the journal *Intelligence and National Security*.[2] Both this work and our earlier article in the *International Journal of Intelligence and Counterintelligence* have proved very popular, testimony to the demand for perspective and a framework for approaching the complex issue of the ethics-intelligence relationship as well as to the enormous interest generated by the Snowden affair. By May 2017 the roundtable discussion had been "viewed" more than sixty-four hundred times and our article more than three thousand times, making them among the most read articles in their respective journals.[3]

We had both written previously about other aspects of intelligence ethics, including intelligence oversight, but felt that a comprehensive treatment of the subject was lacking. We believe in particular that *Principled Spying: The Ethics of Secret Intelligence* is the first examination of the subject that takes into account what has recently been revealed of digital intelligence, the fastest-growing and most controversial part of modern intelligence. For the democracies, retaining such advanced intelligence capabilities is a key part of national security as is retaining long-standing intelligence partnerships, such as between the United States and its close allies, as well as liaisons with many nations around the world. But we believe it is no longer possible to conduct such work without more explicit congressional, parliamentary, and public acceptance of the legal and ethical limits that should be placed on the intelligence agencies lest the manner in which they run their covert activities undermines the national values and freedoms that they exist to help defend. Democratic legitimacy is required for the safe conduct of secret intelligence.

Like the late Lord Bingham's book *The Rule of Law*, this account of how ethics impacts the world of secret intelligence is addressed to those who are inclined to think that ethical behavior sounds like a good thing rather than a bad thing and to those who wonder if it may not be rather important but are not quite sure what it is all about and would like to make up their minds.[4]

Although written in nontechnical terms, we situate the book in the wider academic and practitioner literature on intelligence in general and with that relating to ethics and intelligence in particular. Our objective is to put forward a clear framework for public policy in this vital area by clarifying the relationship between ethics and intelligence (chapter 1) and between ethics, intelligence, and the law (chapter 2). We discuss the utility of concepts drawn from Just War theory (chapter 3), such as right authority, proportionality, necessity, and discrimination, to help in the inevitable balancing exercise in weighing different ethical risks in the approval and conduct of secret intelligence activities. Rather different ethical issues arise that we consider in the traditional practice of running human secret agents (chapter 4) and the management of digital and other technical sources (chapter 5) that involve intrusion into personal data. Questions of the ethics of intelligence are not limited to issues arising in relation to intelligence collection and analysis. The possession of secret intelligence enables taking covert actions that have their own ethical problems, which deserve extended treatment (chapter 6), not least when intelligence allows lethal action to be taken against a located adversary or suspected adversary. We suggest some norms for nation-states to conduct secret intelligence properly, and we discuss how forms of oversight and accountability—internal, judicial, and legislative—can contribute to public confidence that the powerful capabilities of modern intelligence cannot be misused (chapter 7). We conclude with some speculations about the ethical issues that the development of threats and technologies may bring and how far we should look to identify norms of right conduct in global cyberspace.

In each chapter we identify the ethical issues and discuss them in the form of a dialogue between us. Rather than simply presenting our positions, throughout the book we pose key questions to each other and to the reader and offer different responses and perspectives that we hope can stimulate lively debate and thinking.

———————

One of us (David Omand) would like to acknowledge how helpful he found the discussions with many experts in the field while serving as a member of the Global Commission on Internet Governance chaired by former Swedish prime minister Carl Bildt, the openness shown by all the British intelligence and law enforcement agencies in providing evidence to the 2015 Royal United Services Institute's Independent Review of Privacy and Surveillance on which he sat, and the many discussions with David Anderson, the UK government's independent reviewer of counterterrorism legislation.[5]

We would like to thank Luciana O'Flaherty and Matthew Cotton at Oxford University Press and Don Jacobs at Georgetown University Press for their interest in this project and for their support. We are very grateful to Glenn Saltzman, our production editor at Georgetown, and Vicki Chamlee, our copy editor, for their excellent work in preparing the manuscript for publication. Many thanks to the three anonymous reviewers for their close reading of the manuscript and helpful comments, and to all those at Georgetown and Oxford involved in the production and marketing of the book. We would also like to thank Toby Mundy for his hard work and support in seeing this book through from an initial idea to final publication. Both of us are indebted to those former members of the secret intelligence world who have been prepared to engage in academic debate on their former profession. They would prefer, we are sure, to remain nameless, but we hope that more of them in future will come forward and ensure that debates can continue and be suitably grounded in the realities of intelligence work. Much of the credit goes to them, but for any errors and misstatements, the authors accept complete responsibility.

We owe our partners and families more than the customary gratitude for forbearance during the gestation of the book. Thank you.

Introduction

Why Ethics Matters in Secret Intelligence

Why do governments spy on each other and on members of their own populations? The reasonable justification for any intelligence activity is to acquire information that one believes will improve the quality of decision-making by statesmen, policy makers, military commanders, or police officers by reducing their ignorance about their operating environment. Better-informed decisions lead to better government and a safer and more secure society. It is a practice as old as history and one that future governments, armed forces, and police services are not ever going to renounce. What has changed dramatically in democratic societies in recent years, however, is the extent of public questioning about the ethics of methods used to obtain intelligence and thus the extent to which society needs to rein in its intelligence agencies.[1]

Ethics itself can be defined as "a social, religious, or civil code of behaviour considered correct, especially that of a particular group, profession, or individual."[2] Examples of recent behaviors by security and intelligence agencies that have not universally been considered correct abound. Did the US Central Intelligence Agency breach the international prohibition on torture when it waterboarded the al-Qaeda terrorist Khalid Sheikh Mohammed 183 times in attempts to extract intelligence about future attacks on the United States? Is it wrong to spy on friendly foreign leaders, such as the US interception of the mobile phone of German chancellor Angela Merkel? Was it necessary for the NSA to intercept and store communications data on all domestic telephone calls within the United States? Can it ever be justified for undercover officers to use sexual relations with those they are informing on to improve their cover? Is the commercial intellectual property theft

1

by hacking into company networks routinely carried out by the Chinese authorities an unacceptable extension of espionage activity? Is it acceptable to access the Internet communications of ordinary citizens in bulk to try and identify terrorist networks? By recruiting active agents in terrorist and criminal networks, are authorities colluding in serious wrongdoing to obtain intelligence? Did US and UK intelligence officers knowingly allow their governments to exaggerate the threat from Iraqi weapons of mass destruction to justify the 2003 invasion? Was the Russian hacking and other interference in the 2016 US presidential election a systematic subversion of the democratic system and, therefore, as *The Guardian* newspaper concluded, indefensible?[3]

Each of those examples, and many others that have been featured in the news, prompts questions that are at heart ethical in nature; that is, they raise issues of right and wrong conduct. By what standards should we live as members of democracies if we also want to protect our societies from those who do not share our values and wish to cause us harm? Can we license one set of rules for those we employ to defend us that differ from those we apply in our everyday life? Comparable issues have troubled political and spiritual thinkers for centuries while debating when and how the use of armed force to inflict death and destruction can be justified in defending the interests of the state. Today the debate has centered on the morality of intelligence gathering and its use.

That there is a genuine dilemma cannot be denied. Those with the secrets of value—hostile states and terrorist and criminal groups, for example—will go to almost any lengths to keep their secrets safe from prying eyes and ears. To overcome the determination of the person with the secret to keep can require the use of ethically questionable methods. Without activities such as intruding on personal communications, breaking into homes to plant bugs, hacking networks to steal plans, and persuading others to betray their oaths of loyalty to their state or to inform on their colleagues, the real secrets of value to the nation will not be obtained. Furthermore, the sources and methods employed to acquire the secret must remain hidden, or the person with the secret will easily be able to dodge the attentions of those trying to procure it.

Intelligence professionals have always argued that their difficult and sometimes dangerous job requires a license to break normal conventions precisely so that the governments that employ them can have done in the dark what ethically they dare not be caught doing in the day—in particular, stealing other people's secrets. Intelligence officers have thus traditionally been authorized by their governments to gather intelligence under the cloak of secrecy using methods that no democratic government could openly countenance for its everyday activities. Like Richard Wagner's Wotan, the powerful king of the gods who is prevented by the treaties engraved on his spear from doing what is necessary to rescue his kingdom, a convenient solution lies in creating the fearless hero not bound by conventional constraints and thus able to achieve for the king what the king cannot be seen to do himself. That is also the logic of James Bond's 007 license, and although it is as fictional as Wagner's operas, both are expressions of an underlying dynamic of statecraft.

In historical terms, only relatively recently have the ethics of covert intelligence agencies been a subject for public controversy. During the Cold War, for example, both sides conducted intensive intelligence operations against each other in a spy versus spy conflict. Only very episodically with some scandal or publicized triumph did the public become aware of the nature of the intelligence struggle. Not until the 1970s was the part that secret intelligence had played during the Second World War properly acknowledged. Until then the many thousands who had had direct contact with the world of secret intelligence kept quiet about their successes and failures. Most political leaders would not want to know the details of where the intelligence they saw came from, and intelligence professionals would have stared any ethical difficulties straight in the face and walked on.

At the end of the Cold War and the demise of the ideological challenge of Soviet communism, Western intelligence agencies shifted their resources to uncovering secrets and exposing terrorist movements; illegal arms traders; chemical, biological, radiological, and nuclear proliferators; and organized criminal gangs. The emphasis shifted from safeguarding the democratic institutions of the state from external attack and subversion to protecting the public from a variety of serious harms—some external, some internal—in a shift we can track from the concept of "the secret state" to that of "the protecting state."[4]

At the same time, social changes continued a decline in society's deference to authority generally. Intelligence and security activities could no longer rely on the invisibility cloak of national security to protect them from scrutiny when events hit the newspapers. It was to be expected that on behalf of the public, the media would ask whether bungling intelligence agencies had let foreign agents steal national secrets or had let terrorists strike. It was a short step to questioning what the security and intelligence agencies were actually doing to keep the public safe and whether the methods they were using had any democratic legitimacy. In Europe a series of cases from the European Court of Human Rights in the 1970s challenged the traditional view that raison d'état alone could justify the surveillance of citizens by secret agencies that did not legally exist. The rule of law, fundamental to a liberal democracy, requires that laws accessible to the citizen must prescribe when rights could be intruded on, by whom, and with what safeguards.

Professions such as medicine, law, and education are partly defined by having ethical codes of conduct that regulate their activity according to generally accepted standards of right behavior, with severe sanctions for those who do not conform. The public can therefore have reasonable confidence that psychoanalysts will protect the confidences of their patients, as do priests of their parishioners. Lawyers will not steal their clients' money. Teachers will not have sexual relationships with their pupils nor will doctors with their patients. Company executives will not obtain contracts by bribery. By contrast, secret intelligence might appear at first sight to be the one profession that has to be governed by a code of *anti-ethics*, a code of behavior with few, if any, rules so as to allow activity that most people would consider unethical if applied to their everyday lives.

It is certainly the case that an everyday morality that rules out theft, bribery, and corruption and emphasizes the value of honor and the duties of confidentiality and privacy rights cannot simply be applied to the business of getting and using secret intelligence. However, that does not have to mean there should be no limits on what should be sanctioned when trying to obtain secrets of value. In this book we aim to provide a vade mecum, or working guide, to thinking about norms of right conduct for intelligence activity. We believe that is essential since liberal democracies will certainly go on trying to obtain secret intelligence to defend themselves just as their adversaries must be expected to deploy secret intelligence to undermine them.

We do not believe there are any simple answers to the interlaced set of complex questions around the ethical standards we would want applied to modern intelligence activity. Dangerous times will call for different measures than peaceable ones. The technologies that can be harnessed to intelligence gathering will continue to change. International patterns of cooperation and competition may shift, along with recognition of the value of accepting norms of good conduct in cyberspace. Societal attitudes to values such as privacy may also continue to evolve.

Clearly these issues are important and deserve increasing attention. The approach we recommend is engaging in patient and rational debate that recognizes there is always more than one point of view and that each has validity and deserves consideration. Only through the clash of ideas informed by a consciousness of historical experience will the best approach for the moment appear. Nor do we believe that any single ethical methodology that moral philosophy can supply—such as the teleological, the deontological, and the aretaic—can be brought to bear on its own.[5]

Most of our debates in this book are informed by consequentialist arguments drawing on teleological schools of thought—that is, judging acts by their consequences. It matters that intelligence officers act with good intent and that they think hard on the unintended as well as intended outcomes from their actions. The degree of ethical risk of harm to others that they judge acceptable must bear a relationship to the harms they are trying to prevent through authorizing intelligence operations. For example, "dog fouling" is unpleasant and unhealthy but does not justify the intrusive surveillance British local government authorities used to identify the dog owners who fail to pick up after the dogs.[6] The principle of proportionality, however, should not mean that when the potential harm to society is very great, any method, including torture, would be justified. Nor does the value of anonymity to protect free speech mean that child abusers could claim a right to view anonymously criminally indecent images of children, even in private.

In talking to intelligence officers, it becomes clear that most of those who serve the interests of democratic nations implicitly follow an aretaic moral philosophy of life that emphasizes personal virtues and good character. They have ways of behaving well, even when knowingly encouraging betrayal or intruding on the privacy of private communications and family life. But experimental psychology amply demonstrates that even those who see themselves as highly moral actors can be led to behave in unacceptable ways when placed in an unhealthy environment.[7] So ethical issues in intelligence have a situational as well as a personal dimension, not least when it comes to designing safeguards to ensure that future governments cannot misuse intelligence capabilities.

ROADMAP OF THE BOOK

To unpack the issues, this volume takes the form of a debate between us, where in each chapter one of us puts forward a set of arguments, the other responds, and we engage in discussion designed to encourage reflection on how far the arguments and counterarguments resonate. One problem in seeking to debate the ethics of intelligence is the absence of a framework that takes us beyond debating the rights and wrongs of torture. This book, it is hoped, will provide such a framework.

In chapter 1 we examine the relationship between intelligence, the state, and the citizen to explore how far we can speak in terms of an inherent tension between ethics and intelligence. The rule of law is a fundamental principle by which liberal democracies set store, and in chapter 2 we examine how far intelligence activity with its moral exceptionalism can fit under the rule of law, and the nature of the relationship between law, ethics, and intelligence. Just because a valid legal justification can be found for an intelligence operation does not necessarily make it ethically sound. Recent advances in digital technology in particular have opened up new prospects for gathering intelligence on suspects from their Internet use but may have rendered much existing legislation ineffective as a means of controlling this data collection. Another question, which addresses the need for international reach in providing national security, concerns how far intelligence in the future can be left as a matter for national legislation exclusively and how far international norms, or even laws, can be expected to bear on the matter. International human rights obligations in particular are likely to constrain what democratic nations can do to access the personal data of each other's citizens and the personal data of their own citizens held by companies based in a foreign jurisdiction.

Having concluded that applying the rule of law is a necessary but not sufficient guide to intelligence ethics, we turn in chapter 3 to consider the application of the Just War approach. We examine how the concepts that underlie the ethics of military combat might be applied to the practice of intelligence. We distinguish between the classes of target that an intelligence agency may justly plan its collection capabilities around and the manner in which intelligence officers conduct themselves thereafter in much the same way as classic Just War theory distinguishes between just causes of war and the just conduct of war. From such considerations, key vocabulary emerges—such as "necessity," "proportionality," "right authority," and "last resort"—that can be employed to inform debates around ethical issues in intelligence. We consider the usefulness of these principles to the realm of intelligence.

In chapter 4 we address the ethical issues that arise in human intelligence activity that result from recruiting and managing secret agents and covert human sources. Not only is the use of coercive recruitment methods to blackmail individuals into cooperating generally disapproved of on consequentialist grounds, since such agents are likely to be unreliable, but also aretaic or behavioral constraints hold good intelligence officers back and make them feel morally responsible for the safety of their agents and their families. Collusion in wrongdoing is an ethical risk almost always associated with the recruitment of informants and agents within terrorist and criminal organizations, yet the information such active participants can provide may be the most likely to save lives.

The well-placed human source will always have an important role and be very highly regarded by an intelligence agency. Nevertheless, signals and technical intelligence since the Second World War has had an increasing importance in providing complementary information about potential adversaries and their armed forces. The end of the Cold War saw a distinct shift from a concentration on such state targets to gathering intelligence on non-state actors such as terrorist and criminal groups, proliferators, narcotics gangs, human traffickers, and pirates. At the same time, in an extraordinary historical coincidence, the development of the Internet and the World Wide Web created new supply opportunities for information about individuals: identities, communications, locations, movements, and methods of financing. In chapter 5, therefore, we look at the dynamic interaction between these demands for information on individuals, and the ability of the digital world to supply it, and the consequential major ethical concerns over mass surveillance and loss of privacy in personal communications.

Another area of ethical controversy over the last decade that we explore in chapter 6 concerns the uses that have been made of secret intelligence. Modern digital intelligence, for example, can pinpoint the location of an individual, and that intelligence can then be used to capture or kill the individual if he or she is believed to be an active terrorist in the context of the "find, fix, and finish" logic of intelligence-led counterterrorism. Less dramatic examples can also have serious consequences for individuals who may find themselves on a watch list or no-fly list as a result of covert intelligence gathering on their Internet use or from the "weaponization" of stolen information that can be used to harm them.

In contemporary liberal democratic contexts, the operation of oversight and accountability mechanisms mitigate the ethical risks that arise from the collection and use of secret intelligence. In chapter 7 we examine how confidence in democratic societies could be built that it is safe to provide these intelligence-gathering tools and techniques, that they are not being misused, and that taxpayer funds are being spent wisely and to good effect. Ethical issues abound here. For example, when intelligence activity is carried out in the public's name, how can it be truly subject to the public's consent when so many details of the activity must remain secret?

We conclude by looking ahead to some of the ethical dilemmas of the future as intelligence responds to changes in threat and technology. We illustrate the ethical issues that arise in liberal democratic contexts from the tensions between the value of secrecy and of transparency, between domestic and overseas intelligence gathering, between reliance on the use of open sources and of secret sources, between conducting surveillance on known suspects and intelligence gathering to uncover new threats, between the interests of law enforcement and of national security, and finally between the use of military and civilian assets. We end with an appeal for a new social contract between the public, their representatives in elected government and its intelligence agencies, and the private corporations that increasingly manage and use our personal information. In the end, liberal democracies need the consent of the public to confirm the ethical soundness of the activities carried out in their citizens' names and in their interest.

1

Thinking about the Ethical Conduct
of Secret Intelligence

Mark Phythian: Those setting out to think about the relationship between ethics and secret intelligence are immediately confronted with a serious problem—the absence of a clear framework within which to proceed. The starting point in the construction of a framework needs to be the concept of intelligence itself. As the study of intelligence has developed, a range of definitions have been offered. Some are pithy but consequently partial; some others are elaborate but fail to capture the essence of their subject. There is at present no consensus over how intelligence can best be defined. One of the better shorter approaches involves the idea that intelligence is about stealing secrets. As former US director of central intelligence George Tenet explained in a 1998 interview, "Let's be blunt about what we do. There is no dishonor in it. We steal secrets for a living. If we do not steal secrets for a living, then we ought to shut the doors and do something else for a living."[1] Definitions are, of course, significant to any discussion of the relationship between ethics and intelligence because they determine the boundaries of the subject. Writing during the interregnum between the Cold War and the "war on terror," Michael Herman offered the view that "intelligence is information and information gathering, not doing things to people; no one gets hurt by it, at least not directly. Some agencies do indeed carry out covert action, which confuses the ethical issues, but this is a separable and subsidiary function."[2] Whether covert action is regarded as part of intelligence or as something separate clearly impacts the ethical landscape we are considering.

One thing both definitions have in common is that they treat intelligence as a process; however, it is important not to lose sight of the functional

9

dimension of intelligence. One should not only focus on what intelligence does but also think about its purpose—that is, why it gathers information or steals secrets—and in so doing consider the context from which this functional requirement arises. Peter Gill and myself have offered a definition of *intelligence* as "the mainly secret activities—targeting, collection, analysis, dissemination and action—intended to enhance security and/or maintain power relative to competitors by forewarning of threats and opportunities."[3] This definition has the advantage of bringing together process, function, and context. It also emphasizes the reality that the environments in which intelligence is required are fundamentally competitive ones.

All three of these definitions contain elements that hint at the ethical tension at the heart of the practice of intelligence. At its most basic level, intelligence involves theft, or acquiring things whose owners do not want them shared. Some consider the implications of whether covert actions, or "doing things to people," are part of intelligence, and how far the function of intelligence and the context in which it operates impose limits that mark intelligence as a special realm where ethical guidelines that would otherwise apply can be suspended or are considered irrelevant. In addition, the third definition introduces the potential for intelligence to have not only a defensive purpose but also an offensive one, reflecting the reality that throughout history the international system has contained what realist scholars have termed *status quo states*, or those that seek to preserve the existing international system and its distribution of power, and *revisionist states*, or those that are dissatisfied with the existing international order and seek to change it.[4]

In this opening section I want to focus on intelligence as a function of the state and argue that this generates an inherent, and so inescapable, ethical tension. Moreover, such a focus on the relationship between intelligence, the state, and the citizen provides a framework from which we can navigate the various shores of the ethics-intelligence debate. At the international level the ethics-intelligence tension is rooted in understandings of the nature of the international system that are shared, either explicitly or implicitly, by intelligence professionals and that are essentially neorealist in character. The core principle from which they have proceeded is that the international system is anarchic. In this context states can never be certain about other states' intentions; thus, states must provide for their own security. Alliances can be useful, but they can only ever be marriages of convenience. History shows that "today's alliance partner might be tomorrow's enemy, and today's enemy might be tomorrow's alliance partner."[5]

This logic even extends to states whose foreign relations were formally guided by Marxism rather than neorealism. As Soviet colonel Oleg Penkovsky of the Main Intelligence Directorate (Glavnoye Razvedyvatel'noye [GRU]) explained in the 1960s, "We are engaged in espionage against every country in the world. And this includes our friends, the countries of the people's democracies. For, who knows, some fine day they may become our enemies. Look what happened with China!"[6] This state of affairs, with low or qualified trust, gives rise to the requirement for national security intelligence in the first place to reduce uncertainty, improve understanding, and so aid timely and effective decision-making. Numerous memoirs by US intelligence professionals attest to the prevalence of this understanding of the operating environment, its implications for their role as the early warning arm of the United States, and, in some cases, how it impacted the framing of ethical considerations.[7]

As a number of these memoirs also indicate, exceptional times have been considered to legitimate exceptional responses in defense of the state, even where they existed in tension with deeply entrenched norms. In the aftermath of the 9/11 terrorist attacks, it was widely believed that the requirements of US security needed redefining and that US intelligence would have an offensive, or frontline, role in this effort.[8] In his 1985 memoir, *Secrecy and Democracy*, former US director of central intelligence Stansfield Turner directly addressed a question that this post-9/11 approach begs regarding whether "those who are well informed about the threats posed to our country should make ethical decisions on behalf of the citizenry, not merely reflect the opinion of less informed citizens."[9] Turner thought not and, writing after the hearings of the Senate's 1975–76 Select Committee to Study Governmental Operations with Respect to Intelligence Activities (Church Committee), argued that "there is one overall test of the ethics of human intelligence activities. That is whether those approving them feel they could defend their decisions before the public if the actions became public."[10] In terms of liberal democratic values, his position was a significant advance on what the former counterintelligence head of the Central Intelligence Agency (CIA) James Jesus Angleton had offered the Church Committee: it was "inconceivable that a secret intelligence arm of the government has to comply with all the overt orders of the government."[11] However, Turner's stance was still a limited concession to public opinion and normative values, and he was clear about what he was *not* saying: "This guideline does not say that the overseers should approve actions only if the public would approve of them if they knew of them. Rather, it says that the overseers should be so convinced of the importance of the actions that they would accept any criticism that might develop if the covert actions did become public, and could construct a convincing defense of their decisions."[12] What Turner was proposing here was essentially a national interest test that attached a high value to questions of national security and citizen protection—which is the job, after all, of national intelligence agencies and the purpose of state investment in intelligence—and that, in turn, informed the price it was considered worth paying in ethical terms. Thus, the national interest test (or Stansfield Turner test) was one governed by a utilitarian ethic.

However, even as Turner was writing his memoirs, a broader normative development—that is, the rise of the ideology of universal human rights—was challenging its core state-centric logic. Until the 1970s and despite the rhetorical promise of the Universal Declaration of Human Rights of 1948, the advent of the Cold War and post-1945 wars of decolonization had worked against the development of an international agenda around individual human rights. In the West the ideology of anti-communism exerted a far stronger pull than that of human rights. In this context, the concept of national security, based around the need to "protect core values from external threats," did not necessarily require the advancement of those same values abroad.[13] Instead, it was held to justify a range of secret wars, assassination attempts, and other ethically dubious enterprises involving intelligence organizations—principally the CIA—in what former US secretary of state Dean Rusk termed "the back alleys of the world."[14] The second Hoover Commission in 1954 provided perhaps the clearest contemporaneous statement of what this meant for US intelligence and for the ethical conduct of intelligence:

> It is now clear that we are facing an implacable enemy whose avowed objective is world domination by whatever means and at whatever cost. There are no rules in such a game. Hitherto acceptable norms of human conduct do not apply. If the U.S. is to survive, long-standing American concepts of "fair play" must be reconsidered. We must develop effective espionage and counterespionage services. We must learn to subvert, sabotage and destroy our enemies by more clever, more sophisticated and more effective methods than those used against us. It may become necessary that the American people will be made acquainted with, understand and support this fundamentally repugnant philosophy.[15]

Thus, the ends justified the means. However, understandings of human rights and the importance attached to the idea of universal human rights had evolved by the late 1970s to bring them closer to the formulation contained in the Universal Declaration of Human Rights. The consensus underpinning the Cold War liberalism of the 1950s and 1960s was shattered by the US military commitment in Vietnam. The erosion of popular support for the Cold War variant of liberalism, with its emphasis on a global competition in which liberal standards (the "hitherto acceptable norms of conduct," in the words of the Hoover Commission) could be compromised, created a space that was filled by the ideology of human rights. They came to be understood "as entitlements that might contradict the sovereign nation-state from above and outside rather than serve as its foundation."[16] Thus, individual human rights transcended states; neither state given nor state defined, they instead existed independently of states. Further, states had an obligation not only to avoid engaging in activities that would infringe on these rights but also to intervene where these rights were being denied or seriously compromised by other states. The broadly concurrent development of international law provided a framework for promoting and protecting human rights. These developments posed a challenge for Western intelligence agencies with fundamentally neorealist understandings of the international system and with Cold War mind-sets.

The source of the ethics-intelligence tension at the international level, then, is clear. In the context of what is understood by intelligence professionals to be an anarchic, self-help international system, it arises from the clash between the pursuit of national security and the development of expectations around universal human rights that are underpinned by international human rights law. In short, national intelligence agencies are precisely that, *national*. Their primary responsibilities and obligations are understood to be to the state, but they are also bound by wider obligations. Pursuing the former can result in ethical tension in relation to observing the latter, a possibility heightened at times that are held to be exceptional and/or in the context of more offensive intelligence strategies. How far can, or should, states combine a national interest focus with respect for wider norms in the conduct of intelligence? What will determine the limits of the feasible here, and who should determine them? Do times of exception justify abrogating from commitments to wider normative values in pursuit of intelligence? Questions such as these became pressing in the post-9/11 context and still require further thought.

The state is most usually conceptualized as operating at two levels—the domestic and the international—however, globalization eroded this simple binary distinction. Although intelligence structures were often slow to adapt to the changed realities of a rapidly globalizing environment, much contemporary intelligence work is "intermestic" in character; that is, in the context of risk and threat development, the international and domestic levels exhibit considerable degrees of convergence and so are intermeshed. In terms of the security and ethical dilemmas that have accompanied its growth, the Internet constitutes the intermestic phenomenon par excellence. Conceptualizing this intermestic space as an increasingly ragged frontier, US political scientist James N. Rosenau explained it in terms of an international system, where "state sovereignty has been eroded, but it is still vigorously asserted. Governments are weaker, but they can still throw their weight around. . . . Borders still keep out intruders, but they are also more porous. Landscapes are giving way to ethnoscapes, mediascapes, ideoscapes, technoscapes and finanscapes, but territoriality is still a central preoccupation for many people."[17] This, then, is not simply to point out that the international and national are linked and that the international plays a role in shaping the domestic, even though this reality has been a feature of state security concerns in England from at least the age of Elizabeth I, through the post-1917 focus on left-wing domestic subversion that was largely held to justify the existence of the Security Service (MI5) for much of its history, and to the post-9/11 focus on Islamist terrorism.[18] This inevitably involves a focus inside the state on residents and citizens, and as such the ethical dilemmas it raises can be somewhat different from those that exist at the international level.

At this domestic level the ethics-intelligence tension needs to be understood in relation to the question (or problem) of the state. There are even more approaches to defining the state than there are to defining intelligence, but one of the most enduring, and one on which much subsequent scholarship in the field is based, is that provided by the German sociologist Max Weber. His original 1919 definition held that a *state* could be considered to exist "if and insofar as its administrative staff successfully upholds a claim on the monopoly of the legitimate use of violence [*das Monopol legitimen physischen Zwanges*] in the enforcement of its order."[19] Political theorist John Hoffman has suggested that the implication of this view is that "the very need to exercise a monopoly of legitimate force arises only because states are challenged by rebels and criminals who themselves resort to force, and who (either implicitly or explicitly) *contest* the legitimacy of the laws they break. . . . The state which actually *succeeds* in imposing a monopoly of legitimate force thereby makes itself redundant since a gulf between ideals and reality is essential to the state's very *raison d'être*."[20]

In other words, the fate of the state is to assert its monopoly but, in light of the inevitable challenges it must constantly face, never fully achieve it.[21] For example, all states face potential challenges from those who contest their territorial claims and reject the territorial identity ascribed to them. In addition, individual policies—whether economic, political, or ethical— can all result in challenges to this claim to legitimacy. This situation creates a tension that is particularly acute in the contemporary liberal state. Here, as in all states, it generates a requirement for domestic security intelligence, which, in turn, constitutes a recognition that the state will potentially always face challenges to its legitimacy. Just as in the international sphere, the future is uncertain domestically as well, and the state must be capable of providing for its own security. Not only are states uncertain as to whether they will face future challenges, but also their investment in domestic intelligence can be seen as a clear indication that they *expect* them. Levels of trust, it seems, are low here as well as at the level of the international system, and the extent to which they may have been lowered further over recent decades may be attributed to the growth of the intermestic space or frontier.

In a sense, then, domestic intelligence is a functional response to the problem of state legitimacy. To reiterate, the problem is that while legitimacy is regarded as a sine qua non of statehood, it can only ever be limited. As the political theorist Rodney Barker has argued, the state "will generally enjoy legitimacy with its own personnel and with those who enjoy the privileges of the non-political institutions of society, but it can if need be get by with the acquiescence of the rest, provided that it does not antagonise them too much. Often it gets by with little more than acquiescence."[22] But he warns that legitimacy may be "less intense at the political margins."[23] This gives rise to state suspicion of elements within its borders. As a result, at any one time even the contemporary liberal state will be involved in surveilling some as a potential risk or actual threat to others and the political order of the state, although the composition of the "some" will shift over time and by issue. I would argue that this surveillance can be considered a part of the coercive apparatus of the contemporary state and a core tension at the heart of liberal thought. In this vein Hoffman talks of the "schizoid malady" built into the liberal state.[24] Even for Jean-Jacques Rousseau, who opened *The*

Social Contract with his warning that "man is born free; and everywhere he is in chains," ultimately a coercive apparatus was inevitable, as "some of the people all of the time and all of the people some of the time will need to be 'forced to be free.'"[25] As a consequence, then, states understand that they will need to keep watch on, and intervene in the lives of, some of the populace to safeguard the rest and to secure the state itself.

These are the structural contexts in which the need for intelligence arises and the inescapable ethics-intelligence tensions are generated. However, while international relations and political theory provide us with useful frameworks, they are largely silent on the actual implications with regard to intelligence and on the relationship between state, intelligence, and citizen. If domestic challenges to the legitimacy of even the liberal state are inevitable, then how can the state counter them without further eroding its legitimacy among both the target groups and the wider populace? How should contemporary liberal states seek to arrive at "intelligence by consent"? How far is this aim feasible?

David Omand: I agree that a good starting point is the concept of intelligence itself. A useful way to think about intelligence and its enduring value to the human animal is, as you suggest, to see its purpose as being to improve the quality of decision-making by reducing ignorance of the situation being faced (on the assumption, and it is a strong assumption although with exceptions, that the more a decision-maker knows the better the decision is likely to be). If the noise in the undergrowth is known to be from a tiger, then a hunter can better make the judgment call between fight or flight. The information need not be certain: if a diplomat who knows from scientific evidence that the coming years are on balance likely to see increasing drought in the country where he or she is stationed, then the despatch supporting a call for long-term international aid can be more persuasively drafted. Nor does the information need to be a "secret" that must be stolen, especially in these days of open sources being available through the Internet and personal data accessible with lawful authority. By contrast, the defining quality of what is termed *secret intelligence* is that it helps achieve that objective of improving decision-making but crucially with information that other people—dictators, terrorists, and criminals— really do not want us to have and will go to great lengths actively to prevent our acquiring it.

Secret intelligence therefore continues to play a small but essential part in the much wider support system needed by those who have to make security and public safety decisions—be they presidents and prime ministers, diplomats, military commanders, police officers, or border officials—by providing at least the minimum of information they need to make rational choices. To be more precise, we should refer to *national* security and public safety decisions since those decisions have to be taken within the nation-state, even if subsequently they are debated and concerted in international bodies such as the United Nations (UN) and the North Atlantic Treaty Organization. Even where aspects of sovereignty are shared, as with the national signatories of the Treaty on European Union bound by majority voting on common policies and the judgments of the European Court of Justice, national security is an area of exempted competence. That does not mean anarchic relations between the member states; the European Council exists as the intergovernmental forum in which common foreign and security policies can be hammered out. The threats from terrorism, proliferation, piracy, human trafficking, narcotics smuggling, and cyber attacks are ones where European nations have agreed on common policies and where cooperation between police and intelligence services is increasingly evident, including the role that Europol plays. But the final decisions on such matters rest, at their insistence, with nations.

When we think in that context about making wise decisions in light of their ethical consequences, as earlier suggested, often the controversial covert actions associated with intelligence agencies first come to mind. Of course, we would expect a wide range of international activity (ranging from military operations to airline security to major diplomatic initiatives seeking to resolve conflicts) quite properly to be supported by secret intelligence. The related ethical issues are likely to be associated with the choice of policy behind the actions (including whether to work with regimes with very different ethical outlooks) rather than with the intelligence support itself.

Some actions, however, are possible only because of the existence of relevant secret intelligence (ranging from counterterrorist sting operations to lethal drone strikes to support for overseas coups to information operations exploiting stolen data). The ethical issues involved reach into the heart of the intelligence community, and often only the ability of intelligence agencies to act covertly enables the action to be contemplated (such as opening channels for talking to terrorist groups). But before addressing the ethics of covert and clandestine actions (in chapter 6), it is important to recognize that the tasks of accessing, analyzing, and assessing secret intelligence themselves also provide plenty of ethical dilemmas of interest, especially those that arise when the authorities are trying to manage risks to public safety and security.

The reasoning is simple: an inevitable consequence of the defining characteristic of secret intelligence—accessing information that another is actively seeking to prevent the authorities from knowing—is that ethical risk will have to be run to overcome the will of the other with the secret. That observation would have struck a mid-twentieth-century reader as so obvious as to not need saying. Much of the effort of state intelligence has always been devoted to the old-fashioned business of trying to steal other people's secrets, despite theft at the same time being universally disapproved of as an immoral mode of private conduct and with savage sanctions being imposed on the thief if caught. As is described in chapter 2, that was true when Sir Francis Walsingham was trying to uncover the secret plans of the sixteenth-century European continental monarchs who sought to overthrow Queen Elizabeth I.[26] It is still true today as, for example, the intelligence agencies of the United States, Israel, Turkey, Saudi Arabia, Iran, the United Kingdom, France, Germany, and no doubt many others try to fathom the real motivations that lay behind the entry of Russian forces into the conflict in Syria in 2015. What has changed over the last few decades is the democracies have recognized the importance of considering the ethical stance of those involved.

Chapter 2 tracks that evolution in terms of different legal constructs for the practice of secret intelligence. Behind the legal framework sits the ethical code of the leaders and legislators. It would always have been recognized from the earliest days that the twin rationale for choosing covert methods was an inherent need for secrecy (so as not to alert the adversary, and it must be said at times so as not to alert those domestically who might object to the action and mobilize opposition to it) and the need to employ morally exceptional methods (stealing secrets, bribing opponents). A (teleological) ethical stance of judging by results would tend to predominate. Importing a moral code, such as religious injunctions not to steal or kill, in earlier times would have seemed quixotic given that the point of having secret agents was that they would not be bound by everyday morality. Nevertheless, as we discuss in chapter 2, even warfare evolved to adopt a code of chivalry and with "Just War" theory providing both ethical justification for and limitations on the use of extreme violence. Shakespeare critically portrays Henry V's decision to order the slaughter of French prisoners as vengeful.

As we explore in succeeding chapters, an ethical approach to intelligence today is likely to involve a combination of the *teleological*, or consequential, in which the value of success and the risk of failure, exposure, and criticism weigh heavily in the balance; the *deontological*, with the importation of the domestic rule of law and of international human rights standards to set bounds on the application of consequentialist thinking; and the *aretaic*, with its stress on the importance of promoting a culture of virtue ethics within intelligence agencies to shape the self-image of a nation's intelligence officers and to develop their moral character.

The ethics of human intelligence has its own special issues (which we explore in chapter 4), not least the methods used to recruit agents and the duty of care toward sources and their families both when the sources are being run and long after they cease to be active. These issues also involve sharing and receiving human intelligence with foreign agencies, including those suspected of applying very inadequate ethical standards.[27]

Some of these ethical concerns also arise with the handling of digital intelligence work (discussed in chapter 5). Most of the controversy surrounding digital intelligence, in light of the publicity given to the material leaked by Edward Snowden, concerns the invasion of privacy from intruding on data in motion, the content of emails and social media postings, and other communications, and from analyzing the communications data that ensures their transmission across the Internet. But ethical concerns also arise from the mining of data at rest in digital databases containing information that individuals would regard as personal.

As noted earlier, ethical issues are not just for the collectors of intelligence but also for the analysts. For instance, they must consider the degree of certainty required before reaching a conclusion on a piece of intelligence that could result in action being taken that might harm others (such as when determining the location of a terrorist hideout in an urban area).

The opening section of this chapter identified the importance of the ethics-intelligence tension at the international level. An important distinction that nations have historically felt justified in making and that still persists is between what they feel they are able to do to gather intelligence overseas and what they would be prepared to authorize to surveil their domestic population, where tougher justification is usually demanded. A simple example is contained in the still controversial (2016) British investigatory powers legislation: if necessary and proportionate, authority may be given for bulk interception of large amounts of Internet data through a "bulk interception warrant" signed by the secretary of state and approved by a senior judge but only provided that the communications being sought are overseas and not domestic.[28]

Nations with intelligence capabilities all make domestic-overseas distinctions, and most organize their intelligence communities into domestic and external services, often under the authority of the interior or justice minister for the former and the defense or foreign minister for the latter. Part of the original rationale for making the distinction in the democracies lies in the different personal characteristics sought in the intelligence officers, careful and rule abiding in the former and more adventurous and self-starting for the latter. As we discuss in chapter 2, no substantive international law bears on foreign espionage itself, nor is such likely. Nevertheless, civilized nations are increasingly recognizing that the international order is the national order writ large in terms of applying the principles of the rule of law, including transparency over laws regulating external as well as domestic intelligence activity, and in providing for democratic oversight.[29] That is now the case for the United States, the United Kingdom, Canada, Australia, New Zealand, Germany, Sweden, the Netherlands, France (dating from 2015), and most other European nations.

After the Second World War, the decision by the nations of the Council of Europe to bind themselves to the principles of the UN Universal Declaration of Human Rights and then to make themselves legally subject to the European Court of Human Rights (ECHR) in Strasbourg is hugely significant for the legal framework of the intelligence gathering of those nations, as we shall see in chapter 2. In the 1980s citizens of European nations took their own governments to the court and launched important legal challenges, alleging privacy violations such as unlawful telephone tapping. Not only has the Strasbourg court held member nations accountable for their actions in relation to their ECHR obligations, such as ensuring respect for privacy and freedom of speech, but it has also respected the duty of the state to keep those within its borders safe from criminality. The court's jurisprudence nevertheless respects the principles of national sovereignty. At its simplest, the United Kingdom does not have an obligation to act to safeguard the privacy rights of a French citizen in France but does have that duty toward its own citizens and, for example, when a French citizen is visiting the United Kingdom. Democratic governments, in particular, will always feel a special direct responsibility for the welfare of those in their territory over and above any general responsibility that may be felt for others, such as might be suggested in the "responsibility to protect" norm that is often discussed in UN circles but not generally accepted as international law.[30]

The development of the digital economy has created new ethical issues over privacy at both a national and an international level. Delivering products and services in a modern economy, and enabling global communications, inevitably involves both governments and private companies keeping large quantities of personal data about individuals, and this information is of obvious interest to intelligence and law enforcement in relation to their targets. Normal business practice now is for such information to be stored in digital form, with much of it captured directly as digital data from mobile devices such as smartphones and tablets. Digitized data lends itself to easy storage and rapid access, including as bulk data. The techniques of data fusion, data mining, and complex analysis can reveal patterns of behavior and previously unsuspected linkages between suspects. The digital form of the data, however, facilitates both lawful access and theft of data at scale by hackers.

Concern about data privacy rights and unauthorized access or theft of data has led to extensive national data-protection regimes, including in some cases asserting extraterritorial application, with the objective of protecting personal information about individuals that can be identified with them (ranging from their banking details to their movements as revealed by applications, or "apps," on their mobile phones). Most national data protection legislation (and the European Union–wide regime[31]) recognizes the needs of law enforcement and national security for information about their suspects. Under safeguards to ensure respect for privacy, nations are increasingly legislating to permit lawful access to such data for those purposes. Controversy has been most acute when nations legally under international human rights obligations legislate the extension of lawful access to acquire data in bulk, with the defining feature of a bulk power being that it allows public authorities (in particular, law enforcement and intelligence) for specified purposes to access large quantities of data, a significant portion of which is not associated with current targets.[32]

In the private sector, personal data (such as records of web purchases, transactions with loyalty cards, websites visited, and credit card transactions) has a monetary value and is gathered and processed for marketing purposes, with the user having given consent, in theory at least, in return for the benefit of those services. Ethical issues arise for the companies concerned, of course, over the extent to which the user's consent can be genuine and unforced when the service is one the citizen needs, and in practice alternatives also involve the monetization of one's data. The individual citizen who wishes to use the Internet to its maximum potential, and thus participate fully in modern society, also has no choice but to accept that the overall social benefit to the interests of national security and law enforcement justifies the authorities' ability to access his or her personal data. We consider the issues further in chapter 5.

The globalization of Internet-based communications and Web-based commerce creates additional ethical issues. A contested issue is when and how an intelligence agency or law enforcement investigator should be able to access information properly that may be of vital importance to inquiries but has been gathered as part of doing business by a company that is either headquartered overseas or holds the data on a server overseas (and backs it up on servers in a third or more countries).

Lying alongside the small, closed world of traditional secret intelligence and the large universe of open source information is therefore a category of intelligence that can be inferred, given the authority to access it, from personal digital data. Access to "big data" sets is now regularly used to meet the increasing demands for key intelligence on terrorist or criminal suspects such as their true identities, locations, movements, associates, communications methods, finances, and even intentions. I have coined the descriptor "PROTINT" (by analogy with SIGINT for signals intelligence and HUMINT for human intelligence) for intelligence derived from such protected personal information.[33] This intelligence activity certainly raises ethical concerns about personal privacy, but it need not involve stealing secrets, as highlighted in the opening section of this chapter, since government agencies can access this information with lawful authority. Therefore, PROTINT extends what we should define as intelligence activity.

A special category of PROTINT concerns intelligence derived from lawful access to records of telephone and Internet communications use. In the past the registered location of a fixed line telephone was obvious from a reverse lookup of the telephone number in the telephone directory. Anyone seeking to hide his or her identity when making a call would have used a public telephone booth. With modern mobile communications, however, the location of a device—mobile smartphone, tablet, or laptop—can be derived even when the user is out and about and even when the device is not being used. The growth in Internet communications has already led the United Kingdom to pass legislation compelling the communications service providers to retain their customers' records of Internet connections in a form accessible (with the appropriate legal authorization) by the authorities, even when the providers have no commercial reason for keeping this data. Such Internet connections data about "when they communicated, where, how and with whom" can be information that is also capable of revealing facts that the individual regards as highly personal or secret for any one of a number of lawful reasons.[34] Perhaps an individual has been in contact with a sexually transmitted disease clinic and does not want his or her employer to know or does not want his or her partner to know where he or she spent the night. Ethical issues arise immediately over the circumstances in which the authorities should be able to access personal data that is capable of revealing such secrets and what they should be permitted to do with the information.

Another useful concept in considering ethical issues over accessing personal information is SOCMINT, or social media intelligence.[35] Where users of social media want confidentiality, they can choose privacy settings to exclude those with whom they do not want to share their postings. Accessing such information would therefore involve the authority to seek both to override the freely made choice of the user and to gain cooperation from the Internet company. Both may be problematic, as discussed in chapter 5. Terrorists and violent extremists as a result quickly have realized the potential for communicating out of sight of the authorities by using apps that are secured by end-to-end encryption.

Ethical issues also arise over freedom of expression concerning the monitoring of social media where the content may be thought to breach hate speech laws or counterterrorism laws. Internet companies will usually comply with requests from democratic governments to take down material or close accounts where the content is clearly unlawful (such content will most likely have breached the companies' own regulations for use), but they will not accept a responsibility themselves to monitor compliance with either the law or their own ethical codes partly on practical grounds, given the speed and volumes of Internet traffic, and partly because in some cases of over-the-top services they will not have access to the content. For some undemocratic regimes, monitoring the social media use of the general population is part of their internal control structure, giving rise to serious questions over violations of freedom of speech as well as of privacy. Rights issues also clearly arise where nations (such as China, Russia, and Iran) seek to regulate their populations' Internet use by blocking or restricting access to overseas sites that might contain content the authorities consider undesirable.

The impact of any intelligence operation may well not be confined to its legitimate target. The concept of collateral damage is well established in the humanitarian law of conflict, but a similar risk of potential harm through collateral intrusion gives rise to ethical issues in intelligence work. In warfare, international law outlaws the deliberate targeting of civilians who are not participating in the conflict, but it recognizes that in armed conflict civilians may well find themselves in the line of fire, sometimes inevitably so. That possibility need not stop the commander from ordering the attacks that carry a risk of civilian casualties, but the commander is legally bound to reduce that risk consistent with achieving the legitimate military outcome. An analogy can be made with collateral intrusion into the privacy of those who are not the targets of the intelligence operation. Often some collateral intrusion is inevitable even in targeted intelligence operations. A tap on a telephone or a bugging device in a dwelling or vehicle will pick up innocent conversations with family members or third parties that the monitors should not record or should delete as soon as their nature is established. A suspect's computer being monitored may well be used by other family members or friends; thus, a human agent may learn sensitive information about family members or innocent third parties. Respect for the privacy not only of those targeted but also of those who may be swept up in the operation, and acting to minimize that risk, is now an important part of justifying the proportionality of an intelligence operation. The total potential intrusion must be justified by a consequentialist argument that balances the societal good against the risk of individual harm.

A different form of collateral intrusion can also arise in digital intelligence. It may be that the only way of accessing wanted communications overseas is by tapping relatively large quantities of Internet communications overseas and then applying filters and discriminating search terms to pull the wanted needle out of the haystack. Inevitably most of the communications initially accessed are of no intelligence interest. Whether such techniques are compatible with privacy rights depends on how discriminating and efficient are both the algorithms used to filter and discard unwanted material unseen (including the communications of those not the subject of the operation) and the selectors that pull out communications of intelligence interest from what remains. If innocent people are unaware that their communications have been intercepted, stored, and filtered out by computer—thus not ever seen by a human analyst—then the intrusion is potential, not actual, and the potential for harm to the individual negligible. If, however, as in some totalitarian nations, domestic surveillance is sufficiently widespread, then a point could be reached in which the extent of collateral intrusion becomes so great that knowledge of even its possibility could have a chilling effect on public behavior, and thus on freedom of speech, for fear of being intercepted.[36] Such mass surveillance would be unlawful for the United Kingdom. The task of oversight, both judicial and legislative, in the democracies must be to ensure that point is very far from ever possibly being reached. In the words of Liberty, a leading UK human rights organization, privacy has a wider value for society: "The concept of a right to a private life encompasses the importance of personal dignity and autonomy and the interaction a person has with others, both in private or in public."[37]

Extracting intelligence from open source information, meanwhile, should be free of substantive ethical concerns. Open sources are those that are available to all those who know where to look. The value of open source intelligence has been revolutionized over the last few years as Internet search engines have become steadily more sophisticated in how they can conduct complex searches given Boolean logic and provide more complete coverage through the automated Web crawlers, or spider programs, that are constantly indexing the visible part of the Internet. Sometimes the information will nevertheless be hard to find (including from sites on the so-called Dark Net). Also, the information may not always be available free of charge. Many newspapers now hide their content behind paywalls so that only subscribers can access anything beyond the headlines. Many private security firms provide for a fee daily, weekly, or monthly bulletins that inform their readers of the relevant news in regions of interest and on topics ranging from terrorism to market trading.

An excellent example of the use of open sources to derive valuable information is BBC Monitoring, which started in 1937 as the shadow of war approached to provide insights into German thinking and public attitudes through the open study of broadcasts and newspapers. Today BBC Monitoring provides the BBC itself, the government, and other paying customers both instant reporting of newsworthy events and in-depth analysis, covering more than 150 countries and derived from more than seventy languages, of digital broadcasting and websites as well as traditional print, radio, and television sources (a task carried out in very close partnership with its US counterpart, formerly the Foreign Broadcast Information Service and now part of the US Open Source Enterprise). All the source material involved is of a broadcast nature and thus available to anyone who tunes in or follows a blog or social media feed.

The only ethical issue that might arise with open sources concerns the ability of an analyst examining such broadcast information over a longish period (six months of an individual's social media posts, for example) to infer information that the person concerned had not *intended* to reveal through individual utterances. As one scholar puts the point in relation to modern imagery, although unable to assert the right not to be seen in a public place, the individual demands the right not to be watched.[38] But the ethical issue at stake in that case is minor, as reflected in the low threshold of approval British law provides for the police who visually surveil public places.[39] Analysis of broadcast communications can be regarded as comparable to the work of the political scientist or political party analyst who infers from the language a leader uses in a series of speeches that some unannounced change in attitude to an issue has occurred or is imminent, or who simply points out inconsistencies.

Police officers and intelligence officers traditionally have approached their targets differently. For the former their work starts with the discovery of a crime that needs investigating, the identification of principal suspects, and the preparation of a case with evidence to place before a court. Intelligence gathering may play an important part in the investigation, but it must be based on probable cause in relation to the suspect being investigated. For the intelligence officer, the gathering of intelligence on potential threats comes first, preferably before the threat has crystallized or a crime is committed. An unresolved ethical problem, which is highly topical given the presence in Europe and the United States of supporters of the so-called Islamic State (ISIS, or Daesh, as it is also called), is determining what steps society should take to protect itself against individuals whom intelligence reporting (including that passed on by nations overseas) has identified as potentially highly dangerous but who have not (yet) committed an offense or where the hard evidence is lacking to bring a charge of conspiracy to commit a criminal offense. For some nations, detention without trial would be an option. Others use house arrest and, in the United Kingdom, the device of a temporary order under which the individual can legally be subject to measures designed to make surveillance easier, such as limiting Internet use or requiring the wearing of an electronic tag.[40]

A principal task of any intelligence community is counter-surprise and "to tell the Prime Minister what he does not want to hear," in the words of a former chief of Britain's Secret Intelligence Service (SIS). The British Security Service, for example, has the statutory mission of "the protection of national security and in particular its protection against threats such as terrorism, espionage and sabotage, the activities of agents of foreign powers, and from actions intended to overthrow or undermine parliamentary democracy by political, industrial or violent means."[41] Tensions are bound therefore to arise when legitimate protest or other groups discover they have been investigated, for example, through infiltration by undercover officers who seek to examine whether they do pose the possibility of a threat that falls within the MI5's definition. The ethical as well as legal issues for those authorizing such an operation are whether it is necessary to protect the public and, once the operation is in progress, whether enough information has been gathered to enable an informed judgment of when surveillance can reasonably cease.

Intelligence has always, certainly since biblical times, been a valued enabler for military operations. It has thus until very recently enjoyed respectability as an ethically justified part of warfare on the grounds that it can reduce casualties, avert surprise attacks, and help minimize collateral damage. Much of traditional military intelligence has come from the reconnaissance of the battlefield, the study of weapons systems, and the passive collection of radio signals rather than agent running or other intelligence gathering that might carry greater ethical risk, although that has changed in recent years with counterinsurgency and counterterrorism operations. Part of the explanation may also lie in the esteem often granted to the uniform wearer and the standard of personal conduct associated with the warrior ethic. It was no accident that the heads of the first civilian British secret agencies were service officers and that the 1909 cover designations for the Security Service and the Secret Intelligence Service, Military Intelligence Branches 5 and 6, survive today as their popular acronyms "MI5" and "MI6." For some peaceable nations such as Norway, the external service is formally part of the defense establishment. In France the defense minister oversees the external service. And all military forces worldwide have their own intelligence staffs or corps.

It is when military intelligence capability is deployed to support civil power that the potential for clashes of civilian and military ethical outlooks on intelligence activity are most likely (as chapter 4 illustrates with the UK campaign of the 1970s and 1980s in Northern Ireland). Service officers are usually educated to think strategically in terms of ends, ways, and means to achieve a military outcome; thus, they are more likely to take a strictly consequentialist view, with the more enthusiastic officers calling for fewer restrictions. The history of the French paratroopers in Algeria, the British forces in Kenya, and other conflicts involving a colonial power fighting independence movements provide ample illustrations of the ethical dilemmas.[42]

Within each category of intelligence operation—human, digital, visual, technical—the risks both to the individual from being the subject of intelligence attention and to society from the lack of it, on the facts of each case, are liable to vary far more than between categories themselves. There is no obvious common standard against which to weigh the different moral risks other than by looking at the harm that might potentially result to the individuals concerned and at the harm that might result from *not* approving the activity, a difficult counterfactual question but one that cannot be ignored when looking at the ethics of the matter. As Professor John Finnis has written (about Article 3 of the ECHR),

> One can control what one intends in a way one cannot control the side-effects [*sic*] of what one chooses, especially if the side effects involve the choices of other persons. This is well-known to philosophers, whether like me they accept that there are some moral absolutes or like utilitarians and sceptics they deny that there are any true moral absolutes. . . . The risk creation forbidden by the Court is to the applicant; the risk thereby created by the Court (and any state compliant with it) is to the State's citizens, visible to the Court, if at all, only as an undifferentiated mass—despite their one-by-one fate if and when the Court-imposed risk materialises.[43]

Mark Phythian: In my previous section I focused on the ethics of intelligence as a set of issues arising from the nature of the state in general, but it seems to me that the overarching theme that is emerging is the question of how far the ethics of intelligence constitutes a distinctively liberal problem. It is not unreasonable to suggest that liberals have a natural suspicion of intelligence because of their concern over its potential to erode the very liberal values it exists to protect. Arguably this liberal suspicion has been heightened by the rise of the ideology of individual human rights, the expectations it has created, and the difficulties intelligence agencies have in justifying surveillance of the citizenry in light of this ideology. Hence, liberal commentators recognize a range of threats that individuals need to be protected against—hacking, cyber attacks, terrorism, pedophilia, and so on—but at the same time they see a "struggle for the private sphere and how much unseen access we let into our lives." In short, various hostile forces out there can threaten individuals, but at the same time individuals "need to be safe from a prying state."[44] It seems that a concept of "liberal intelligence" is, at least for some liberals, as inherently contradictory a concept as "democratic centralism" proved to be in the Marxist lexicon.

David Omand: Being suspicious of any potential to erode liberal values is a healthy instinct, but it is not the same as concluding in advance that the activity must thereby be banned as incompatible with liberal values. I argue therefore for what Max Weber called an ethics of responsibility (*Verantwortungsethik*) in which there is a political process involving weighing the means available to promote social good and to counter harms.[45] A balancing act is conducted over how to apply them. But we should stop short of being solely driven by what Weber called the ethics of conviction (*Gesinnungsethik*) in which value-driven conduct excludes consideration of the consequences of *not* adopting certain means (such as the risks to society from refusing surveillance of suspected terrorists) and thus is liable to produce outcomes in which the public would severely criticize the authorities for placing citizens in unnecessary danger when bad things happen. I would draw a parallel with the support of the liberal state that we see on the public's part for maintaining the armed forces despite their potential to inflict considerable death and destruction. The ethics of responsibility recognizes that there will be circumstances in which the application of violence through armed combat is the lesser evil, but the ethics of absolute conviction would lead to pacifism and the refusal to accept the legitimacy of the profession of arms. That is why I am attracted to applying to intelligence the concepts that have emerged from Just War thinking, such as proportionality and necessity (see chapter 3), that have motivated the taming of much unnecessary violence and cruelty in warfare through the Geneva Conventions and international humanitarian law.

Mark Phythian: If we consider liberalism as comprising seven core interacting concepts—liberty, rationality, individuality, progress, sociability, the general interest, and limited and accountable power—then we might view one dimension of the ethics of intelligence problem in terms of how it assists in the achievement and maintenance, and even enhancement, of them without eroding any of them.[46] This problem is made more difficult because some of these principles that are core to liberalism contain contradictory tensions. For example, liberalism can be seen at one and the same time as being a "theory of restrained power aimed at protecting individual rights and securing the space in which people can live without governmental oppression," a theory of "mutual interdependence and state-regulated welfare that is necessary for individuals to achieve both liberty and flourishing," and a theory that recognizes "the diversity of group life-styles and beliefs and aims for a plural and tolerant society."[47] Surveillance or other intelligence-based interventions aimed at securing any one of these might well erode another. As I suggested earlier, given the nature of the state, it is to be expected that some groups will always be targets of its surveillance. That the discussion of the nature of liberalism necessarily takes place at a high level of generality, which does not facilitate consideration of micro-level dilemmas and how they might best be navigated, does not help either. We aim to address this dimension of the problem.

David Omand: I certainly recognize that the greater need to respect human rights is an advance for liberal civilization. With the exception of the universal prohibition of torture (certainly a rare example of a justifiable conviction-driven ethic), all the principal human rights in the UN Universal Declaration of Human Rights (and their equivalents in the US Constitution and the European Convention on Human Rights) are qualified rights that must always be respected but can legitimately be infringed under certain conditions. (For critics of intelligence agencies, of course every infringement is a violation; the language used is itself value laden.) I do see the need therefore to talk of a balancing act within the basket of human rights while exercising the ethics of responsibility. Governments have responsibility for seeing that the law is upheld so that the citizen can live without fear under the rule of law. Protecting the innocent, for example, might lead to intruding into the privacy of the home when a family member is suspected of a serious crime against a child, as the consequences of inaction may be very serious. That leads me to argue that there will be cases where we should accept some erosion of one right (in that case, the privacy of family life) that may be justified by the enhancement to others (such as the right to life of a child at risk). Similar considerations of protecting society from harm suggest strongly that outlawing intelligence-gathering techniques such as bulk access to digital data would be a mistake and instead argue in favor of allowing their use under strict controls and oversight (as discussed in chapter 7).

Mark Phythian: That is a logical argument, but it serves to push back the ethical considerations down to the individual authorizing an operation.

It thus introduces a considerable element of subjectivity and the influence of the prevailing culture.

David Omand: Once some element of consequentialist ethics is introduced, as I believe it must be, inevitably human judgment (carrying with it also the possibility of human error) will have to be applied to individual cases. As in the common law, hard decisions are unavoidable. Arrangements for both macro- and micro-balancing acts are needed. Society, through its democratic processes and in light of high-level policy considerations, must provide the macro rules under which ministers, judges, and officials can exercise their micro judgments in individual cases. The macro policies that provide the justification for the relevant law must be publicly available, but the considerations in any individual case cannot be public at the time and possibly long thereafter. A parliament cannot be expected to authorize individual intelligence operations. Thus, an example of a macro rule would be the restriction in UK law that only the gathering of national security intelligence relating to individuals outside the United Kingdom can justify an application for a warrant to access communications in bulk. An example of a micro decision taken under the rule would be the acknowledged use in 2014 to access the bulk communications of ISIS extremists in Syria to track down and prevent an individual from executing a bomb attack in Europe.[48]

Mark Phythian: To pursue this sense in which the ethics of an intelligence problem constitutes a distinctly liberal one, the high level of generality at which understandings of liberalism exist has been useful for intelligence. During the Cold War the simple equation of liberal democracy with freedom, in contrasting the values it represented with the totalitarianism (or slavery) of the Cold War foe, extended claims first made for liberal democracy earlier in the century that created a narrative of the ethico-political superiority of the West.[49] This was reflected in the sense of mission that legitimated for the intelligence professional some practices that might otherwise have been considered ethically dubious.

Illustrative of this is a study of professional intelligence ethics undertaken by Kent Pekel and published in 1998.[50] It was based on structured interviews with a cross-section of fifty CIA professionals, who were each asked ten questions. The first was, "Please agree or disagree with this statement by a career CIA officer: 'Espionage is essentially amoral.' How do you think about the ethical implications of your job?" The second was, "What inputs shape your own sense of ethics and morality?" Pekel found that eight themes regularly surfaced. The first was "belief in and awareness of the moral purpose of the Agency mission."[51] Pekel found that during the Cold War there was "universal clarity about the ideals and commitments to which the Agency was dedicated," and an awareness of them and a commitment to these shared values were "the driving forces behind the CIA's operating culture." The importance of this narrative is clear in the comment of one CIA senior manager, who told Pekel: "In this business, you start to get soiled when you *want* to do the 'dirty' part of espionage rather than feeling that you *must* do it to achieve noble ends."[52] However, Pekel also found that immediate post–Cold War threats lacked the "obvious moral dimension presented by the expansionist ideology of the Soviet Union," and so they were "less compelling motivators for doing a difficult job with integrity." As one case officer told Pekel, "Now the only thing that matters is: Is it good for the United States?" Whereas, "during the Cold War, what was good for the United States was seen to be a matter of *principle* . . . today it is often more clearly seen as an issue of national interest."[53]

Pekel found some were concerned that "this cloudier sense of moral purpose might in the future also have ethical implications. They worried that, if the [Directorate of Operations] case officers of tomorrow are less clear about the goals to which their profession is dedicated, they will be more likely to become 'soiled' by the 'dirty' aspects of their craft."[54]

David Omand: The date of the Pekel survey, 1997–98, is illuminating. That was a time of uncertain transition from a largely unitary threat to the state itself to what we now see as a multiplicity of dangers to the public. A similar CIA survey today—in the age of al-Qaeda and ISIS, Chinese cyber espionage, and resumed Russian aggressiveness—I suspect would produce a completely different result. Today intelligence work has a strong and obvious moral dimension based on the dominant narrative about protecting the public from a variety of harms and on the shared sense among Western (and not just Western) agencies that they are fighting common enemies. That sense is reflected in the huge rise in intelligence sharing since 9/11. As long as that narrative is compelling, then the intelligence function is seen by professionals and accepted by citizens as being necessary and to which the critiques after alleged intelligence failures to protect the public—from the 9/11 attack (2001) in the United States, to the July 7 (7/7) Underground bombings (2005) in the United Kingdom, to the 2015 terrorist attacks in France, Denmark, Belgium, and Germany—all bear witness.

Mark Phythian: I agree. So long as the narrative is compelling, then the intelligence function is seen by professionals and accepted by citizens as being necessary. But the strength of narratives can fluctuate. Moreover, the narratives themselves can change. At these times, perceptions of intelligence might focus less on, say, limited power protecting individual rights and more on unaccountable power eroding core liberal values of individual freedom, pluralism, and tolerance. I would make a general point here: the sense of mission is a key legitimating factor and needs to be present for all intelligence professionals to commit fully to the role. One consequence is that they will usually reject any suggestion of moral equivalence between their mission and those of their targets.[55] However, there is a risk that it gives rise to a thin view of the role of ethics in intelligence, reinforcing a sense that the international system is a competitive one in which opposing sides have separate ethical values and thus embedding an "us and them" dichotomy that provides little or no ethical common ground for cooperation and progress. In short, there is a risk that the practice of intelligence does not simply reflect neorealist understandings of the world, in which trust is low and suspicion is a natural state, but that it reinforces them.[56]

Historical assessments of specific intelligence operations or interventions will vary depending on the acceptance of the validity of the mission and how perceptions of this change over time. For example, opinion remains divided as to whether the CIA's Cold War covert funding of writers and artists was ethically acceptable. The critique of Frances Stonor Saunders—that this activity distorted reality and risked producing "a kind of *ur*-freedom, where people think they are acting freely, when in fact they are bound to forces over which they have no control"—is rooted in the liberal values outlined earlier.[57] So too is the alternative view of the distinguished CIA historian Nicholas Dujmovic, who referenced the CIA's role in the publication of Boris Pasternak's *Doctor Zhivago* and concluded "that the CIA's role in making available literature for people otherwise denied the freedom to read it is a positive chapter in the Agency's history."[58] Ethical judgment here would need to be informed by the aims of the operation and whether it was simply designed as an act of altruism to make otherwise banned literature available in the Soviet bloc—the CIA is estimated to have distributed some ten million books and periodicals in the Soviet bloc during the Cold War, so on this reading it was a particularly altruistic organization—or whether it was a means of achieving a broader Cold War end.[59]

David Omand: Clearly distributing literature subversive of Soviet norms was not simply designed as an act of altruism. In fact, these exercises, such as the translation and promotion of George Orwell's *Animal Farm* and

Arthur Koestler's *Darkness at Noon* (and even more so the spreading of the truth about the Soviet Gulag), were means of achieving a broader Cold War end in exposing the nature of the Soviet regime. As you say, ethical judgment needs to be informed by the justification of the operation (what we describe as the *jus ad intelligentiam* in chapter 3). Black propaganda was not involved; rather, the reverse was used in overcoming the restrictions imposed by the secretive Soviet authorities and with a defensive aim of preventing Soviet propaganda from taking root in Western and third world societies. Reading today a work such as Sidney Webb and Beatrice Webb's *Soviet Communism*, with its extravagant praise for all things Soviet, including collectivism, but omitting entirely any consideration of the human cost of liquidating the kulaks, reminds us why such information operations were needed.[60] For all the excesses of zeal, and occasional inanities, of Western anti-communism in the early Cold War, the motivations of the two sides remain fundamentally ethically different.

Mark Phythian: I suspect that even broad agreement on this question would not result in an ethical consensus, with different approaches (for example, deontological and consequentialist) likely to generate different answers. Nevertheless, it is worth noting that while the West rightly criticized the Soviet Union heavily for its treatment of Boris Pasternak, at the same time MI5 was coordinating the surveillance of key British and UK-based literary and artistic figures who were, or were suspected of being, communists.

David Omand: International communism was rightly seen at the time as a serious external threat to the Western democratic model, as the fate of Eastern Europe showed. And the Soviet Union was engaged in a major covert effort to recruit sympathizers and to infiltrate activists into positions of influence in British society, including the trade unions. The government used covert surveillance to identify and assess communist activity. In part because such coverage provided reassurance that the Soviet model had limited appeal, the United Kingdom never thought it was necessary to make being a communist an offense or to ban the Communist Party, and the government never lapsed into McCarthyism. But Parliament imposed overt sanctions so that if you were a communist (or fascist), then you could not join the armed forces, the police, or the senior civil service. And we now know from the archives that the governments of the day used their influence behind the scenes to prevent known communist sympathizers from obtaining high positions in broadcasting and the more prestigious parts of academia.

Mark Phythian: I suspect that accessing the membership records of the Communist Party of Great Britain should have been sufficient to prove that it never had anything more than minority appeal. Nothing in the surveillance record suggests that the scale and expense of state surveillance of communists and suspected communists were necessary. At the same time, was there any way the state could find this out for sure without casting its net quite widely? This takes us to the question of necessity, which we return to in chapter 2.

How far does this suggest that the liberal problem of intelligence in a domestic context is rooted in the fact that it represents a state function common to all states—that is, seeking and neutralizing challenges to the state—and, despite the existence of a narrative binding it to core liberal values, can at times seem to undermine the values that the liberal state notionally exists to uphold? If we are to accept that all state intelligence agencies are based on a necessarily strong legitimating narrative, and if we observe that they tend for the most part to be *national* rather than universal *normative* narratives, then what distinguishes liberal intelligence from intelligence in the service of other state forms?[61] How significant are the differences?

David Omand: Yes, the liberal problem lies in the potential for excessive zeal on the part of those who regard themselves as guardians of the democratic state (although I would not accept that the early Cold War surveillance to check whether covert communists had penetrated British institutions was in fact unjustified). The function of securing the state (today often expressed in terms of safeguarding the public) is legitimate. The means that may have to be used are necessary and include intrusive investigation, but they carry the potential for misjudgment of two kinds. The first is in an exaggerated belief in the seriousness of whatever threat is being faced, so that even when applying the principle of proportionality, the means employed become excessive—for example, watching those who pose no real danger. The second is in mission creep, as the very existence of the security and intelligence apparatus could create temptations. For example, ministers could find excuses to seek information on political opponents on the self-serving grounds that opposing the current regime itself is tantamount to sedition since the current regime has the best interests of the nation in mind. That latter example would today be prohibited in the United States and the United Kingdom by law, and any intelligence officer who complied would be committing a criminal offense. That takes us back to the ethical climate within a domestic security service that would make such a crime unthinkable. So a key problem lies in the effectiveness of the democratic control mechanisms.

Mark Phythian: To what extent then were the high levels of secrecy that were attached to UK intelligence services before the Cold War ended designed to conceal an illiberal dimension of the liberal British state?[62]

David Omand: The secrecy was certainly designed to conceal the existence of the work of the UK agencies. Part of an answer to this line of questioning lies in the way that the United Kingdom, for so many years, sought to conceal the very existence of its intelligence agencies, as we discuss in chapter 2. As I have previously suggested, all secret intelligence gathering will involve ethical risk since by definition it entails finding some way of overcoming the will of the person with the secret to keep it. But one defining difference between the practice of domestic intelligence collection in liberal democratic states and that in totalitarian states is the *extent* of it, and that in turn relates directly to the *motives* for it. The liberal state has accepted a responsibility for providing a reasonable level of protection of the public through the rule of law, which subjects, for example, intrusive surveillance to strict necessity and proportionality tests that limit the extent that it can be used. As the former senior judge who serves as UK interception commissioner concluded in respect of UK digital intelligence activity, the United Kingdom does not, as a matter of fact, conduct "mass surveillance" (he added that such surveillance would be comprehensively unlawful).[63] That judgment provided public reassurance that the surveillance taking place is consistent with the privacy rights that the citizen enjoys under the European Convention of Human Rights. In short, the authorities have no interest in the doings of law-abiding citizens (and every interest in not wasting time on them given the real tasks to be achieved). The authorities in totalitarian states, on the contrary, have every interest in the doings of ordinary citizens since they will reveal threats to the regime itself.

Mark Phythian: These questions were also the kinds that occurred to the historian Timothy Garton Ash after he gained access to the file the East German Ministry of State Security (Stasi) kept on him while he was a postgraduate student in Cold War–era Berlin, and he talked to those who worked for the Stasi and those whom he had considered to be his friends but were revealed in his Stasi file to have informed on him. "What," he asked, "*is* the essential difference between the Security Service of a communist state like East Germany and the Security Service of a democracy like Britain?"[64] Garton Ash noted similarities in collection techniques on both

sides and in the approaches to and values placed on the officer-agent relationship. He was somewhat skeptical of the argument that the West's methods during the Cold War were by definition more scrupulous than those
of the Eastern bloc. He seemingly accepted the argument of Markus Wolf,
the former head of the East German Foreign Intelligence Service, that the
methods employed by both sides were similar in the relatively "civilized"
context of Cold War Europe and that their differences were a consequence
of the methods used by the CIA in Latin America and by the Mossad and
other intelligence agencies in the Middle East.[65]

David Omand: The observation is correct that most of the techniques
of surveillance, such as bugging or telephone tapping, are common to all
security services. The same knife in the hands of a butcher and of a violent
jihadist, however, carries very different risks to society. What differentiates
acceptable from unacceptable intelligence activity are the constraints of the
legal regime under which it is conducted; in the former case they include
the elements of transparency of law, independent authorization according
to principles of lawfulness, necessity and proportionality, oversight, and
the ability to have abuses independently investigated and redress secured.
Even where the motive on both sides might be the same and legitimate
(say, tracking down a serious criminal), the ethical consideration brought
to bear on the methods used and their scale might well be very different
(such as pressure put on associates to inform on one another).

I would incidentally challenge the view you cite from Markus Wolf
regarding the recruitment of human agents. The major Cold War successes
of the West were largely due to Soviet and Warsaw Pact officers and officials
who grew disenchanted with the growing failures and repressions of the communist bloc (while many of the successes of the "Committee of State Security" and its predecessors in recruiting ideologically motivated agents inside
Western societies before the Second World War played on disillusion with
social divisions, mass unemployment, and poverty of the interwar years).
Cold War recruitments by the likes of Markus Wolf instead had to rely largely
on finding targets with sexual weaknesses or money troubles that could be
ruthlessly exploited.

Mark Phythian: Having arrived at the conclusion that the means were
essentially similar, Garton Ash was left with the possibility that the difference lay in the ends and that surveillance and spying were "good when done
for a free country."[66] But even here, he recognized that there was a slip-
pery slope, and the bright, clear ethical lines that would allow for reliable

judgments are absent. This recognition may have resulted from a meeting he had with David Cornwell, better known as the author John le Carré, who had spied on fellow students during his time at Lincoln College, Oxford, in the 1950s. Wasn't what Cornwell had done in Oxford exactly what those who Garton Ash had assumed to be his friends in Berlin, but reported on him to the Stasi, had done? Cornwell subsequently wrote to Garton Ash, telling him that "I betrayed, in your terms," but also arguing that "it was justifiable to betray the trust of people whom you have befriended in order to gain information for the British state, as it helped to defend a free society."[67]

David Omand: We can only assess the ethical choices of a generation by the standards of their time, not by retrospectively applying our own, shaped as they are by very different circumstances. As I pointed out previously, a function of the Security Service is to investigate potential threats to national security. In the 1950s it had become embarrassingly clear that prewar Soviet intelligence had been actively recruiting young radical students (famously Kim Philby, Guy Burgess, Donald Maclean, Anthony Blunt, and John Cairncross from Cambridge, and it was feared a spy ring was inside Oxford University[68]) and persuading them to go under cover to penetrate British (and thus US) intelligence, governmental, and diplomatic circles. It would have been a dereliction of duty in those days for the Security Service not to have taken steps to keep watch.

Mark Phythian: We return to the problem of intelligence within liberalism as Garton Ash goes on to consider the "real and unavoidable" contradiction involved in infringing freedoms in the name of their preservation. He writes that "if the infringement goes too far, it begins to destroy what it is meant to preserve."[69]

David Omand: To talk of contradiction goes far too far. A tension between security and liberty is unavoidable, but in the end we need enough of both since without security there will never be freedom and protection of rights (as those who live in the Middle East have experienced time and again). Absolute security, in the terms you cited at the outset of an absence of a threat sufficient to wither away the state itself, is not a desirable end since the means to secure it will indeed undermine the liberal values of society (as the United States discovered during the post-9/11 war on terror). Absolute freedom likewise is not a desirable state since it gives free rein to those who profit from exploiting the innocent and the weak. Garton Ash's formulation is interesting because it suggests that he sees, as I have always, that liberalism can accommodate a certain level of infringement of freedom, perhaps of the kind that you pointed out Frances Stonor Saunders objected to, for example. This begs a key question, which he asks: Who decides what is too far? Another key question that this begs, but he doesn't ask, is that of who guards the guardians, and we address these questions in chapters 2 and 7.

Mark Phythian: At the end of this reflection on the essential difference between Western and Eastern bloc spying, Garton Ash's conclusion comes in two parts. The first is to restate the essential contradiction that surveillance in a liberal democracy generates: "The domestic spies in a free country live this professional paradox: they infringe our liberties in order to protect them."[70] This, then, is a consequentialist ethical defense. The second is that "we have another paradox: we support the system by questioning it."[71] In other words, the ethics of intelligence also rely on information, on the possibility of informed debate, and on the clear granting of consent, all supported by effective oversight. Those who question liberal intelligence are not its enemies but its natural constituency.

David Omand: Ultimately, that is how we have to see things today. It was not always thus, and in chapter 2 I chronicle the development of this way of thinking about the secret activity of the British state. This struggle to manage the paradox today most clearly distinguishes liberal intelligence— not the practice itself but the liberal architecture in which it is contained and that defines the limits of the practice—from other forms. When these standards are not met, liberal democratic values are undermined. To answer Garton Ash's question, this is how we recognize what going "too far" means in practice. And this makes consideration of the relationship between law and intelligence both very important and multidimensional, as we see in chapter 2.

2

Ethics, Intelligence, and the Law

David Omand: In the summer of 1586, imprisoned behind the battlements and moats of Chartley Hall in Staffordshire, the exiled Catholic Mary, Queen of Scots, plotted her escape to reclaim her Scottish kingdom. With the help of one of her courtiers skilled in cryptography, Thomas Phelippes, she carefully penned an encrypted secret message of encouragement to her supporters. The substitution cipher was elaborate and, she was assured, secure, with individual hieroglyphs denoting key words such as the king of France and the king of Spain. She looked to them to invade England, restore the Catholic religion, and return her to her Scottish throne. In the message she rashly implied her approval of the first part of the plot, the assassination of Queen Elizabeth I.

She was, however, up against Europe's first true spymaster, Sir Francis Walsingham (whose portrait still hangs today in the office of the chief of the British Secret Intelligence Service [SIS]). Walsingham's network of agents had provided preemptive intelligence of the plot that had enabled him to place double agents, including Thomas Phelippes, in the household of Mary. Knowing the content of her letters through Phelippes (who, the story has it, was not above embellishing the deciphered plaintext to make it more damning of Mary), Walsingham allowed the letters to be smuggled out of the castle (in the bungs of empty beer barrels) and then intercepted as evidence of treason. This covert intelligence operation provided the crucial evidence for Mary's arrest, her trial and conviction for treason, and her eventual beheading.

The case demonstrates how human and communications intelligence can support each other—always the most effective combination—to enable covert operations, literally secret agency.

Today it would be natural to pose a series of questions about how the law should govern such an operation. Was there legal authority for the collection of this intelligence through a covert human intelligence source? Was the threshold of necessity reached, and were the methods proportionate? Did sufficient national security justification exist in terms of the need to protect the lawful regime in England from the threat of external aggression (especially with religion playing its part as an accelerant in the fires of treason)? Was the operation carried out within the legal conventions of the day, including the authority to use prerogative powers to operate in secrecy to defend the ruling power? Was the rule of law upheld when action was taken? There was a trial by her peers according to custom (even if Mary resisted on the legalistic grounds that as a crowned queen she had no equals in the realm). We would recoil from the harshly coercive interrogation of fellow conspirators and witnesses to provide corroborative evidence, but that was lawful at the time. Certainly deception was used, as it always is in sting operations, but the historical record shows that Mary could not have run a credible defense of entrapment. Insurgents seeking the violent overthrow of the regime knew the legal risks they were running and the penalty for treason.

Having effective intelligence support was, and still is, an important part of the survival kit of any ruler, be they caliphs, emperors, monarchs, or their republican successors. Uneasy was the head that wore the crown then and sometimes now. We might call this the *prerogative agent model* of security and intelligence work, where the rulers lawfully exercise their prerogative powers, often by decree, to protect themselves and thus the nation.

Authority thus rested with the ruler (whether an anointed sovereign or a revolutionary committee) who could command the ends, ways, and means to conduct any activity that he or she, and the close counselors, felt necessary. Secret funding could be commanded for exercising prerogative intelligence work (including funds obtained outside normal tax gathering) with powers of arrest over individuals (followed when necessary by torture), an important tool of the trade. This prerogative model would therefore in most cases be subject to no specific statutory restraint other than the whim of the rulers and the inclinations of their close advisers and agents.

The prerogative agent system of maintaining national security is heavily results oriented since failure to deliver to the ruler would lead to a falling out of favor. Worse yet, it could lead to a loss of one's head, as Thomas Cromwell, one of Walsingham's predecessors, found when his secret plan to marry King Henry VIII to Anne of Cleves to strengthen Protestant influence backfired.[1]

A few nations today still operate in this way, where the autocratic ruler along with the head of secret police exercise personal control over secret

activity, including political corruption, assassination, and torture, to maintain national security and to advance their personal security and prosperity.
The model, unsurprisingly, sits ill with governments that are accountable to
democratic legislatures that now exist in the majority of nations. Once legislatures are established, the exercise of prerogative authority in the name of
the security of the nation when such power impinges on domestic liberties
is bound to become a legitimate subject of parliamentary interest. We can
see this in the English experience of the seventeenth century when Parliament confronted the king, for example, and in 1640 abolished the Court
of Star Chamber, which received evidence obtained by torture. (It took the
Act of Union in 1707 for Scotland to copy this, and it was only in 1789 that
France took equivalent steps.)

The ultimate challenge to the divine right of the king and the assertion
of the sovereignty of Parliament came nine years later with the execution
of Charles I in 1649 and the institution of the commonwealth. The protec-
tor Oliver Cromwell nevertheless still needed secret intelligence to counter
royalist plotting. So Parliament funded a network of agents that provided
support to the new regime and was run by Cromwell's secretary John
Thurloe and assisted by the cryptographic skills of the Oxford professor of
geometry John Wallis. With the restoration of Charles II and as Parliament
consolidated its new role, intelligence remained valuable, and agent running continued with Professor Wallis serving the state as the "cryptographer royal" with parliamentary approval. A proclamation of May 25, 1663,
for example, was the first public reference to the authority of the secretary
of state to warrant the opening of letters.

What evolved from this struggle between the Parliament and the king
was a model for the practice of security and intelligence in which the legislature recognized three points: such dirty work was necessary for the
security of the nation, it had to be funded, and to be effective it had to be
conducted in secret. This way of thinking about security and intelligence
work we might label as the *hidden guardian model*. Parliament recognized
that even a democratic government needed a few people who could operate
away from public gaze, with sufficient money, and with no awkward questions asked to uncover plots against the state and to help the conduct of
international diplomacy.

After the Restoration, Parliament controlled taxation, the issue that had
forced the original rupture with the king. Parliament established a Secret
Service fund and within a few years routinely granted an annual Secret

Service vote. Parliamentarians knew they were funding covert intelligence activities and implicitly accepted that the votes ought not be questioned, let alone openly debated or subjected to the normal scrutiny of public expenditure.

During the eighteenth century the British Secret Vote was spent gathering intelligence on continental threats to the realm and conducting covert actions, including bribery in support of British foreign policy and promoting the expansion of British interests overseas. But the fund was used at times for domestic bribery to secure votes and as an all-purpose government slush fund for minor but embarrassing payments such as to former royal mistresses.

On the other side of the Atlantic, the use of a network of agents, the Culper spy ring, greatly assisted George Washington's successful campaign against the British Army. As one defeated British officer is quoted as saying, "Washington did not really outfight the British. He simply outspied us."[2] Meanwhile, conventions developed in the British Parliament as it insisted on at least some audit of the secret expenditure with the results reported to the chair (but not the members) of the influential Public Accounts Committee, which was set up in 1861. But convention also gave the clerks of the House of Commons the authority to minimize the tabling of awkward questions to ministers about secret services for which the prime minister (and the president in the United States), by the nineteenth century, was seen as carrying political responsibility. It was part of what Walter Bagehot called the efficient part of the Constitution that, behind the scenes, made government actually work as opposed to the dignified part that the public could be invited to admire.[3]

The hidden guardian model subsequently served the United States and the United Kingdom well for the latter part of the nineteenth century and the first half of the twentieth century, including the crucial part that intelligence played in the world wars. What seems extraordinary to modern sensibilities, however, is that the men and women who had worked in wartime intelligence kept quiet about the existence of these extralegal capabilities. Occasionally the prosecution under the Official Secrets Act of an espionage case against the UK agencies would reach the courts, or a scandal would reach the newspapers. Many in the UK establishment of senior politicians, parliamentarians, judges, prosecutors, lawyers, senior police officers, university dons, and senior newspaper editors knew from their personal wartime experiences that intelligence and security services must still be engaged in ongoing activities, be funded from the public purse, and be under general oversight from the elected government of the day but without any public acknowledgment or specific legal authority for the activities in which they were engaged.

In the United States, intelligence had remained a military function, with the forerunner of the CIA, the Office of Strategic Services (OSS), having been founded in 1942 as an agency of the Joint Chiefs of Staff. The UK government, meanwhile, was one of the first to see the value of creating civilian organizations to conduct secret intelligence activity and to recruit intelligence officers, train them, and deploy them under a formal management structure. Departments with no legal status, but staffed by crown servants, were created. (In 1909 a Secret Service Bureau split within a year into the domestic Security Service [MI5] and an external intelligence service [MI6], and in 1919 building on the experience of the First World War, a cryptographic and signals intelligence organization, the forerunner of Government Communications Headquarters [GCHQ], was established.) The details of individual operations were usually kept from ministers to protect them should there be a scandal, although in 1937 a system of executive authorization was introduced with Home Office warrants signed by the home secretary for all telephone intercepts.

Many countries today (probably the majority) continue to operate their security and intelligence or secret police organizations under such a hidden guardian model. Funds are voted and staff employed, but the locations of their offices and listening posts are mostly not declared, questions are discouraged, recruitment is not an open process, and the secret agencies have no legal personality and cannot be taken to court. The latitude, with plausible deniability, available to the secret servants of the state under this model is wide.

An evident danger was that the "hidden guardians" would come to see themselves as an elite group that alone possessed an understanding of the threats facing the nation (the evidence for which would of course be secret) and thus would be prone to paranoia—for example, self-authorizing whatever seemed necessary to deal with perceived postwar threats from Soviet and Warsaw Pact agents subverting democratic processes (and that was certainly their intention).[4] This tendency was seen in the anti-communist investigations by Senator Joseph McCarthy, supported by J. Edgar Hoover's Federal Bureau of Investigation. Even if Soviet operations were often clumsy, they did succeed in penetrating wartime British intelligence and the US atomic bomb project and in recruiting a few postwar legislators and lead-ing British trades unionists, academics, and broadcasters both to provide information and to exercise influence. It was perhaps inevitable therefore that postwar security and intelligence work in the United States and Europe would naturally attract many with an inherently rightist political outlook and that those of a more leftist or liberal disposition would be screened out or self-select themselves out by not considering such careers.

In the United States, the National Security Act of 1947 provided for the administration of the National Security Council and of the Central Intel-ligence Agency, and the CIA Act of 1949 exempted that organization from most of the usual limitations on the use of federal funds and consequent disclosure of its organization and operations. In the United Kingdom, these postwar years saw the development of increasing executive regulation of secret activity, leading to what might be called an *executive rules model*.

In 1951 the Home Office updated the 1937 guidelines and included the provision that an interception for law enforcement purposes required that the offense being investigated must be really serious and that investigators have good reason to think that the interception would result in a conviction. In 1952 responsibility for the sensitive domestic work of the British Secu-rity Service was transferred from the prime minister to the home secretary, who stamped his authority with a direction that the role of the service was the defense of the realm as a whole from internal and external espionage and sabotage, and "against the actions of persons and organisations which may be judged subversive to the State."[5] It maintained the well-established convention that ministers would not concern themselves with the detailed information gathered by the service but would be "furnished with such information only as may be necessary for the determination of any issue on which guidance is sought." After the 1956 Commander Crabb scandal and the forced resignation of the chief of the SIS, the foreign secretary took the opportunity to tighten control of all sensitive intelligence operations that might have foreign policy repercussions.[6] This contrasted with the US prac-tice where the president, assisted by his White House staff, exercised this authority. From 1952 onward, President Harry Truman authorized the CIA to provide intelligence briefings to presidential candidates and help the CIA establish a close working relationship with the new president and his close advisers (President Donald Trump being an exception in that regard).[7]

The prime minister commissioned a report from the former appeal court judge (and Nuremberg war crime judge) Lord (Norman) Birkett, who recommended in 1957 that for the Security Service's justification to pursue a case, it had to be a major subversive or espionage activity that was likely to injure the national interest. Further, the material likely to be obtained by such interception had to be of direct use in compiling the necessary information for the Security Service to carry out the tasks laid on it by the state. Finally, normal methods of investigation must have been tried and failed or, by the nature of things, must have been considered unlikely to succeed if tried.

When nations conduct secret activity under an executive rules model, the temptation may arise to use secret funds and powers to serve the political interests of either the leaders of the day or of the minister in charge of a secret service. Postwar reviews of the British Security Service emphasized the importance of the nonpolitical nature of its work (a provision later embodied in 1989 in the first statute governing the service) but concluded that "there is no alternative to giving the Director General the widest possible discretion in the means he uses and the way in which he applies them." The report added the caveat "always provided he does not step outside the law."[8] But since the powers were not defined in law, what that caveat might mean would be a matter for the discretion of the director general.

The executive rules governing secret activity may have been strict, but the fact was that in the United Kingdom (unlike the United States), they were largely extralegal. There was no immunity from the normal criminal law for those involved in telephone tapping or in breaking into a house or vehicle covertly to search or to plant a listening device. Intelligence officers of the Security Service of the day therefore had to rely on a nod and a wink to local police if caught in the act, and the aggrieved citizen had no effective remedy in the courts against mistakes or excesses.

A white paper presented to Parliament in 1980 (without mentioning the Security Service) confirmed that interception might be undertaken only with the authority of the secretary of state, given by a warrant under his own hand. The government did not introduce legislation to cover the exercise of these powers, but it promised a continuous independent check on how interception was being conducted. Lord Diplock, the senior judge appointed for that purpose, listed six conditions that he felt had to be observed:

(a) The public interest that will be served by obtaining the information, which it is hoped will result from the interception of communications, is of sufficient importance to justify this step.

(b) The interception applied for offers a reasonable prospect of providing the information sought.

(c) Other methods of obtaining it such as surveillance or the use of informants have been tried and failed or, from the nature of the case, are not feasible.

(d) The interception stops as soon as it has ceased to provide information of the kind sought or it has become apparent that it is unlikely to provide it.

(e) All products of interception not directly relevant to the purpose for which the warrant was granted are speedily destroyed.

(f) Such material as is directly relevant to that purpose is given no wider circulation than is essential for carrying it out.[9]

The implication of condition C, and maintained since, is that the ethical risk of telephone interception is greater than that from the use of informants, perhaps on the grounds that the latter can be more closely targeted on the suspect whereas the former may well capture conversations from family members as well.

Executive regulation of secret activity, domestic and foreign, and an acknowledged element of independent judicial oversight for the most intrusive techniques available at the time were therefore important parts of the mid-twentieth-century British executive rules model. As the twentieth century drew to a close, however, the absence of a statutory legal basis for the model became a serious problem. It became harder in the United Kingdom to maintain the plausibility of denial that had to follow media exposure of security and intelligence activity by agencies that did not formally exist. And as public deference to authority waned and intelligence scandals occupied front pages (such as the revelation in 1967 that the United Kingdom was routinely monitoring traffic on the transatlantic cables[10]), it became harder to keep the lid on exposures. Even the highly secretive signals intelligence agency GCHQ (officially its cover story was as a communications research establishment) found itself embroiled in controversy when Prime Minister Margaret Thatcher in 1984 banned its staff from trade union membership and thus from joining wider civil service industrial action that might compromise the relationship with the US intelligence community.

As noted earlier, matters regarding internal security had been arranged differently in the United States. It had been the assertion of British parliamentary sovereignty that had so upset the colonists in America in 1773, who suffered under a tea tax insisted on by a British legislature in which they were not represented. The founding fathers therefore constrained the law-making powers of the US Congress within a binding Constitution, making supreme the rule of law, not the rule of a parliament.

In the 1791 US Bill of Rights came the famous words that no person shall "be deprived of life, liberty, or property, without due process of law," and that the people have the right "to be secure in their persons, houses, papers, and effects, against unreasonable searches and seizures"—except "upon probable cause." When it became necessary, following the assassination of President William McKinley in 1901, to set up a federal security capability (that eventually became the FBI), it had to be from the outset a law enforcement agency bound by the law and with legislation to give its agents law enforcement powers. When in 1947 under the pressure of tensions with the Soviet Union—and influenced by the successes of British intelligence in World War II—the United States set up a central external intelligence capability (the CIA), it was by an act of Congress. The US Congress was therefore seeking to have intelligence and security activity operate under what we could call a *legal compliance model*. (Such was the sensitivity around the interception of communications, however, that the National Security Agency was set up by presidential directive as an agency within the Defense Department. It was only in 1979, after the scandals investigated by the Church Committee, that legislation established the Foreign Intelligence Surveillance Court [FISA] to regulate some of the activity of the NSA.)

An important component of the US legal compliance model is the protection of the basket of rights guaranteed under the US Constitution to American citizens, including a respect for privacy, that the country's courts are obliged to uphold. English common law did not recognize a comparable right to privacy. By the 1980s Parliament had still not legislated for such a right, although the United Kingdom had endorsed the 1948 Universal Declaration of Human Rights, including the rule of law, the right to life, the prohibition of torture, and the right to liberty and security, as well as the right to respect for private and family life. The UN declaration may not have been legally binding, but it set the template for the subsequent European Convention on Human Rights of the Council of Europe. The legal protection of human rights for European nations (including the United Kingdom) was then linked with the rule of law through the jurisdiction of the European Court of Human Rights in Strasbourg. The British executive rules model for security and intelligence work would not long survive the potential for challenges in Strasbourg.

A key article in the ECHR provides that "there shall be no interference by a public authority with the exercise of" the right to privacy "*except such as in accordance with the law* and is necessary in a democratic society in the interests of national security, public safety or the economic well-being of the country, for the prevention of disorder or crime, for the protection of health or morals, or for the protection of the rights and freedoms of others."[11] Yes, the court acknowledged that a state has a right to defend its citizens, but it could only do so under the rule of law (including clear legislative authority), respecting the principles of proportionality and necessity, with proper authorization, independent oversight, and independent investigation of allegations of abuse.

After the Strasbourg court upheld a number of complaints of privacy abuse, the UK government finally legislated through the 1985 Interception of Communications Act to provide a legal framework for the interception of telephone calls.[12] Further ECHR challenges followed, and with the landmark 1989 Security Service Act, the UK government finally accepted that Parliament should place the Security Service itself on a statutory footing, limit in primary legislation its purposes in accordance with the ECHR, and provide for ministerial accountability. The 1994 Intelligence Services Act similarly avowed the Secret Intelligence Service and GCHQ, placed their activities on a statutory footing, and created an oversight committee of parliamentarians. The Regulation of Investigatory Powers Act (RIPA) of 2000 later provided for not only telephone interception but also all forms of intrusive electronic powers then being used—including visual surveillance, bugging, and interference with property—and made them subject to oversight by former senior judges acting as independent commissioners.

The model the United Kingdom had evolved by 1994 could therefore be labeled, like that of the United States, legal compliance under which the executive (in the United Kingdom, the secretary of state) was required to account for the activities of the security and intelligence agencies, with legislation regulating the most intrusive domestic surveillance powers and providing for independent oversight and a court to examine allegations of abuse of these powers. UK legislation itself, however, was opaque, for example, about the legal authority the act gave the foreign secretary to authorize bulk access to overseas communications.

Challenges to these UK and US legal compliance models were not long in coming. After 9/11 the focus of security and intelligence work moved from the protection of the democratic institutions of the state to the safety and security of the public. Intelligence was urgently sought on the individuals behind threats such as terrorism, proliferation, and serious international crime. In facing the threat from al-Qaeda, President George W. Bush as commander in chief under the Patriot Act of 2001 authorized the NSA to conduct secret data collection outside the normal confines of the FISA Court.[13] The CIA was ordered to conduct extraordinary rendition measures to seize al-Qaeda suspects and coercively acquire intelligence from them, activities that might be better described as befitting a hidden guardian model. (These programs were later scaled back, and in a few cases stopped, by President Barack Obama.)

Coincidentally, as new technology developed, intelligence about individuals and their associations, locations, and movements was becoming increasingly available from digital sources, not least Internet communications and mobile devices, including bulk access to Internet data, hacking, and computer network exploitation. Consistent with the legal compliance model, UK ministers privately authorized such activity using a variety of preexisting legal powers.

When the NSA contractor Edward Snowden in 2013 leaked to journalists large quantities of classified information about the digital intelligence activity of the United States and the United Kingdom, motivated by fears that the United States was in breach of its constitutional safeguards on privacy, he also exposed the way that the legal framework and definitions of traditional interception legislation had been stretched to accommodate the latest powerful digital intelligence practices. Independent inquiries were commissioned, first in the United States and then in the United Kingdom. The United Kingdom then embarked on a national debate that formed the basis of new legislation, the Investigatory Powers Act 2016.

What has finally emerged from this turmoil in the United Kingdom (and to a lesser extent in the United States) is what might be called the *social compact model* of security and intelligence work. The model is based on an ideal of a democratic license to operate being given, after open debate, to the security and intelligence authorities and their law enforcement partners that defines their lawful purposes, regulates their intrusive methods, provides for independent oversight by judicial commissioners and by a committee of senior parliamentarians, and establishes a specialist court (the Investigatory Powers Tribunal) to investigate and adjudicate on allegations of abuse. Under President Obama a similar US process led to comparable conclusions. France has embarked on legislation aiming eventually to reach a similar point, as has Germany, although less wide in scope. Other European nations undoubtedly will follow suit.

The essence of the social compact model is that through open debate, Parliament and the public can come to accept the secret parts of the state are necessary to the functioning and protection of an open society and that they require powers laid down in legislation. At the same time, Parliament and the public must also accept intelligence operations themselves cannot be more than minimally transparent without defeating their own purpose. However, these operations are tolerated only on three conditions (three Rs): all activity is conducted within *the rule of law*, there is *regulation* and proper democratic accountability, and authorities exercise *restraint* to respect the privacy of the individual and apply the legal principles of proportionality and necessity at every stage.

Mark Phythian: Identifying these historical eras provides a very useful framework for thinking about the evolution of the official bases of intelligence work in democratic contexts. It highlights in the case of the United Kingdom, but to varying extents elsewhere as well, the democratic deficit that has been a factor in the relationship between intelligence, the state, and the citizen. But this account of the evolution of the relationship between intelligence and legality also raises a number of ethical issues that highlight how the law can itself be a source of ethical tension.

Until the relatively recent emergence of the legal compliance model, intelligence practice was officially authorized rather than governed by statute. This state of affairs had significant ethical implications. The absence of statute and oversight aided the development of a space sealed off from external scrutiny. The combination of official authorization combined with secrecy shielded intelligence agencies, and operating behind this shield, intelligence agencies did not have a pressing need to give a great deal of thought to questions that would have provided ethical guidance for work that was, after all, authorized. Because groups that operate in secret are less susceptible to external challenge or to regular reviews, they are often more likely to exhibit recurrent patterns of behavior and tend not to have the same incentives to review issues, including ethical issues, around their conduct. As a consequence, consideration of ethical questions becomes secondary to the organizational mission.

Secrecy is at the heart of the intelligence-ethics tension. Secrecy is not only a widely recognized requirement of effective intelligence but also a potential obstacle to democratic legitimacy. It has necessarily created a distance between those charged with conducting intelligence work and those citizens whom, through its conduct, intelligence aims to protect. Secrecy also creates potential problems in that it means intelligence organizations must mostly forgo the wider input that could provide a counter to possible groupthink in assessment and decision-making arising from poor reasoning.[14] It also creates a private space within which intelligence encounters law. In other words, if the *law* constitutes the set of rules governing the conduct of the intelligence "game," then *secrecy* provides a space for game playing. In practical contexts, the law is not simply applied; first, it has to be interpreted, and how that has been done in the recent past has been far from clear to the public.

We can see something of the impact of secrecy, and of the space it creates, in the personal files that MI5 maintained on individuals during the early Cold War period, in which ethical reflection and questioning are notably absent. MI5 targeted many of these individuals because they were known or suspected communists. One was the Oxford historian Christopher Hill, who came to be regarded as one of the leading historians of the seventeenth century. Hill joined the Communist Party in 1936 and came under the close attention of MI5 around 1944. Consider, for example, this source report from August 1950 that provides an account of Inez Hill, Christopher Hill's first wife (and on whom MI5 kept a separate personal file), that is worth quoting in full:

> Inez HILL is described as a somewhat neurotic, rather emotional and unstable person. She has stated that she has been until recently a member of the British Communist Party, and has also announced quite recently that she is sick to death of the Party and of Communism and no longer wishes to belong. It is difficult to say whether this resolution represents her fixed political determination, boredom with her husband's political activities or merely the result of a gush of emotionalism. There seems to be some reason to believe that she is in fact bored with her husband's activities, especially since his political sympathies lead him, according to her, to give a considerable amount of his money to the Party. Since he is reputed to give

his wife a very small sum as a dress allowance or pin-money, Inez HILL may well resent the Communist Party absorbing what would otherwise go towards a new Summer dress for herself.

Another source has often suggested that Inez HILL is not only fed up with her husband's politics, but also with her husband. She may, of course, be pretending to have finished with Communism on account of the hardening of the Public's attitude towards Communists. But it seems that neither she nor her husband took any pains to hide their politics, and in fact publicly upheld their adherence to Communism.

Christopher HILL himself has been described in the past as somewhat mean-minded, pompous and tiresome.[15]

Beyond providing support for the argument that intelligence is the plural of anecdote, it is hard to see the value of this report or the many more like it contained in the MI5 personal files.

David Omand: As in experimental science, even a negative result can have value. As we discussed in chapter 1, there were well-grounded reasons for suspicion of the interest Soviet intelligence showed in young students at Oxbridge and for the use of open communist sympathizers in the universities to spot promising potential recruits and pass on their names (without themselves necessarily being otherwise involved). It would have been dereliction of duty in those days for the Security Service not to have taken steps to assess a prominent figure in British communist circles such as Christopher Hill, noted historian though he might have been.

Mark Phythian: Nevertheless, the case does help illustrate the difference between legality and ethics. The monitoring of Hill's phone calls, intercepting his letters, gleaning trivial information from acquaintances, supplying accounts of his lectures—all of these were done legally insofar as they had been officially authorized using prerogative powers. But was this the right thing to do? Was any of it necessary? Was the full range of this monitoring really necessary? Did Christopher Hill represent a potential threat? A minute from his MI5 case officer, J. L. Vernon, from December 1951 provides an answer to this last question: "HILL is one of the leading Communists at Oxford University and plays a prominent part in all the Party's cultural work. He is one of the persons whom I have selected (in consultation with Thistlethwaite) as deserving further investigation, in order to increase our knowledge of Communism at the Universities."[16] In other words, the intelligence collection net was being cast widely.

David Omand: Given the remit of the Security Service and the evidence of Soviet subversive activity across Europe in the late 1940s and early 1950s that was of great concern to the Clement Attlee government, assessing whether there was an emerging espionage or subversion problem in the United Kingdom would have been fully justified. Your point has also, I suspect, even more force in relation to the hidden guardian era, where intelligence officers would have felt freer to make their own judgments of what they thought necessary to do in the interests of national security.

Mark Phythian: Even if we were to accept that overall rationale in terms of necessity, was the degree of intrusion proportionate? After all, as Simon Blackburn has noted, "One of the moral signatures of a society will be the extent to which the law allows liberty to do, feel, or think the wrong things."[17] These ethical questions, operating in a culture shaped behind the barrier of secrecy, were never formally asked but were implicitly answered in the affirmative via the official authorization provided by the Home Office warrant.

David Omand: It cannot of course be assumed that the politicians and senior officials overlooked ethical considerations of what constituted a free society, for example, in deciding against banning membership in the British Communist Party or the promulgation of its views. Ethics did not just start with the codification of modern human rights that we might consider today as the touchstone of ethical state behavior. Nor do we know from the files how far privacy considerations really entered into their thinking when considering whether to authorize intrusive intelligence activity in that era of executive rules in the twentieth century. What historical cases such as Hill's show, from what has been released to the National Archives, is that in those days after the Second World War the approach to privacy (not a concept ever recognized under English common law) differed from that taken today under the protection of the ECHR and our own 1998 Human Rights Act.

Mark Phythian: What I think this case helps illustrate is that the relationship between legality and ethics is more multidimensional than is sometimes suggested. The conflation of legality and ethics that can occur regarding intelligence issues can constitute a conscious strategy that serves to limit discussion of a range of questions, such as those posed here in relation to the surveillance of Christopher Hill; his first wife, Inez; and his wider associates. Authorization in this way serves as a proxy for ethical consideration, and actual ethical consideration is bypassed.

David Omand: The point is very well made. It might well be lawful, if the necessity were to arise, to authorize the interception of the mobile telephone communications of a friendly foreign leader. It would not be hard to devise scenarios in which a friendly foreign leader might be having undisclosed conversations with other leaders to explore issues of national security concern, but it may nevertheless simply not be sensible to run the risk of damaging foreign relations should the operation become exposed, as the US interception of Chancellor Merkel's telephone demonstrated. In the 2015 independent surveillance review on which I sat, in addition to the expectation that the investigative work of government agencies must be conducted under the rule of law, we insisted that it must be restrained; that is, it should never be routine for the state to intrude into private lives.[18] It must be reluctant to do so and then restrained in the powers it chooses to use—an ethical judgment—and properly authorized when it deems it necessary to intrude. And there must be effective oversight, judged by the capability to supervise and investigate governmental intrusion, by the power to bring officials and ministers to account, and by the transparency it embodies so that the public can be confident it is working properly. In Hill's day, with memories of the war still very raw, the public would have been readier to accept that these matters were for the authorities and demonstrated a higher level of trust than we see today in the integrity of politicians. Conscious of the danger of romanticizing the past, I would nevertheless argue that today's media-driven political world leads to a less reflective, coarser form of government in which short-term expediency and a concern to be seen as responding to popular opinion risks less ethically thought-through policies.

Mark Phythian: This, then, leads to a second issue I want to discuss—the way in which politicians use assertions of legality to close down the ethical discussion of intelligence issues. Understandably, some ethicists view the invocation of law in relation to ethical issues as politicizing a question. However, I would argue that assertions of legality in the sphere of intelligence ethics have been intended to *depoliticize* the issue; they are an act of de-contestation.

David Omand: I agree that it is good to be reminded that an act may be legal but not necessarily what is morally right in the circumstances. That is the consequentialist case for secretaries of state to apply political and foreign policy judgment—with an ethical dimension—to the wisdom of intelligence operations and not to rely just on senior judges and lawyers to certify their legality. John Finnis argues, for example, that to this day some domains of executive responsibility, especially but not only in international affairs, are rightly reserved by law for the responsibility, discretion, and political accountability of the executive government.[19] In any case, however, the boundaries of the law are not always clear cut. A margin of ethical appreciation is always sensible rather than always acting right up to the boundary of the law. We do not admire those who go to extraordinary lengths to exploit loopholes in the law, for example, to pay less tax.

Does the logic run in the reverse direction? Is what is unlawful always unethical? Is there a margin of appreciation in the other direction we should allow those in the secret world? A principle may appear to be absolute in law—for example, one must not steal—yet be of limited moral validity since we would not, I hope, condemn a parent for stealing food to feed a starving child.[20] We might think badly of Victorian courts for handing down sentences of transportation for such hard cases, lawful though they were at the time.[21] I am not arguing for giving any discretion to intelligence officers to disregard domestic law, but my example nevertheless should remind us that we have to take care in applying the moral attitudes of today—for example, to privacy—to mount general criticisms of the past.

Mark Phythian: Let me take a much more recent example. Consider British foreign secretary William Hague's initial response to the revelations arising from the June 2013 leaking of top secret GCHQ documents by Edward Snowden. Hague sought to assure members of Parliament and the public of both the robust legislative framework in the United Kingdom and the strength of intelligence oversight via the parliamentary Intelligence and Security Committee. This was, Hague said, "one part of the strong framework of democratic accountability and oversight that governs the use of secret intelligence in the United Kingdom, which successive Governments have worked to strengthen. At its heart are two Acts of Parliament: the Intelligence Services Act 1994 and the Regulation of Investigatory Powers Act 2000." Overall, the United Kingdom had "one of the strongest systems of checks and balances and democratic accountability for secret intelligence anywhere in the world."[22] The message was clear: move on, there is nothing to see here and no need to be concerned.

David Omand: Following the Snowden allegations William Hague was first and foremost giving reassurance, from his own knowledge in his privileged position as foreign secretary, that the media's accusations against the GCHQ of operating without lawful authority and oversight were untrue. He was right to make that clear and in particular to stress not only that the staff of the GCHQ had obtained the individual authorizations required under domestic law but also that oversight had shown they were behaving ethically in their assessments of necessity and proportionality in individual operations. As we discuss in chapter 5, the underlying issue, which Hague did not address in his speech, was a different one. How should that confidence be "future proofed" in light of rapid technological change, and what additional checks and balances would be needed to cater for the enhanced power of modern digital tools? The government's first response, the so-called Snooper's Charter, did not survive scrutiny.[23] The political reality was that the government had to move on from what I described in the opening section of this chapter as the legal compliance model to that of the social compact; starting afresh with independent reviews and extensive open debate led to brand-new legislation that became the Investigatory Powers Act 2016.

Mark Phythian: I think that Hague's assurances need to be understood in the context of Jan Goldman's observation, made with regard to the United States but that applies equally to the United Kingdom: "For most Americans, law and ethics are intertwined, leading most people erroneously to believe that if it is legal it must be ethical and all things ethical are legal."[24] The important point here is that there is a relationship between legality and what we might term social acceptability. To be able to demonstrate, or argue with a degree of plausibility, that something is legal impacts the way people come to view it—that is, on the perception of its social acceptability.[25] In some cases, asserting the legality of a practice preempts (or, at least, is intended to preempt) the ethical question; in light of an assertion of its legality, it does not even need to be asked. Ethical cover is provided by the legal judgment; a separate ethical judgment is superfluous. The ethical issue is thus neutralized.

David Omand: The overriding assumption, I think we agree, is that the pursuit of intelligence in liberal democracies should always be governed by the rule of law. Strict adherence to the rules, in the sense of not straying beyond them, is an obligation of intelligence professionals. If intelligence practice falls within legally prescribed parameters, then a necessary (but not a sufficient) condition for a civilized society has been met.

Mark Phythian: So far, so good. However, let's unpack this a little further. The force of the law in liberal democracies is drawn from the legitimacy it enjoys with the public. This, in turn, is based on the assumption of informed consent; that is, an activity sanctioned by statute has been subjected to informed debate, and so to appropriate amendment arising from this debate, by legislative representatives. In this way, the legislative light to which it is subjected acts as a safeguard against ill-thought-out practices that could have undesirable future consequences. But as your outline of the evolution of the law-intelligence relationship shows, the emergence of intelligence into the liberal-democratic light has been a relatively recent development and should be regarded as an ongoing process in even those states where it occurred earliest of all (as we discuss further in chapter 7).

Historically, the operation of intelligence has not been characterized by bright legislative light applied on behalf of voters/taxpayers. We can see various proxies for this level of accountability were introduced, and became progressively more thorough, during the twentieth century. Moreover, these processes were joined by the increasing professionalization of intelligence practices. What we referred to in chapter 1 as the Stansfield Turner test is an example of one such proxy. However, such proxies cannot overcome the fact that they are precisely that—proxies for the granting of informed consent. This means, for example, that contextualizing the environment in which Christopher Hill and Inez Hill were surveilled in terms of the prevailing ethics of their time raises the question of whose ethics we are talking about. There is no sense that at this point even the Stansfield Turner test was applied. The general public would have been unaware of the existence of MI5 and of its methods; thus, it would have been unable to express an opinion as to the necessity or desirability of them.

David Omand: I agree that the guardians of those days were indeed hidden. But I do not doubt that the postwar majority, had they known, would have supported security work to contain the threat from communism (just as, even after Snowden's revelations, the majority today supports digital intelligence gathering to contain the threat from terrorism). But your point is helpful as another way of putting my argument for the desirability of shifting to the social compact model.

Mark Phythian: We agree therefore that in a liberal democratic context, assertions of legality have not always been sufficient to forestall ethical disapproval if the secrecy that surrounds some intelligence activities fails and the public becomes aware of them, especially where laws understood, however vaguely, to have been introduced for one set of purposes are extended to another without public debate. These cases, in turn, can lead to reassessments of the legal bases on which these actions rest and to the recognition of their inadequacy. Hence, the relationship between law and ethics is a dynamic one.

David Omand: I agree that the objective must be to align as far as possible legal and ethical considerations, at least until circumstances change with future technical developments that raise different ethical issues and require new regulation. An example might be the future combination of small drones with high-resolution digital imaging coupled with effective facial recognition software managed by artificial intelligence algorithms, where existing surveillance legislation may within the next decade prove to be inadequate to reflect the privacy concerns that such developments may raise. Another example, in the opposite direction, would be if a major new threat to national security were to emerge requiring the government to return to Parliament for additional powers.

Mark Phythian: It is worth pointing out that in the case of the United Kingdom, it has often been thanks to media exposure rather than the industry of formal oversight mechanisms that the public has been made aware of cases of legally sanctioned mission creep. For example, during 2008 and 2009 media reporting made apparent that some local councils in England and Wales were using the Regulation of Investigatory Powers Act 2000 in ways that raised concerns about slippage and excessive state surveillance. Councils in Derby, Bolton, Gateshead, and Hartlepool had used it in relation to dog fouling, and the Poole borough council had used it to spy on people collecting shellfish in Poole harbor and on a family to see if it was really living in the catchment area of a particular school ("curtains open and all lights on in premises"). Kensington and Chelsea used RIPA 2000 to look into disabled parking placard abuse. In the context of the outraged public reaction to these and other similar cases, Sir Simon Milton, chairman of the Local Government Association, wrote to all council leaders and reminded them that RIPA 2000 "requires that the powers only be used when 'necessary or proportionate to prevent or detect a criminal offence'. You will all know of the example where councils have been criticised for using the powers in relation to issues that can be portrayed as trivial or not considered a crime by the public." Shortly afterward Home Secretary Alan Johnson moved to curb the ability of local councils to use RIPA 2000.[26]

David Omand: And he was right to do so, as was the government in making the current legislation, the 2016 Investigatory Powers Act, much more restrictive in that respect. The intention in RIPA 2000 was to give local authorities the minimum powers they needed for child protection and to deal with serious public health issues (allowing such techniques as carrying out visual surveillance; they never had power to seek a warrant for telephone interception or bugging). When cases came to notice that unintended uses were being made of covert surveillance (made public following oversight but of course then amplified by the media), it was right to clamp down. That shows the system, including the role of a free press, was working.

Mark Phythian: It is significant, nevertheless, that although the GCHQ had followed statutory provisions authorizing the obtaining of intelligence on UK citizens from the US PRISM global interception program, when the GCHQ was taken to court (the Investigatory Powers Tribunal[27]), the government itself was held to have failed the rule of law test since citizens could not have known exactly what safeguards existed and how they were applied. It is striking that three successive high-level reports (including the one you sat on) recommended that RIPA 2000 be replaced. One report by David Anderson, the independent reviewer of terrorism legislation, commented that RIPA 2000, "obscure since its inception, has been patched up so many times as to make it incomprehensible to all but a tiny band of initiates." This state of affairs, Anderson continued, "is undemocratic, unnecessary and—in the long run—intolerable."[28]

David Omand: That is another point well made and one that reflects the underlying importance of the implicit shift the British government (and this author) has made in moving from a legal compliance to a social compact model for regulating secret intelligence. We can regard *ethics*, as the dictionaries would guide us, as a social, religious, or civil code of "correct" behavior, especially that of a particular group, profession, or individual. And we can regard the *law* as its complement—that is, a system of rules a particular country or community recognizes as regulating the actions of its members by criminalizing certain actions and that it may enforce. So in a well-regulated society there should be a consistent mapping of the boundary between the behavior sanctioned by law as criminal and the behavior considered ethically acceptable, always allowing for the inevitable time lags between changes in public attitude and in legislation. If there is a significant, persistent gap or underlap between behavior that the law prohibits and that society believes to be ethically acceptable, then campaigns to expand the boundary of the law must be expected, as we have seen in England over foxhunting. If, however, there is a significant overlap, with behavior criminalized that many in society feel should be allowed, as was the case for many years with divorce law, then civil disobedience must be expected. Very significantly, in light of recent public concerns over privacy and in a first for Europe, the UK government has taken the public step of avowing all the modern forms of digital intelligence including equipment interference (hacking) and the use of bulk personal databases. In that way, any under- or overlap between ethics and law for the time being has been minimized.

Mark Phythian: That may be true for domestic law, but what of the impact of international law in relation to national intelligence gathering? The importance of the ability to make a plausible assertion of legality is arguably even greater here than at the domestic level. This may fall some way short of a consensus view of the legality of an action but nevertheless provide legal cover and generate a degree of social acceptability by utilizing what US lawyers term a colorable or legally available argument.[29] The reason for this lies in a development noted in the previous chapter—that is, the rise of the ideology of individual human rights together with a supporting legal framework. There is potential tension between domestic law and international human rights law in an intelligence context, and for the United Kingdom the impact of European law adds a further dimension. As we have noted, the prospect of the UK government continually falling foul of the European Convention of Human Rights with respect to its own citizens after a string of adverse judgments led to the introduction of the 1989 Security Service Act, placing MI5 on a statutory footing for the first time, and the subsequent Intelligence Services Act (1994) doing the same for MI6 and GCHQ.[30]

David Omand: In addition to regulating domestic surveillance, the law in most democratic nations now provides a national legal basis for espionage conducted overseas. In the case of the United Kingdom, that legal basis includes compliance with the 1998 Human Rights Act, which is itself based on the ECHR. Nevertheless, intelligence officers are at constant legal risk overseas. Although no treaty recognized in international law bears on the ubiquitous practice of espionage (nor will one ever likely do so since nations will not agree on what constitutes espionage), every nation makes espionage against it a criminal offense, and some still consider it a capital offense. The general international practice arose out of placing intelligence officers overseas under diplomatic cover precisely so that diplomatic immunity to prosecution could be claimed if allegations of espionage were made. Without such cover, a jailed officer could only hope that a spy swap might be in the interests of the countries concerned.[31] Some offenses committed overseas, such as bribery of a foreign official, are also offenses in the United Kingdom (under anti-bribery and anti-corruption legislation).

British officers planning an operation that involved breaking a law overseas could also technically be guilty of a conspiracy in the United Kingdom to commit a criminal offense. For such reasons section 7 of the 1994 Intelligence Services Act provides for the foreign secretary to sign a certificate of authorization of acts outside the British Islands such that if "a person would be liable in the United Kingdom for any act done outside the British Islands, he shall not be so liable if the act is one which is authorised to be done by virtue of an authorisation given by the Secretary of State under this section."[32] Thus, being able to say that British intelligence officers at all times comply with *domestic* law is important. And that includes being human rights compliant.

Mark Phythian: That is reassuring in light of controversies involving alleged UK complicity in torture. The dilemma facing intelligence officers is in having to be human rights compliant yet still undertake activities such as using bribery, deception, false identities, and all the rest as routine activities. To carry out these activities, they are provided with explicit legal and implicit ethical exemption from standards that society otherwise applies. Those methods may be made lawful in domestic law under section 7, but there also has to be an ethical boundary beyond which they do not stray. I am reminded of the scene in Graham Greene's (pre–section 7) novel *The Human Factor*, where the head of MI6 (known as "C") and two officers are discussing the existence of a mole inside the organization. One suggested solution to this problem that would avoid a trial and the inevitable attendant publicity is to "'draft whoever it is to some innocuous department. Forget things.' 'And abet a crime?'" asks one of the officers. "'Oh, crime,'" replies the other officer, "and smiled at C like a fellow conspirator. 'We are all committing crimes somewhere, aren't we? It's our job.'"[33]

The rise of the ideology of universal human rights has created difficulties for national intelligence because it has been accompanied by the development of frameworks of international human rights law that exist in tension with national laws legitimizing otherwise unlawful intelligence actions and perhaps rendering them invalid. This reality has also meant that US intelligence conduct in the war on terror could not simply ignore the law. In a scene in the memoir of former US director of central intelligence George Tenet, al-Qaeda "big fish" Abu Zubaydah had been captured in a raid by Pakistani and US authorities in Faisalabad in March 2002. He was shot three times as he attempted to evade capture, and the CIA arranged for private jet to fly a leading surgeon from Johns Hopkins Medical Center to Pakistan and save his life. Once stabilized, he was handed over to the CIA for interrogation. But how far could they go in interrogating him? As

Tenet explained in his memoir: "Despite what Hollywood might have you believe, in situations like this you don't call in the tough guys; you call in the lawyers."[34]

Let us be clear: the purpose of consulting the lawyers was to protect those applying interrogation techniques from a future risk that international human rights law might pose to interrogators who were deemed to have used torture. But the law here seems to have been decided by taking what the administration wanted to do and then generating an argument for its compliance with the law. A July 2009 report by the US Justice Department's Office of Professional Responsibility was highly critical of two Justice Department lawyers who provided the arguments that facilitated the waterboarding that followed—Jay Bybee, by then a federal judge, and John Yoo, by then a professor at the University of California–Berkeley. The report found that both had engaged in professional misconduct by failing to provide "thorough, candid, and objective" analysis in memorandums regarding the interrogation of detained terrorist suspects. David Margolis, the deputy associate attorney general responsible for reviewing the report, rejected this conclusion in his own subsequent report, and even though he did not think it was done in bad faith, he still commented that what became known as the "torture memos" were based on "poor judgment" and seriously flawed legal analysis. Margolis found that "Yoo's loyalty to his own ideology and convictions clouded his view of his obligation to his client and led him to author opinions that reflected his own extreme, albeit sincerely held views of executive power while speaking for an institutional client."[35]

David Omand: We may know that now, but it does appear that the United States deliberately kept all that from the United Kingdom at the time (including the operations in Europe with a "black site" in Poland for interrogating detainees, including Khalid Sheikh Mohammed[36]), recognizing that the United Kingdom could not lawfully cooperate and that the UK law officers would never have accepted the Bybee and Yoo interpretation of international law and would thus have had to oppose the policy. The United States would have known that the United Kingdom had previous experience. The British Army had coercively interrogated (although thankfully not involving waterboarding) a small number of Irish Republican Army suspects in 1971, and the Irish government had taken the case to the European Court of Human Rights, which found the British Army guilty of inhuman and degrading treatment of the detainees. Prime Minister Edward Heath had subsequently banned such practices from use by intelligence or service personnel for all time. After an investigation the parliamentary Intelligence and Security Committee unsurprisingly confirmed in 2007 that the United Kingdom had not been complicit in that US policy of extraordinary rendition and coercive interrogation, but it did note that the United Kingdom had been slow to detect what the United States was doing.[37] So it is important to recognize that after 9/11 the UK government or its agents did not themselves engage in torture or directly authorize torture, nor has that been alleged.

In the post-9/11 circumstances, I regard the leaders and members of the UK agencies and armed services as having acted very responsibly and of having shown considerable ethical awareness in not being drawn into wrongdoing alongside their US counterparts as information gradually seeped out about what they were doing. I should add that a section 7 certificate, had an agency requested it, could not have lifted the responsibility from intelligence officers to refrain from participating in, soliciting, encouraging, or condoning the use of torture or cruel, inhuman, or degrading treatment for any purpose. I should add that there is the separate matter of the ethics of receiving intelligence from a state whose services are suspected of ill-treating suspects. That is not itself wrong, provided it is not part of a collusive relationship (such as asking a foreign intelligence service, known for its systemic use of torture, to detain and question a terrorism suspect). The House of Lords (acting as the predecessor of the UK Supreme Court) in *A and Others v Secretary of State for the Home Department*, while deciding that evidence obtained under torture is not admissible in legal proceedings, nevertheless made clear that in certain circumstances the secretary of state can use information obtained under torture to take action to save a life.

Mark Phythian: There is no doubt that some intelligence practices associated with the Bush administration's war on terror lie at the extreme end of a range of scenarios where the fundamental question of "How far can intelligence go?" in the collection of information is begged. What happens if the latitude afforded by national and international law is held to be insufficient to address risks or threats to the state and its populace? That such questions are posed reflects the way in which the contemporary transnational terror threat has extended the range of response scenarios by also extending the range of modes of challenge that the state faces. Such terrorist attacks are unlikely to be so severe as to amount to the "supreme emergency" situation that Michael Walzer has discussed.[38] In talking of supreme emergency, Walzer was invoking Winston Churchill's characterization of the situation facing Britain in 1939. In the face of such a dire *and* imminent threat, where the very future of the entire political community is at risk, this therefore "may well require exactly those measures that the war convention bars."[39]

Nevertheless, such terrorist attacks certainly represent a potential threat to large numbers of a state's residents. As Bruce Hoffman noted as long ago as the mid-1990s, the rise of terrorism justified by reference to religion has represented "a significant loosening of the constraints on the commission of mass murder," with religion being used "as a legitimizing force sanctioning if not encouraging widespread violence against an almost open-ended category of opponents."[40] Hoffman recognized that the terrorist who invokes religion as justification "sees himself as an outsider from the society that he both abhors and rejects and this sense of alienation enables him to contemplate—and undertake—far more destructive and bloodier types of terrorist operations than his secular counterpart."[41] The contemporary terrorist threat has evolved in a number of ways since the mid-1990s, but this remains at the heart of the security dilemma it generates and is fundamental to debates about the response of intelligence in its role as an early warning arm of the state. In practice the 9/11 terrorist attacks gave rise to an intelligence-led response on the part of the United States that fits Walzer's characterization of how, when deep values are at risk, a "utilitarianism of extremity" can supplant the "rights normality."[42]

However, there is no clear guide as to what is regarded as acceptable here or how to balance the demands of national security and universal human rights. Moreover, the human rights requirement is absolute and so allows for no balancing. What is the most appropriate ethical course in these circumstances? Utilitarian approaches accord a low priority (if any at all) to values such as freedom and autonomy, values that "include a respect for life, whereas utilitarian thinking by itself justifies too easily the sacrificing of someone's life to promote the good of others."[43] Even setting that consideration aside, the way in which this balance is determined is inherently subjective. Who applies this judgment? How can we be sure that these judgments, taken in secret, reflect wider societal values?[44]

David Omand: The United Kingdom's own post-9/11 counterterrorism strategy, CONTEST, was very different from the Bush administration's war on terrorism in that it stressed the objective of normality. In the words of the UK strategic objective, it sought to reduce the risk from international terrorism so that people could go about their normal lives, freely and with confidence. The British approach to countering terrorism incorporated a strong element of ethical thinking, drawing on the (sometimes painful) experiences of previous campaigns. One important lesson was that utilitarian thinking has to be long term as well as short term. There is an obvious difference between judging the rightness of an operation in terms of its short-term justification and by its possible longer-term consequences. The proponents of the Bush era's coercive interrogation program immediately after 9/11 understandably felt justified by the need to get intelligence to prevent further murderous attacks. Had the measures been less extreme (the legal advice at the time from the White House that they did not amount to torture now looks, as you point out, distinctly shaky), such a program could have been held to be both necessary and proportionate to the harm to be prevented. But even so, looked at in terms of a longer-term counterterrorism strategy, the program risked playing into the terrorists' own agenda and certainly alienated moderate opinion both domestically and overseas, making any long-term prosecution of the campaign harder.

A fundamental lesson that those such as myself working on devising the UK counterterrorism strategy after 9/11 had learned from experience was the value of preemptive intelligence. That is as true today as it was then. With good intelligence the authorities can act against the terrorists with the rapier; without it the recourse has to be to the bludgeons of emergency powers, house-to-house searches, and even detention without trial, thus alienating the community and creating new recruits for the terrorist groups. That is a lesson that continental European partners are having to learn in light of the wave of jihadist attacks over the last few years.

As a leading Oxford philosopher once pointed out to me, upholding the rule of law is at the heart of a civilized society. The United Kingdom has rightly incorporated a legal prohibition on torture into domestic law, since the right not to be tortured is absolute and cannot be justified even on grounds of national security. The prohibition is clear under the UN Universal Human Rights Declaration, agreed after the horrors of the Second World War, and under the subsequent European Convention to which the United Kingdom is subject. But as the Oxford philosopher continued, were your child to be kidnapped and were you genuinely convinced that his or her survival depended on immediate rescue and the only person who knew the child's location was the kidnapper, sitting in front of you silently and smugly, with time to save the child running out, then you have, as an individual, the responsibility to weigh your moral duties both as a law-abiding citizen and as a parent. Not acting also has consequences. As John Stuart Mill wrote, "A person may cause evil to others not only by his actions but by his inaction, and in either case he is justly accountable to them for the injury."[45] We are independent, autonomous moral actors in a free society, and an ethically defensible result might well be to inflict a clearly unlawful act of violence on the kidnapper to try and persuade him to talk. As I suggested earlier there can be unlawful acts that can be ethically justified. The difference between this thought experiment, of course, and the cases of post-9/11 US coercive interrogation lies in the absence of preemptive absolution. There is no White House "keep out of jail free" card to play. You would, and should, confess to the violent crime and take your chance of a plea in mitigation when it came to sentencing. Most of us would consider the life of our child to be worth a spell in prison. But no instruction to another to commit the violence could be lawful; therefore, there can be no ethical case whatever for maintaining a state torturer.

Mark Phythian: Former director of the US National Security Agency and the CIA Michael Hayden discussed enhanced interrogation techniques in his memoir, *Playing to the Edge*.[46] In their memoirs, both Hayden and his deputy director for operations Jose A. Rodriguez Jr. defend the techniques used in attempts to extract information from terrorist suspects in essentially utilitarian terms by emphasizing the value of the techniques in eliciting information. In judging such utilitarian arguments, the public needs to place considerable trust in the accounts of senior intelligence managers, because the secrecy that attaches to the evidence means the public cannot access the primary material for themselves. However, these memoirs are not dispassionate summaries of a game now over; instead, they are interventions in an ongoing game, one in which there is a contest for the dominant narrative within which CIA conduct in the first decade of the twenty-first century will be understood in future histories.

Dianne Feinstein, chair of the Senate Select Committee on Intelligence, which published a highly critical five-hundred-page executive summary of its inquiry into CIA detention and interrogation practices in the war on terror in December 2014, responded to Hayden's memoir by producing a thirty-eight-page guide, "Factual Errors and Other Problems."[47] For example, in his book Hayden wrote, "No one with any knowledge of this program doubted that it had provided unique, actionable intelligence."[48] Feinstein's office reached a different conclusion:

To the extent that "this program" is intended to signify the use of the CIA's enhanced interrogation techniques, CIA records demonstrate that numerous individuals with knowledge of the program doubted that it had provided unique, actionable intelligence. The Inspector General [IG] concluded that "it is not clear whether these plots have been thwarted or if they remain viable or even if they were fabricated in the first place," noting that the IG's review "did not uncover any evidence that these plots were imminent." In several examples, CIA officers identified inaccuracies in the CIA's representations that the program had produced "unique, actionable intelligence," but the CIA failed to take action to correct those representations. Finally, the CIA agreed "in full" with the Study's conclusion that the CIA never conducted its own comprehensive analysis of the effectiveness of its enhanced interrogation techniques.[49]

David Omand: To return to your earlier remark, this is the context in which the lawyers whom George Tenet referred to in his memoir entered, stage right. It was clearly essential to Tenet and to Jose Rodriguez and their staffs that they were given a determination that the practices were lawful. According to the findings of a review by the CIA inspector general into the CIA's counterterrorism detention and interrogation activities from 2001 to 2003, a number of CIA officers were concerned about the reliability of these findings and were also aware that they offered no protection in international law. As the inspector general reported:

> During the course of this Review, a number of Agency officers expressed unsolicited concern about the possibility of recrimination or legal action resulting from their participation in the CTC [Counterterrorism Center] Program. A number of officers expressed concern that a human rights group might pursue them for activities [Redacted]. Additionally, they feared that the Agency would not stand behind them if this occurred.
>
> One officer expressed concern that one day, Agency officers will wind up on some "wanted list" to appear before the World Court for war crimes stemming from activities [Redacted].[50]

Mark Phythian: My argument is that in addition to providing an apparent guarantee against prosecution, the assurance of legality makes more ethically acceptable something that would otherwise be regarded as ethically impermissible (and which many in the wider US intelligence community, we now know, had severe doubts about). The White House lawyers conferred state legitimacy on a practice and gave those directing the practice an authority they would otherwise have lacked. One tactic of senior CIA officials familiar with the rendition and torture of terrorist suspects in the immediate post-9/11 period is that, following the ruling of the Bush administration lawyers, they consistently refer to CIA interrogation practices as "enhanced interrogation techniques" and resist the suggestion that they amounted to torture.

A good example of this can be found in a 2012 interview with Jose Rodriguez, who played a key role in the development of these enhanced interrogation techniques. He explained to his interviewer, Amy Davidson, that "the practices the CIA used were not torture. . . . These actions were . . . judged to be legal and not torture by the Department of Justice, and briefed to appropriate members of Congress."[51] Asked why he felt that "the word 'torture' matters so much," he replied, "Well, because torture is illegal." He went on to explain: "We at the CIA did not have the luxury of shopping around for a legal opinion. We went to the Justice Department asked then, Is this legal? Can we do this? And they came back to us two months later and said, Yes it is. So we went with the opinion that we received. Had they said that we couldn't do it, we would not have done it."[52] Similarly, looking back to the time when he became director of the CIA in 2006, in his memoir Hayden recalled that "in the world as it was seen from Langley, folks there believed they had done the right things morally, legally, and operationally."[53]

To reiterate, my argument is that those who believed they had done the right thing morally could arrive at this conclusion only because they had been given legal approval. The morality of the tasks at hand would have seemed different absent the conferment of this legality. It is also clear that for some, such as Rodriguez, the moral question and the legal question were one and the same thing.

In terms of the relationship between intelligence, law, and ethics, the title Hayden chose for his book, *Playing to the Edge*, is interesting. As he explained, "The reference is to using all the tools and all the authorities available, much like how a good athlete takes advantage of the entire playing field right up to the sideline markers and endlines."[54] It is interesting because the location of "the edge" is clearly legally rather than normatively defined.

David Omand: One of the arguments in deterrence theory against laying down redlines that an adversary must not cross is that it implies that there will be no sanction if the adversary creeps right up to the line and "plays to the edge" with all the risks of being misinterpreted as having strayed over it. The ethical implication of identifying legal boundaries is that it is hard to act against those who end up operating as closely to them as possible. I cited earlier the problem with aggressive tax avoidance that, by definition, still involves operating *within* the law.

Mark Phythian: Yes, and this is the clear meaning conveyed by the title Hayden chose. In the realm of intelligence, especially in the post-9/11 context, what are the ethical implications of identifying legal boundaries and then operating as closely to them as possible? Are there any? By definition it would still involve operating *within* the law. A number of philosophers, though, have declined to involve themselves in discussions of precisely what constitutes torture on the grounds that this effort does set up a boundary; it does define "the edge" in this context and so suggests a range of ethically questionable practices, which could be held to fall short of any definition, is permissible.[55]

Moreover, to extend the sporting metaphor, athletes can cheat or explore gray areas at the boundaries of the permissible to gain an advantage while claiming adherence to the rules of the game and trusting that the precautions they take will ensure secrecy. The sport of cycling provides one very good example.[56] However, athletes don't have one advantage in determining the boundaries that national intelligence agencies possess. In the realm of national security, we have seen that it is possible for players to hire referees to redefine the boundaries and so extend the location of the edge.

David Omand: The point is a fair one. That is why when the "Yellow Card," giving the rules of engagement for British Army soldiers during the Northern Ireland campaign, was drawn up (and published) in the 1970s, it was deliberately drafted with a margin of appreciation. If soldiers did play to the edge of the rules in the card, then they would still remain well within the actual boundary of the law. In the intelligence world, the inevitable secrecy toward adversaries—dictators, terrorists, and criminals—surrounding our sources and methods makes such an open approach difficult when it comes to publishing detailed internal instructions or rules for intelligence operations.

Mark Phythian: Perhaps then the historical evolution of the law-intelligence relationship has not been quite so linear and sequential as your initial outline suggests. Perhaps these cases show us that in parts of the intelligence and law enforcement communities, the executive rules and legal compliance models have persisted and actually coexisted in a state of potential and occasional actual tension. If so, then oversight bodies have a vital role in addressing the executive branch's resistance on which the continuation of the elements of an executive rules culture is based. We shall return to the question of oversight in chapter 7.

3

From Just War to Just Intelligence?

David Omand: Whenever an intelligence officer identifies a potential agent to recruit or devises a way to access digital communications, ethical risks are likely to arise at some point. As was discussed in chapter 1, it is in the nature of secret intelligence gathering to find a way of overcoming the will of the person with the secret who wants to prevent us from knowing it, and that is likely to involve using deception or other methods that we would scarcely regard as suitable for the everyday interactions of civilized human behavior. Yet without obtaining the secret, greater harms may result. We might insist today that intelligence activity be conducted within legal constraints, but on what moral foundation should those constraints be based?

The general shape of the problem of determining how to secure a just outcome while having recourse to the use of ethically risky methods has been with us for centuries. Establishing conditions for the just use of violence had been the preoccupation of thinkers in the Just War tradition from Aristotle, Augustine, and Thomas Aquinas to Martin Luther and John Locke. Such reasoning tries to reconcile different propositions that are in tension: (1) states have a positive duty, as part of their contract with their citizens, to protect the population when the need arises and to uphold justice and law; but (2) protecting the innocent and defending moral values sometimes demand using force in response to an aggressor who is prepared to use violence; and yet (3) all but psychopaths would agree that causing deliberate harm to others is at heart ethically wrong and to be avoided.

If we substitute "the harms caused by the direct use of force" with "the lesser potential harms caused by intelligence activity," such as invading someone's privacy or placing the family of an agent in danger, the general line of reasoning still makes sense. For the originators of Just War thinking, their reasoning was theological and remains so for those in more recent times such as Reinhold Niebuhr and others who have written in the tradition of Christian realism.[1] The concepts of the Just War tradition are, however, equally powerfully applied in the humanitarian thinking of philosophers such as Locke, who steer between realism and pacifism while accepting war at times as a lesser evil but placing limits on it. (Luther notably departed from the original Catholic Just War tradition by excluding wars of religion from those that can be considered just.) Modern theories of rights and their applicability to all people and at all times also have a deep root in this tradition.[2] As the Jesuit Francisco Suárez wrote in 1610:

> Although a given sovereign state, Commonwealth, or kingdom may constitute a perfect community in itself, consisting of its own members, nevertheless each one of those states is also, in a certain sense, viewed in relation to the human race, and member of the universal society; for these states when standing alone are never so self sufficient but they do not require some mutual assistance, association, and intercourse, and times for their own greater welfare and advantage, but other times because also of some moral necessity or need.[3]

International humanitarian law now allows for a balance of these competing moral demands of permission and limitation. Thus, for armed conflict the purpose must be considered just. The military actions must be necessary in achieving the military aim and must be proportionate, and the tactics and weapons employed must be capable of discriminating between legitimate targets and those that the warrior has a duty to protect. The Geneva Conventions of 1949 therefore provide legitimacy for states to use lethal force in conflict but on the condition that commanders provide for the mitigation of suffering both to those who are inevitably the target of military operations and to those who should be protected from its effects. In particular, Additional Protocol 1 limits attacks only to "objects which by their nature, purpose and use make an effective contribution to military action."[4] For actions under international human rights law outside armed conflict, the use of lethal force must be no more than is absolutely necessary in defense of any person from unlawful violence. The addition of "absolutely" recognizes that in peacetime the authorities will usually have more options open for protecting the public, and lethal force should not be used when there are reasonable alternatives open.[5]

It is thus not the case that in peacetime while faced with the armed criminal or terrorist or in war amid the clash of arms, the law need be silent, as Cicero claimed in his dictum *Silent enim leges inter arma* (in times of war, the law falls silent). In 1998 US chief justice William Rehnquist alluded to Cicero when he suggested that "the least justified of the curtailments of civil liberty" were unlikely to be accepted by the courts in wars of the future. "It is neither desirable nor is it remotely likely that civil liberty will occupy as favored a position in wartime as it does in peacetime. But it is both desirable and likely that more careful attention will be paid by the courts to the basis for the government's claims of necessity as a basis for curtailing civil liberty," the chief justice wrote. "The laws will thus not be silent in time of war, but they will speak with a somewhat different voice."[6]

Following the Just War tradition, conduct must be considered at two different levels. The first outer test concerns the initial decision to enter into conflict, the *jus ad bellum* (justification of war), or the justness of the cause on which lives and human welfare will be hazarded. The second inner test relates to the ethical acceptability of the methods chosen to prosecute the war once it has been embarked upon, or the *jus in bello* (justice in war). We can consider in turn whether there could be intelligence equivalents—the *jus ad intelligentiam*, which would limit the purposes considered legitimate for secret agencies, and the *jus in intelligentia,* which would place ethical restrictions on the methods for gathering it.[7]

FROM JUS AD BELLUM TO JUS AD INTELLIGENTIAM

The possession of significant military capabilities can provide a state with legitimate security and the ability to exercise the innate right to self-defense, but it could also bring the capacity to enrich itself at the expense of its neighbors or to derive other selfish advantages by threatening the use of force. Augustine termed such conflicts wars of desire rather than wars of necessity, and Hugo Grotius in 1625 ruled them out as illegitimate wars in the first codification of the law relating to international relations.[8] Just War thinkers such as Aquinas emphasized restraint and the regrettable necessity of war. If a peaceful outcome to a dispute could be obtained, then it was one's moral duty to seek it before resorting to arms.

The mere possession of military superiority can give rise to unjust outcomes if it is believed that the state concerned will use its power irresponsibly. Legitimate steps taken by a state to build up a defensive capability can trigger insecurity in other states, leading them to try to regain their former sense of security, and can provoke an arms race, creating what is known as the *security dilemma*. In the same way, the possession of a significant unconstrained digital capability (such as an advanced cyber attack capability) may give a state the ability to steal an unjust advantage over others, as well as legitimately to protect its interests, and may trigger a version of a cyber security dilemma.[9]

Unlike, however, the contemporary jus ad bellum, which in the end can be traced to the UN Charter and the legitimizing role of the Security Council, there is no equivalent fount of authority for the jus ad intelligentiam. No significant international law bears on espionage, although as we saw in chapter 2 every country makes spying against it a criminal offense. Nevertheless, efforts are under way to identify norms of behavior in relation to digital intelligence gathering that democratic countries might consider following and that might, were sufficient states to follow them, in time be regarded as customary international law. The Global Commission on Internet Governance chaired by former Swedish prime minister Carl Bildt has published recommendations to that effect, as has a UN working group of experts.[10]

The 1948 UN Declaration on Human Rights, discussed in chapter 2, recognizes the need to meet the just requirements of morality, public order, and general welfare in a democratic society. The Council of Europe's Convention on Human Rights, which entered into force in 1953, incorporated that principle and provides a starting point for jus ad intelligentiam: "There shall be no interference by a public authority with the exercise of this right [i.e., respect for one's private and family life, one's home, and one's correspondence] except such as is in accordance with the law and is necessary in a democratic society in the interests of national security, public safety or the economic well-being of the country, for the prevention of disorder or crime, for the protection of health or morals, or for the protection of the rights and freedoms of others."[11]

Drawing on that language, the founding 1989 and 1994 legislation for the British security and intelligence agencies therefore limits the work of the agencies to only three statutory functions: upholding national security, detecting and preventing serious crime, and safeguarding economic well-being (the latter is qualified as having to originate from outside the nation and be of national security concern). These three purposes provide for the

UK agencies an outer ethical limit for their work, as part of a statutory jus ad intelligentiam. The use of national intelligence for any other purpose would be unjust (and unlawful).

If we accept that states will still have primacy in the international order, then protecting their individual national security interests is an obvious legitimizing purpose for intelligence activity. National security is nevertheless not defined anywhere in any nation's statute law (and the judiciary have traditionally deferred to the executive when the claim is made that cases before the courts engage national security interests). Of course, disagreements will inevitably arise over what counts as national security because states will have different thresholds of interest under different social and economic systems. On the one hand, Chinese and Russian cyber espionage against US defense companies represents a significant violation of intellectual property rights for the United States. But espionage against national security targets is only to be expected, and it is accepted that the onus is on the United States to defend such secrets. On the other hand, we might surmise that for the Chinese and Russians, whose armaments production is in the hands of the state, acquiring information about new advanced weapon systems, even if developed in the US private sector, is first and foremost a matter of national security. That appears to be the import of the 2015 understandings reached between the government of China and those of the United States and the United Kingdom.[12]

Most democratic governments in recent years have taken to publishing National Security Strategies, which highlight those threats to national security that are felt to be important. For example, the 2015 UK strategy identified four top risks to national security that will drive UK intelligence priorities for the coming decade:

1. the increasing threat posed by terrorism, extremism, and instability;
2. the resurgence of state-based threats and intensifying wider state competition;
3. the impact of technology, especially cyber threats, and wider technological developments; and
4. the erosion of the rules-based international order, making it harder to build consensus and tackle global threats.[13]

In the first category, terrorism is treated as a crime but one that may in its extreme form affect national security, so in the United Kingdom the

Security Service has primacy in gathering intelligence. The same can be said in France, where after the 2015 and 2016 terrorist attacks a parliamentary commission emphasized the importance of national intelligence and law enforcement working more closely together in fighting terrorism.[14]

For the United States, the founding National Security Act of 1947 provided a single purpose for the CIA—"to correlate and evaluate intelligence relating to the national security." It allowed the director of the FBI to "make available to the Director of Central Intelligence such information for correlation, evaluation, and dissemination as may be essential to the national security," with the proviso that the CIA must have "no police, subpoena, law-enforcement powers, or internal-security functions."[15] The resulting relationships between the externally facing CIA and the federal law-enforcing domestic FBI have always been a source of congressional concern, as noted, for example, in Congress's criticism of intelligence sharing prior to the attacks on 9/11.[16]

In every jurisdiction where the rule of law has sway, it has always been accepted that the prevention of crime is a legitimate objective for law enforcement. Prevention involves anticipation, and that in turn depends on prior knowledge of criminal intent through some form of intelligence gathering.

In recent times law enforcement has increasingly used techniques, such as the recruitment of long-term agents inside criminal gangs and the use of the most sophisticated tracking and eavesdropping equipment, that in the past would have been associated with national intelligence. In some jurisdictions, such as the United States and Germany, this building of an intelligence capability within law enforcement is a deliberate response to the need to keep the worlds of secret intelligence and of law enforcement constitutionally separate. For other nations, such as the United Kingdom, that dividing line has never been as sharp, and law enforcement has increasingly looked to the intelligence community to use its advanced global capabilities for intelligence support in tackling serious crime such as narcotics, human trafficking, and cyber crime. The rise in jihadist terrorism and the consequent interaction between domestic threats and those originating overseas can be expected to encourage the worlds of policing and national intelligence to move closer together, as it has done in the United Kingdom, and the increasing problem of cyber crime is likely to accelerate this trend. Thus, the ethical principles applied to the work of intelligence agencies ought also to apply to law enforcement intelligence activities while accepting that the details of authorization procedures and oversight may differ.

The UK provision for national intelligence to be deployed for the purpose of safeguarding economic well-being should be seen as part of the broad national security area of responsibility. While it excludes commercial espionage for the competitive advantage of national companies, it would include tackling serious cyber attacks from overseas aimed at destabilizing markets or hostile activity that might threaten the continuity of energy supplies. After the Snowden revelations, the US president reconfirmed publicly that commercial espionage was not allowed under the procedures of the National Security Agency.[17] The same has also been the case with respect to the signals intelligence UKUSA Agreement, comprising the United States, the United Kingdom, Canada, Australia, and New Zealand, that dates back to the Second World War.

A further ethical restriction has been placed in US and UK legislation that makes it a criminal offense to seek to use national intelligence assets for a political party or personal advantage. Categories of persons whose privacy deserves special protection, such as elected representatives, ministers of religion, lawyers exercising legal professional privilege, and journalists with their sources, have also been identified. At least among the United States and its close allies (i.e., the Five Eyes community of the UKUSA Agreement) and among the thirty-seven members of the Council of Europe and signatories to the ECHR there are therefore the beginnings of an implicit jus ad intelligentiam that might in time form global norms to govern the purposes for which secret intelligence may be regarded as a proper activity by states (even if not governed by international treaty).

FROM JUS IN BELLO TO JUS IN INTELLIGENTIA

The Just War tradition can provide ethical considerations to guide intelligence activity in individual cases, the jus in intelligentia. If the just cause criterion discussed earlier is added, then the tradition provides a usable set of concepts for examining ethical risks in the intelligence world, namely:

- *just cause*—being in accordance with the constraints of statute law, transparent to the public, and with the intended meaning of terms such as "national security" explained in published government documents
- *right intention*—acting with integrity and having no hidden political or other agendas behind the authorization of intelligence activity or

the analysis, assessment, and presentation of intelligence judgments to decision-makers

- *proportionality*—keeping the ethical risks of operations in line with the harm that the operations are intended to prevent
- *right authority*—establishing the level appropriate to the ethical risks that may be run and that will then allow for accountability for decisions and oversight of the process
- *reasonable prospect of success*—having adequate justification for individual operations based on sound probabilistic reasoning that also prevents general "fishing expeditions" or mass surveillance
- *discrimination*—determining the human and technical ability to assess and manage the risk of collateral harm, including privacy intrusion into the lives of those who are not the intended targets of intelligence gathering
- *necessity*—finding no other reasonable way to achieve the authorized mission at lesser ethical risk but still applying any intrusive investigation with restraint

Right Intention

To qualify as just, the activity must have the right intention. In the intelligence business, it could be characterized as integrity of motive on the part of those initiating and authorizing the operations.

The real justification for the operation must be honestly stated in the submission for authorization and not rest on some hidden agenda of the intelligence agency or indeed of the intelligence officers concerned. The chilling 2006 Academy Award–winning film by Florian Henckel von Donnersmarck, *The Lives of Others*, brilliantly dramatized this risk. Its plot revolves around agents of the Stasi being ordered to carry out intimate surveillance of an actress on the grounds she is the mistress of a dissident, but the hidden motive is that the intelligence chief desires her. The US NSA is said to have coined the term "LOVEINT" to refer to the practice of employees illegally making use of monitoring capabilities to check on their spouses or lovers.[18] UK interception of communications commissioner Sir Anthony May described how an employee of the Government Communications Headquarters deliberately undertook a number of unauthorized searches on an individual as "the first known instance of deliberate abuse of GCHQ's interception and communications data systems in this way."[19] The employee was sacked.

Aquinas held that ambushes, as a way by which a military commander could conceal his meaning, were not illegitimate in war (as he pointed out, even sacred doctrine itself often conceals its meaning). The principle of right intention therefore should not rule out deception during an intelligence operation, such as a false-flag recruitment by an intelligence officer posing as a national of a country that the agent might regard more sympathetically. A tolerance of deceit and half-truths may be standard for the professional human intelligence officer, but such wiles cannot be acceptable if applied to one's own side, whether with customers for intelligence, authorizing officers, or overseers.

We might add the same today for the public trust necessary to maintain intelligence capabilities in a democracy. As Immanuel Kant concluded, acts of a furtive or dishonest nature in war will undermine trust necessary for future peace, and nothing should be done that might jeopardize that.[20]

Proportionality

Assessing proportionality must be done as a balancing exercise in which the potential harms that the operation could cause are set against the harms that it is designed to avert, such as helping uncover the members of a terrorist network believed to be planning an attack. There is inevitably subjectivity here, for which the courts have been willing to allow "a margin of appreciation" for the decisions taken by the state agency.[21] In addition, an element of counterfactual thinking is involved. The authorizing officer has to judge not only the potential risks being run but also what risk is represented by *not* conducting the operation. Thus, a computer interference operation might be judged proportionate to frustrate a serious criminal cyber attack, notwithstanding the risk of unintended knock-on effects on other Internet users, if the cyber attack appears to be likely to cause significant damage. But a comparable operation to uncover and disrupt a gang of bicycle thieves could well be regarded as excessive.

Courts are likely to want to be satisfied that national legislation for intrusive intelligence gathering sets out sufficient safeguards against abuse and that those safeguards have been followed in any particular case. Greater confidence in the balancing judgment is likely if it is taken or reviewed at a senior level, so it should be expected that the more intrusive an operation the higher the authority required. The same should hold for the intensity of oversight.

Proper Authority

For the medieval Just War philosophers in a world of warring princes and barons, having only the sovereign being able to give authority for war was essential. As discussed in chapter 2, intelligence activity needs to be conducted in a democracy in accordance with the authority provided by rights-compliant domestic law (the activity is then not "arbitrary," in the words of the UN Declaration, or "unreasonable," as the Fourth Amendment to the US Constitution puts it).

An important part of the rule of law test is that in addition to having some basis in domestic law, the law itself must be sufficiently accessible so that the manner in which it operates or is applied will be properly foreseeable. The principle is clear, although in practice exactly how an intelligence technique is deployed against a specific target is likely to be highly classified. There will inevitably be a tension between an openness to aid understanding on the part of the citizen and a reticence to prevent the target from knowing the exact plans to obtain its secret and thus enable it to frustrate the intelligence operation.

Insisting on legal safeguards to ensure sufficiently senior-level approval on the most sensitive operations is part of building trust on the behalf of the public that the secret world is under proper control. Confidence is quickly eroded when, after some scandal, who authorized an operation is not clear and the paper trail is absent. The inquiries into British Army covert intelligence gathering in Northern Ireland in the 1970s and 1980s provide a case in point.[22]

Domestic surveillance has always been regarded as more sensitive than intelligence gathering overseas. In cases involving domestic interception in the United States for counterespionage or counterterrorism purposes, individual warrants are made to an individual judge of the Foreign Intelligence Surveillance Court. The European Human Rights Court has likewise expressed a preference for judicial involvement: "In a field where abuse is so potentially easy in individual cases and could have such harmful consequences for democratic society as a whole, it is in principle desirable to entrust supervisory control to a judge."[23] Supervisory control in Europe to date has not necessarily meant *prior* judicial authorization, although the more potentially intrusive the technique, such as Internet bulk access, the more judicial involvement might be considered advisable in strengthening the case that the intrusion was a necessary and proportionate interference with privacy.[24] The recent UK intelligence legislation, the Investigatory Powers Act 2016, stipulates that warrants must be judicially reviewed *before* they enter into force, thus significantly strengthening the previous British system.

Reasonable Prospect of Success

A further criterion to be applied in conflict is that there must be a reasonable prospect of success in terms of contributing to the legitimate mission. Even if the purpose is valid and the methods to be used are proportionate to the issue, a hardheaded assessment of the likelihood and consequences of failure is required before the operation is authorized.

That does not mean, however, zero risk of failure. Nature imposes limits on our ability to know how things will turn out. Events have a way of surprising us. But there cannot be reckless disregard of risks or a blanket approach, often characterized as a fishing expedition, in the hope that if enough people are investigated a guilty party will be found.

Discrimination

In the Just War tradition, *discrimination* refers to the ability to distinguish legitimate targets from those that the warrior has a duty to protect (for example, civilians not involved in the conflict and surrendering enemy combatants). Precautions must also be taken to avoid causing incidental loss of civilian life or injury that would be excessive in relation to the concrete and direct military advantage anticipated. For that reason today there is an established principle in international humanitarian law that before a weapons system is acquired or adopted, the state concerned must assess whether it can be used with sufficient discrimination to avoid excessive civilian casualties. It is recognized that weapons systems do on occasions fail, but the system design must be able to minimize faults that could lead to an inability to discriminate.

An analogy can be drawn with bulk access to Internet communications through the interception of a bearer in a fiber-optic cable, satellite, or microwave link. As we explore in chapter 5, seeking the communications of a suspect may involve computerized searching through all the communications that have been accessed but with no certainty of success. The ethical test that must be met is whether the computer algorithms being used are sufficiently discriminating so as to give a high likelihood of picking out the sought-for communication and a lower risk of selecting irrelevant material. The agency must therefore be confident that the filtering and selection processes are suitably refined to minimize the extent of invading the privacy of the innocent.[25]

International humanitarian law accepts that collateral casualties cannot be avoided altogether, although reasonable efforts must be made to reduce the risk. This discrimination principle has its analogy in intelligence. Necessary intrusions into the privacy of suspects must be conducted in such a way that it minimizes the risks to those who are not the object of the surveillance. The risk can be managed, for example, by rules for not recording irrelevant material or quickly discarding it.

Necessity and Restraint

Additional Protocol 1 to the 1949 Geneva Conventions applicable to armed conflict places a requirement on a military commander to justify that an operation is a necessary part of achieving his military aim. Similarly, it might be thought that intelligence operations need to be justifiable to meet an approved intelligence requirement. In the case of the United States and the United Kingdom, these requirements are approved by the nations' respective National Security Councils. "'Necessary' means less than 'indispensable,' but more than merely 'admissible' or 'useful'" was the summary of that legal position by UK reviewer of counterterrorist legislation David Anderson in commenting on future UK interception legislation.[26]

Military necessity can of course include feints and attacks designed to confuse the enemy as to the commander's real intent, but the losses expected in such operations must not be disproportionate, as discussed earlier. A further consideration is the developing concern in relation to armed conflict that there is a moral obligation to reduce the risk faced by one's own forces if technology exists that helps prevent or completely avoid casualties.[27] Those who argue strongly in favor of such a moral obligation rely on what can be called the *principle of unnecessary risk*: "In trying to accomplish some objectively good goal, one must, ceteris paribus, choose means that do not violate the demands of justice, make the world worse or entail more risk than necessary to achieve the good goal."[28] That line of thinking would reinforce the value of using indirect means such as digital intelligence where possible rather than run the risks involved with human agents.

In intelligence work, the preferred way of collecting the relevant information entails a lesser or no ethical risk—for example, from open sources. In that respect running ethical risks could be seen as a last resort although in a different sense from that used when referring to the resort to war itself. This principle therefore is part of Just War restraint since the ethical risks associated with any secret intelligence method are best avoided if less risky alternatives are available.

Mark Phythian: Just as the Vietnam War gave a new impetus to thinking about the relationship between morality, ethics, and war, the character of the post-9/11 security environment (the war on terror) has also given rise to a fresh wave of thinking about the relationship between intelligence and ethics, with an earlier wave having followed the Church Committee's inquiry in the post-Watergate United States. For some, the renewed thinking about just wars that emerged in the early post–Vietnam War years provides a framework that might be applied to thinking about the ethics-intelligence relationship, extending the principles of the justice of war (jus ad bellum) and justice in war (jus in bello) to generate equivalents in relation to intelligence collection—jus ad intelligentiam and jus in intelligentia. On the surface, this seems a promising parallel. Discussion of both war and intelligence is often characterized by a similar kind of realist-idealist dichotomy. Indeed, Michael Walzer's classic account *Just and Unjust Wars* opens with a characterization of attitudes toward war that could similarly be applied to intelligence; simply substitute "intelligence" for "war" in the following passage:

> For as long as men and women have talked about war, they have talked about it in terms of right and wrong. And for almost as long, some among them have derided such talk, called it a charade, insisted that war lies beyond (or beneath) moral judgment. War is a world apart, where life itself is at stake, where human nature is reduced to its elemental forms, where self-interest and necessity prevail. Here men and women do what they must to save themselves and their communities, and morality and law have no place.[29]

The thinking underpinning efforts to extend Just War insights to the practice of intelligence has generated some of the most thoughtful contributions to the developing debate about how we think ethically about intelligence. However, I would argue that there are problems with this line of thinking, not least with the ways in which the parallels being suggested can be misleading and so ultimately unhelpful. Some of the problems that exist are retained from attempts to apply these principles to considerations of war. In addition, though, fresh, intelligence-specific problems are generated. There is, I think, some risk that while the same terms are being used across discussions of war and intelligence, their meaning becomes widely different in each. The extension of the principles could therefore confer a legitimacy that is unwarranted. In light of this, perhaps an ethical framework for considering intelligence needs to develop its own language as well as adopt some of that of the Just War tradition.

Let me illustrate this general problem by dealing first, as you do, with the question of jus ad intelligentiam, the extension of jus ad bellum to the intelligence sphere. One issue that arises in attempting this parallel concerns the fact that war is an exceptional state while, in the contemporary world, intelligence activity is a constant state of affairs. Hence, decisions to go to war involve a shift from a deeply embedded norm that has no intelligence equivalent. We do not talk of "going to intelligence" or "resorting to intelligence" as we do of "going to war" or "resorting to war."

You suggest that, in the UK context, the three statutory purposes of the British security and intelligence services—maintaining national security, detecting and preventing serious crime, and safeguarding economic well-being—provide a statutory jus ad intelligentiam, but what they provide is a very broad-based legitimating mission statement. The equivalent would be to regard the purpose of jus ad bellum judgments as legitimating the maintenance of standing armies. However, jus ad bellum is intended to provide an ethical framework for understanding when it is considered legitimate to engage those armies in acts of war and a test that is designed to allow judgments to be applied in each specific case where this occurs.

As you concede, national security in particular is a rather general catch-all term (an issue both in terms of the latitude it affords in commissioning and the obstacles it erects to overseeing).[30] It does not provide a guide as to precisely when or to what extent it is legitimate to engage intelligence capabilities. The four particular challenges listed in the 2015 UK National Security Strategy that you mention, I think, would also fall short of the specificity required to provide a basis for a jus ad bellum equivalent, if we understand this as legitimating engagement with a particular target. Rather, these challenges provide the context for maintaining an intelligence capability (and informing the configuration of such a capability) in the same way that, at various times, the existence of threats from France, Germany, and the Soviet Union once provided the context for sustaining military preparedness. Even the most thoughtful attempts to apply Just War theory to thinking about intelligence have been rather vague about what jus ad intelligentiam would actually mean in practice.[31] In a sense, this is inevitable if we understand this judgment as relating to specific targets.

The values that states attach to a given category of target are not consistent across the international system but arise from understandings of national security that are forged in a specific strategic environment. For these reasons, I would argue that thinking about the ethics of intelligence in terms of a jus in bello equivalent—that is, how intelligence should be conducted in specific contexts—offers much more promise than a jus ad bellum equivalent, albeit it is not without its own problems. In addition, thinking of jus ad intelligentiam in this way may well reinforce misunderstandings about how contemporary national security intelligence agencies operate. The traditional notion of "targeting" found in the classic model of the intelligence cycle needs to be heavily qualified in an era of large intelligence bureaucracies. As I have noted elsewhere, states do not invest in expensive intelligence collection capabilities and then simply wait for policy makers to identify targets for them.[32]

Another issue arises from the fact that, in practice, intelligence operates in a preventive mode, whereby it seeks to identify risks at the earliest feasible moment, before they can develop into threats. This kind of perpetual horizon scanning has been greatly assisted, for richer states at least, by rapid technological advances (an issue we revisit in chapter 5), requiring us to revise notions of what targeting means for intelligence today. In short, technology has enabled the most advanced users of intelligence to address a challenge set out by the CIA's Ray Cline in 1976, when he warned that "there is no way to be on top of intelligence problems unless you collect much more extensively than any cost-accounting approach would justify. . . . You might think you could do without most of what is collected; but in intelligence, in fact, as in ore-mining, there is no way to get at the nuggets without taking the whole ore-bearing compound."[33] This development, however, has impacted notions of discrimination, with attendant implications for the relationship between intelligence and democracy, particularly given the rise of the intermestic and where domestic surveillance is concerned. It also represents a challenge to attempts to construct an intelligence equivalent of jus ad bellum thinking.

The application of principles derived from jus in bello to the practice of intelligence (jus in intelligentia) provides much more promising ground and, I think, the capacity to establish an important ethical framework for intelligence conduct, but there are problems to be identified and resolved here. For example, the crucial element in discrimination in war is between those who are combatants and those who are noncombatants. This is not always a straightforward matter with regard to war, but distinguishing between combatants and noncombatants in an intelligence context (between legitimate targets and non-targets) is even more fraught with difficulties. In essence this is the crux of contemporary debates around domestic surveillance capabilities and practices where combatants in an intelligence context are domestically based. Moreover, combatants in an intelligence context will engage in acts of resistance; so not only are there (usually) no battlefields or uniforms or other signifiers but also in this sphere of activity denial and deception are routinely utilized. In this context, though, targets are likely to live with families and have work colleagues and social friends. Collateral intrusion seems inevitable. A key question, then, is how we understand and apply the principle of discrimination in this context.

Secrecy and deniability are barriers to judgments about the practical application of discrimination in an intelligence context, making accountability difficult to achieve and allowing for formal rather than substantive adherence to the concept; that is, from public pronouncements it may appear that the principle of discrimination is being observed, but actual practice could be incompatible with the principle. To take an example, by 2011 the Obama administration claimed that its armed drone strikes in Pakistan had managed to eliminate civilian (noncombatant) deaths. However, a *New York Times* report in May 2012 suggested that this feat was attributable to the administration's having "embraced a disputed method for counting civilian casualties" that effectively "counts all military-age males in a strike zone as combatants ... unless there is explicit intelligence posthumously proving them innocent."[34] In sum, discrimination is crucial to notions of jus in bello and should be to its intelligence equivalent. However, much thinking, both internal and external to intelligence agencies, needs to be undertaken to develop an adequate ethical approach in this regard.

Let me make a couple of points about the principles of necessity and last resort regarding how the idea of "military necessity" might translate

into one of "intelligence necessity" and what "last resort" might be understood to mean in the ethical practice of intelligence and, indeed, how useful
the concept is when applied to intelligence. In these areas straightforward
language has been distorted to justify going to war or to carry out acts in
war. Their use with regard to intelligence risks introducing yet further dis-
tortion, to the point where their desired and actual meanings may become
completely independent. In part this is because the principles of Just War
theory are designed to set a very high bar on the resort to war, making it
the exception rather than the norm, precisely because of the seriousness of
the human consequences of going to war. It is also because Just War theory
contains its own contradictions. In particular, claims to military necessity can be taken to override other considerations, such as noncombatant
immunity, and to distort others, such as proportionality. To take examples
from the Second World War, the British area bombing of Germany and the
US use of atomic bombs over Japan were each justified in terms of military
necessity (ending the war at the earliest feasible moment), but these claims
have been seen as problematic and remain heavily contested. Nevertheless,
at the time the invocation of military necessity overrode considerations of
noncombatant immunity and proportionality. In this way, Just War theory
opens itself up to the subjective application and interpretation of principles
drawn from its toolbox in a way that meets national requirements but is
inherently utilitarian. It does not simply provide tools for applying universal ethical standards where an individual life has the same value regardless
of where it is lived or the context in which it is lived.

One way of thinking about necessity in a military context is to understand it as being something akin to the state of "supreme emergency" that
Winston Churchill characterized Britain as facing in 1939 (as discussed in
chapter 2).[35] In terms of intelligence collection, necessity will often mean
something less and thus involve a lowering of the bar as understood in the
context from which it is being borrowed. A skeptic might regard this as
amounting to a sleight of hand in some cases. Michael Walzer has highlighted its misuse in a war context, with the effect that what is being referred
to "is not about necessity at all; it is a way of speaking in code, or a hyperbol-
ical way of speaking, about probability and risk." Even if, Walzer continues,
"one grants the right of states and armies and individual soldiers to reduce
their risks, a particular course of action would be *necessary* to that end only
if no other course improved the odds of battle at all." However, these choices
will always exist, and, as Walzer reminds us, "these are moral as well as

military choices."[36] In this vein, you cite David Anderson's operational definition of the term "necessary" in an intelligence context as meaning "less than indispensable but more than merely admissible or useful." This gives intelligence judgments about what is necessary a latitude that the *Oxford English Dictionary* would not recognize: *necessary* is defined as "indispensable, vital, essential; requisite"; and *necessity* is defined as the "constraining power of circumstances; a condition or state of things which forces a certain course of action." Arguably, Anderson's definition does damage to the term's literal meaning while accepting the legitimating cover that it provides.

Of course, in the case of the 9/11 terrorist attacks, US president George W. Bush declared a formal state of emergency on September 14, 2001, and President Barack Obama subsequently renewed it. No one could deny the horror of the 9/11 attacks. In this context declaring a state of emergency signaled that normal rules of conduct were to be overridden. It opened the way for utilitarian justifications for responses to the attacks because the context was held to justify a departure from preexisting norms (both military and intelligence), and then that required some form of sliding scale to provide an ethical measurement of the extent of departure that would be morally permissible. We discuss some of these departures, in terms of domestic intelligence collection and the war on terror's "action" (i.e., operational intelligence responses), in later chapters.[37] For now, I want to focus on the implications of the inevitable resort to utilitarian calculations. Here, the values involved in the calculation are inevitably understood in subjective terms and are aimed at securing a desired outcome, not achieving some perfect ethical balance. As Walzer remarked, in such contexts involving utilitarian calculation, often "what we are calculating is *our* benefit (which we exaggerate) and *their* cost (which we minimize or disregard entirely). Is it plausible to expect them to agree to our calculations?"[38] In realms where there is no agreed basis for valuation—for example, regarding intrusions of privacy in relation to ameliorating the risk of terrorism, coercive interrogation, or risk of noncombatant deaths—how do we determine the ethical cost?[39] There is no clear answer. Utilitarianism itself certainly doesn't provide one. Using what is deemed legally permissible is one guide, but we have seen from recent history that lawyers are not necessarily neutral arbiters.

In a sense, this "us" and "them" distinction simply involves moving to a heightened distinction that is already made explicit in national legal frameworks. As you point out, they tend to set different standards for the treatment of nationals and nonnationals and, in so doing, attach an implicitly higher value to "us" compared to "them" by offering differing levels of protection. This inevitably feeds into how notions such as necessity and proportionality are understood in intelligence terms. It is not fertile ground on which to attempt to establish a globalized ethics of intelligence.

The idea of "last resort" is another Just War concept whose meaning is contested in discussions of war, suggesting at least similar problems could arise in its extension to intelligence. Taken at face value, the concept is core to the idea that war should not be entered into as a policy preference and that it should not be one of several options; rather, it "should be marked by extreme reluctance and a sense of moral tragedy and foreboding."[40] But the question of how to identify the last resort is still a source of significant debate for Just War theory. For some the last resort will never arrive. For others history is littered with examples where it came and went, and one side found it had waited too long, such as with the British policy of appeasement toward Adolf Hitler's Germany in the 1930s. For others still, there are clear limits that at least partly arise from notions of military necessity. One example concerns how much time was right to allow Saddam Hussein's Iraqi troops to withdraw voluntarily from Kuwait before commencing war in 1991.[41] In an era where arguments for preventive war are regularly advanced, *last resort* can mean intervening at a point significantly in advance of the need to engage in self-defense as understood in Article 51 of the UN Charter.[42] In short, there is a clear risk that in interpretation and application, the term has come to be divorced from its literal and earlier meaning.

What is meant by last resort in the context of intelligence collection, and whether it is compatible with attempts to extend the principle from the war context, raises a similar question of meaning. Notions of forewarning and timeliness are central to definitions of intelligence given that it operates within a preventive paradigm. To wait until arriving at the last resort before beginning to collect intelligence on a threat is obviously too little too late. To understand the term "last resort" as meaning to try to acquire the information being sought by all other means before turning to espionage doesn't get us very far and overlooks the fact that a target's most important secrets are likely to be the ones it guards most closely and so are inaccessible without recourse to some form of espionage. They would not willingly be given if asked for. In these cases, espionage might be regarded as the only, not the last, resort.

In recognition of this circumstance, does this mean that if intelligence agency X did not try to acquire information from target Y by less intrusive and/or less ethically challenging means A through D but instead began its efforts at the more ethically challenging method E that this would still be understood to constitute last resort because, on a balance of probabilities (although this could not be known for certain unless they were tried), methods A–D seemed unlikely to bear fruit? The same questions obviously apply if the aim is to prevent target Y succeeding in course of action Z. Another question concerns how we factor in temporal dimensions (echoes of the "ticking bomb" here[43]) to judgments around last resort. Given all this, asking how far last resort should be considered an appropriate judgment in relation to the ethics of intelligence collection seems reasonable.

We need to consider how all of these principles—from those contributing to jus ad bellum / jus ad intelligentiam judgments through to those constituting jus in bello / jus in intelligentia—might be developed to suggest objective standards for the practice of intelligence without losing sight of the challenges involved. Once again, the nature of the international system will impose limits on the development and consistent application of objective standards. To repeat an earlier point, national intelligence agencies are precisely that—*national*. Thus, all risks and threats and the legitimacy of the range of possible intelligence responses and interventions ultimately are understood subjectively through the filters of national political culture and the strategic environment in which a state sits and that impacts the culture. At the same time, objective international human rights standards are enshrined in the 1948 UN Universal Declaration of Human Rights and the subsequent rise of international human rights law that impact national intelligence cultures, particularly in liberal democratic contexts. Tensions can arise, for example, in the context of what is understood to be an emergency context, and this helps explain contests over language in this area. In this context, developing an intelligence equivalent of Just War approaches as an ethical guide is an important and complex project that requires much more work, and we need to resist its reduction to a tick-box exercise designed to legitimize a preferred practice.

David Omand: I was struck by your vivid phrase to the effect that war is an exceptional state of affairs, and intelligence in the contemporary world is a constant. At first sight that sends a torpedo heading to the heart of my argument for the Just War tradition's being applied to intelligence work. But let me see if I can steer around it. First, the distinction may not be as clear as your phrase suggests today in a world of long-running counterinsurgency, counterterrorism operations, and drone strikes. Indeed, the statement that

war is an exceptional state would have come as a surprise to Europeans during the hundred-plus years of war from 1337 to 1453. If the jus ad bellum is
to cover all the modern categories for the use of armed forces, as it should,
then the difference with intelligence work becomes less stark. Second, the
application of jus ad bellum addresses whether the motive for starting an
armed conflict is to be considered justified, even were its conduct expected
to be in perfect accord with international humanitarian law and jus in bello.

I do agree that there will never be clear answers from Just War theory,
as you put it, if what is meant is a moral calculus that can tell us what is
right to do without applying human judgment and therefore without introducing human fallibility in any given set of circumstances. Apart from the
absolute right not to be tortured, our other human rights are qualified ones
and may indeed come into conflict with each other (for example, freedom
of speech does not cover shouting "fire!" in a crowded theater). It is in how
we talk to each other about the consequential balancing act that the Just
War approach can be most useful. As you say, it should not be reduced to
a set of boxes to be ticked but developed as a set of concepts to disentangle
the issues involved.

The search for jus ad intelligentiam in particular should help guide us
as to whether the use of secret intelligence is justified in the first place for
some disputed purpose (to steal commercial secrets or to spy on a new protest movement, for example) even if we were assured that the methods used
would be deployed to the highest ethical standards.

Mark Phythian: Perhaps ironically, I can see that jus ad intelligentiam
fits better with decisions around initiating surveillance of a target domestically than with foreign intelligence gathering. My argument for caution
in adapting it to this context, though, is that key concerns that the jus ad
intelligentiam requirement sets out to address—competent authority and
right intention—should not arise in the domestic context of the state. The
just cause element of jus ad bellum becomes the relevant test; in essence, it
is the necessity test we have discussed. That the application of intelligence
in a domestic liberal democratic setting relies for its judgments on principles deriving from decisions to go to war would be an unfortunate, and an
unnecessary, idea, I think.

The area of application that most interests me is foreign intelligence,
which has been the focus, explicitly or implicitly, of those who have written most thoughtfully on this question in the past.[44] To respond to the very
good points you raise about the distinction between war and peace, a sense

of the need for perpetual preparedness—the intelligence organization's default position and its riposte to the Kantian notion of perpetual peace—is premised on the real possibility of war. As then US director of central intelligence Robert Gates once told a meeting of junior CIA officers: "This nation is at peace because we in intelligence are constantly at war."[45] For intelligence professionals looking outward, then, the prism through which they view the world is one of omnipresent risks, with their number, range, location, and stage of advancement all being variable. These professionals would all be familiar, as Gates surely was, with Thomas Hobbes's warning that "Warre, consisteth not in Battell onely, or the act of fighting"; but it could be better understood by reference to the weather: "As the nature of Foule weather, lyeth not in a showre or two of rain; but in an inclination thereto of many dayes together: So the nature of War, consisteth not in actu-all fighting; but in the known disposition thereto, during all the time there is no assurance to the contrary."[46] Nevertheless, war—as understood in the Just War literature and as conforming to standard definitions, such as that used by the Correlates of War project (substantial combat, involving orga-nized armed forces, that results in a minimum of a thousand battle-related combatant fatalities within a twelve-month period[47])—clearly remains an exceptional state. Most people in most of the world usually live in a state of peace most or all of the time. However, developments over recent years have served to blur the boundaries between war, covert action, and intel-ligence gathering.

Two developments are particularly significant in this respect. The first is the development of what has come to be termed hybrid warfare, an approach that can be applied by non-state actors, such as ISIS in Iraq and Syria, and by states, as with Russia in Crimea and farther afield.[48] Hybrid warfare is a fluid concept, reflecting the various combinations of techniques that it comprises, but it usually denotes a cyber and a conventional dimen-sion to conflict where the cyber dimension can be utilized to alter percep-tions by penetrating, wrong-footing, and unsettling an opponent in support of a broader political aim.[49] This has impacted the purpose and function of intelligence. The second development relates to the post-9/11 counterter-rorism roles that some intelligence agencies, principally the CIA, have been required to perform and their implications for understandings of intelli-gence. As former CIA officer Charles Cogan wrote in an article published in 2004: "Intelligence operatives in the twenty-first century will become hunt-ers not gatherers. They will not simply sit back and gather information that comes in, analyse it and then decide what to do about it. Rather they will have to go and hunt out intelligence that will enable them to track down or kill terrorists."[50]

These developments have two consequences worth noting here. First, they both heighten the importance of recognizing the need to apply some ethical "rules of the game" to this sphere of activity. Second, they highlight the complications that arise in thinking about the ethics of intelligence in terms of the extension of Just War principles. The advent of hybrid warfare complicates yet further the bases of ethical judgment. Conversely, though, in a sense the war on terror intelligence roles make this simpler insofar as when intelligence plays a frontline military role, as the CIA did in Afghanistan immediately after 9/11, we don't need to trouble ourselves with trying to formulate an intelligence equivalent of Just War theory; we can simply apply Just War theory itself. Halfway house variants of Just War theory have been proposed to address this context, but it is not clear that they transcend the issues and limitations that accompany more traditional Just War theory.[51]

David Omand: I agree with that conclusion. We should maintain a distinction between how we examine the ethics of intelligence activity itself, the subject of this book, and the ethical and other considerations behind the foreign and defense policies that must govern when and how states take action against other states or non-state actors. For example, what are the rules of engagement to be for killing terrorists, whether carried out by assassination, Special Forces raids, remotely piloted vehicles, or other means? The threshold for deliberate killing, for example, would have to be a very high one (as it is for an armed police officer's use of force when confronting a terrorist on the street) and involve considerations of necessity, imminence, and proportionality in relation to the risks to innocent civilians.

Mark Phythian: Notwithstanding the points I raised in relation to the use of jus ad intelligentiam, let's take up your point about thinking through possible bases for establishing guidelines that might allow for meeting the basic requirement enshrined in it, of just cause or necessity, across a range of different cases. One key issue that a jus ad intelligentiam requirement must address is how to reconcile the demonstrable need for an intelligence intervention—that is, proving there is a just cause or necessity—with the preventive mode that intelligence essentially operates in and the inexorable logic that accompanies this and pushes it to make increasingly upstream interventions in contexts of high uncertainty so as not to miss any incipient risks or emerging threats. Interventions that are based on suspicion or intuition, as those in the higher reaches of uncertainty must be, are unlikely to meet any worthwhile test of necessity. So what is the appropriate scale of measurement here?

Following on from this, how specific do you think a legal justification has to be to engage national intelligence capabilities? Earlier you discussed how the United Kingdom has legally defined the work of its intelligence agencies in relation to upholding national security, preventing and detecting serious crime, and safeguarding the economic well-being of the nation, but, as I have suggested, these categories are very broad.

David Omand: I think the work could be held reasonably to include not only what is published in the National Security Strategy but also the determination of authorized *intelligence requirements* by the government—for example, by the National Security Council—as part of a finer-grained legitimizing jus ad intelligentiam. In the case of the United Kingdom and the United States, such requirements do go into much more detail and would form an important part of the justification of necessity for any intelligence-gathering operation. But crucially they are kept secret and not published. If we accept, as we both do, the modern insistence that secret activity must be placed under the rule of law, then detailed intelligence requirements should not define the jus ad intelligentiam boundary since that should have been arrived at after informed open debate in which the public has had an opportunity to participate.

For me, what is important for jus ad intelligentiam is that those running intelligence agencies have a clear sense of both what the democratic society they exist to protect expects of them and what they as secret agencies are not set up to do. That sense comes first from statutory regulation decided on after open public debate and from the published directives and policy statements from the elected government of the day. The heads of the agencies must be able confidently to refuse instructions that fall outside their remit.

To give a historical example from the era before intelligence legislation, in 1936 Director General of the Security Service Vernon Kell initially refused requests from Prime Minister Stanley Baldwin to investigate Wallis Simpson, the American (twice over) divorcée with whom King Edward VIII was smitten, on the grounds that their relationship did not threaten the security of the realm.[52] Baldwin eventually browbeat Kell into complying. The king abdicated shortly afterward. MI5 at the time, of course, did not officially exist and had no written charter. I would distinguish the Baldwin-Kell argument about whether it was proper to engage MI5 from the proportionality and necessity considerations that might govern the authorization of one intelligence-gathering method rather than another against such a target. (In that case, surveillance of Simpson's telephone did reveal at the time that she had another lover, a Ford motor dealer in Mayfair.)

I would agree therefore that an annual set of National Security Council intelligence requirements should not be regarded as a defining document for jus ad intelligentiam. Under the current British legislation, however, a warrant seeking legal authority for an intelligence-gathering operation, the jus in intelligentia, does have to provide a link to an authorized intelligence requirement as justification.

Mark Phythian: Perhaps there are other legal provisions we might see as forming part of jus ad intelligentiam? For example, UK statute law rules out using national security intelligence to promote the political interests of the ruling party. Any use for party political advantage would be unlawful. The US president ruled out using NSA interceptions to benefit the commercial interests of American companies, and a general prohibition on such commercial espionage has always been part of the Five Eyes signals intelligence agreement. To what extent is there a case for the further promotion of such norms internationally as a basis for establishing a shared ethical baseline in terms of jus ad intelligentiam that might be developed in the future? My own assessment would be rather pessimistic, despite the obvious desirability of such a development, given the structural factors that drive the general intelligence requirement in the first place.

For example, there may well be a prohibition on spying on allies as part of the Five Eyes agreement, but it clearly has not extended beyond this (for example, as far as the Fourteen Eyes states).[53] This takes us back to the US interception of German chancellor Angela Merkel's mobile phone, a revelation that has become a widely recognized shorthand for this broader issue of spying on allies. We can see straight away the corrosive impact on trust that Immanuel Kant warned us of in the wake of the Snowden-facilitated exposure of this interception. Merkel's spokesman, Steffen Seibert, said that Mrs. Merkel had told President Obama that "between close friends and partners, which the Federal Republic of Germany and the United States of America have been for decades, there should be no such surveillance of the communications of a head of government" and that such practices "must cease immediately."[54] Hans-Peter Friedrich, the German interior minister, explained that "if the Americans intercepted cellphones in Germany, they broke German law on German soil," and "those responsible must be held accountable."[55]

Yet eighteen months later it was revealed that the German Bundesnach-richtendienst (Federal Intelligence Service [BND]) had also been involved in broad-based spying on allies in collaboration with the NSA.[56] Merkel responded to this revelation by explaining that "there is an innate tension. We must improve what needs to be improved through reports to the parliamentary control bodies. But on the other hand, even if it is not so popular right now, it is part of their job for our intelligence services, especially the B.N.D., that they must and will cooperate internationally to protect the bodies and lives of 80 million Germans as best they can."[57] Subsequent reports suggested that BND spying on allies went beyond its cooperation with the NSA and embraced a range of friendly states such as Poland, Austria, Denmark, Croatia, and the Vatican. This suggests at least a degree of hypocrisy. It also serves to illustrate the ethical complexity of judgments that are made in the context of a competitive international system, where allies might agree on much but by no means on everything and where allies may not be direct competitors in many areas but could still be in key ones.

Nevertheless, this issue also raises questions about discrimination (perhaps better thought of in terms of prudence in examples such as this), proportionality, and necessity. If secrecy could be guaranteed, surveillance of foreign leaders could be argued to be of advantage in the utilitarian terms in which national security intelligence has often been assessed. But there is always some risk that secrecy will falter, either by someone's design or by accident, and that assessments of the utility of an intelligence action will then be made under very different circumstances and in the face of reactions that would never arise to impact the alliance environment if the secrecy could have been maintained. The NSA itself recognized the "grave damage" to alliance relations that could follow any disclosure.[58] Nevertheless, seemingly only when the NSA was required to address the question of prudence as a consequence of disclosure did the additional questions of proportionality and necessity, either unaddressed or under-addressed up to this point, receive the degree of consideration they should have attracted initially.

In addition to spying on friendly states, there has been no prohibition on spying on the United Nations or other international organizations. Ultimately, then, the notion of spying on allies perhaps fails to capture the more complex reality that the international system gives rise to: states can be simultaneously mutually supportive across certain issues and undertake surveillance of a partner state with regard to others. As former director of central intelligence James Woolsey commented in 1999, "We have allies who spy on us for technological and commercial reasons. And we have countries who we co-operate with, Russia is one, on some very important issues like terrorism, but they still spy on us and we on them for other purposes. That's just the nature of the world."[59]

David Omand: At the domestic level an interesting example of a possible further jus ad intelligentiam norm arose during the passage of the Investigatory Powers Act 2016. The British National Union of Journalists argued that intelligence legislation should explicitly protect all communications of journalists as a matter of principle since the safeguarding of their sources is in the public interest. The union suggested that if the authorities ever felt it necessary to do so, then the journalists should be told in advance of the application for a warrant and given the opportunity to argue their case in front of the authorizing senior judge. After much debate, such a fixed jus ad intelligentiam rule was in the end rejected (not least since that would have left the risk that foreign agents could operate with impunity under journalistic cover). But after open public debate Parliament did insist that the act contain special provisions for journalists and lawyers with additional safeguards, and comparable provisions applying to ministers of religion and elected representatives are published in the related codes of practice presented to Parliament.[60] Such open provisions I would regard as forming part of jus ad intelligentiam, leaving the balancing act to the normal process for applying in specific cases the jus in intelligentia principles.

Mark Phythian: A key term here is "after open public debate," which, prior to the publication of the Snowden revelations, we simply did not have in the United Kingdom or indeed elsewhere. It goes to the heart of a modern insistence that secret activity should be placed under the rule of law: the business of setting ethical and legal boundaries has to be arrived at after *open* debate, in which the public has an opportunity to participate, and *informed* debate, with sufficient transparency to make such discussion meaningful. Absent the Snowden revelations, the open public debate that has led to significant legislative reform in the United States, in the United Kingdom, and in several European nations simply would not have happened. We should remember the initial response of Foreign Secretary Hague to the Snowden leaks that I mentioned earlier. Now in the United Kingdom we must hope the enforced openness that has followed the need to pass the Investigatory Powers Act 2016 will be sustained and will represent, as you have suggested, a genuine move to a social compact model. But our discussion still leaves hanging the objection that the jus ad bellum criteria that apply to a just war are of a different order and are necessary for reasons that do not pertain in a domestic intelligence context. My view remains that it would be misleading to try and draw too close a parallel as to what we would consider a just or unjust use of intelligence targets from the experience of what we would consider a just or unjust war.

David Omand: I agree with your note of caution. We must not imagine there is a one-to-one correspondence between the application of jus ad bellum and what we are discussing as jus ad intelligentiam. Of course, in appropriate cases where jus ad bellum is satisfied, then we would expect the relevant jus ad intelligentiam relating to intelligence support to the armed forces would follow on the grounds that, in terms of ethical risk, the greater includes the lesser. But beyond that the parallel can break down since there will be legitimate intelligence requirements that would be justified on different grounds from a consideration of the use of force. An example might be preventing serious crime such as uncovering a major Internet fraud.

Perhaps, therefore, we could also regard part of the essence of the distinction between ad bellum and in bello as lying in the type of respective accountability: the distinction between, on the one hand, the sovereign strategic decision to engage in hostilities for national self-defense (or today in pursuance of a UN Security Council resolution) and, on the other hand, the operational and tactical decisions by many field commanders—some at very junior levels—for which they are individually responsible. The former can be openly debated at the time, the latter only in the light of ex post scrutiny. That would suggest we are on the right track in suggesting that today jus ad intelligentiam can be found in the laws, publicly available codes of conduct, and other public guidance that bear on the justification of intelligence activity, as debated in and passed by democratic legislatures, and the jus in intelligentia representing the application of the (normally highly classified) sets of orders, internal rules, and authorizations by which the general requirements of law are translated into action. So the former represents the social contract reached between Congress or Parliament and the executive and its secret agencies over what secret agencies in a democracy exist to do, a subject that can sensibly be debated publicly at a suitably general level of principle. The latter concerns the day-to-day decisions of intelligence officers and those authorizing their operations on cases that will inevitably be highly classified. Those decisions must be taken of course within the constraints of the law and subsequently be open to oversight, but hopefully they will also be consistent with a set of ethical principles such as those discussed in this chapter.

Mark Phythian: That conceptualization may well be very relevant to intelligence work, but it does emphasize my concern not to have facile comparisons drawn with examples taken from the model provided by the Just War tradition. Nor should we underestimate the difficulties for intelligence officers in practice to apply jus in intelligentia principles. Another concern I have is whether in the end the meaning of these principles will change over time and between cultures. Avoiding harm to the innocent is, we must hope, an enduring principle, but is it possible, for example, in intelligence work to have stable rules to discriminate between legitimate and illegitimate targets for surveillance? As I have suggested, the distinction differs according to national intelligence cultures and the political cultures from which they emerge and, in turn, are influenced by the strategic environment. To illustrate the point further, the extent of agent running in target organizations (and the number and nature of them) can be expected to vary according to the strategic environment, which also influences the importance afforded to agent protection and the kinds of risk agents are asked to run (indeed, their entire risk environment).

David Omand: The Just War tradition is just that, a tradition, and like the common law will evolve over time. The Just War concepts such as discrimination have shown themselves to be of great utility even when applied to military technologies and strategic environments that were unimaginable fifty years earlier, let alone five centuries ago. We should therefore not seek permanence in their application. Your reference to legitimate and illegitimate targets takes us into exactly such an application of the Just War principle of discrimination in the digital world.

I regard the discrimination principle as an important guide to right conduct by any intelligence agency, particularly when contemplating seeking authority to access digital communications and personal data. It is one of the most important ways of distinguishing between the conduct of an intelligence agency in a liberal democracy and that in a totalitarian or despotic state, even when the agencies are using exactly the same intelligence technique. The aim should be to find the communications or data related to the legitimate target of an intelligence or criminal investigation, and the technique used must be capable of making that discrimination. Just as civilians who directly participate in hostilities as irregular combatants can then be considered unable to claim any benefit from the protections that the

Geneva Conventions afford civilians, so the terrorists, cyber criminals, narcotics dealers, or serious criminals cannot claim that their privacy rights should have prevented the authorities from identifying, locating, and gathering evidence on them.

In addition, almost every investigation will likely scrutinize suspects to establish whether they are involved in the criminal activity. Inevitably many of those suspects will turn out in the end to be innocent. That process is part of upholding the rule of law. It is a trope of the detective fiction genre that the guilty party is not uncovered until the end of the investigation and the end of the story. Finally, the great majority in a democracy should be of no interest to the authorities, and their privacy rights are engaged only because it is not technically possible to separate their communications from those of the suspects in advance of interception, filtering, and selection processes or where, for example, bulk communications data has been retained for a period so that specific queries about suspects may be run at a later date. Totalitarian states, on the contrary, have a habit of conducting persistent surveillance on the population at large (including their use of the Internet) and check whether they pose a danger to the regime through their thoughts and writings, as well as actions.

Mark Phythian: The detective novel analogy is an interesting way of thinking about the issue. One key difference, though, comes from the fact that intelligence usually operates in a preventive paradigm. The crime has not yet taken place and, indeed, may never take place. The purpose of intelligence is to ensure, as far as possible, that there is no equivalent of dead bodies turning up in the Rue Morgue. The case for authorizing such operations, in liberal democratic contexts, must therefore strike a balance between casting the net widely enough (bearing in mind the principle articulated by Ray Cline, mentioned earlier) but not too widely. It must certainly include confidence that the methods being applied will minimize privacy intrusion on the innocent. As you suggest, the degree of attention paid to this dilemma should be one of the defining characteristics of what we might term liberal intelligence, but is it enough to ensure that the computer selection algorithms will minimize the chances of a human analyst seeing their communications? For example, we would never accept the authorities' placing a camera in every bedroom, even on the understanding that it would never be switched on or that the material would be examined only with a judicial warrant, in recognition of the potentially chilling effect on private behavior.

David Omand: We should certainly recognize the need to respect privacy rights given the *potential* for intrusion inherent in the design of an interception system. So for all those whose communications are carried on a satellite, microwave link, or fiber-optic cable that are capable of being intercepted, we should acknowledge that their privacy rights are engaged from the outset of the intention to intercept. These privacy rights are not *violated*, however, if the provisions for lawful access (for example, in the ECHR or the Fourth Amendment to the US Constitution) are met. Thus, the design must allow effective filtering and selection as far as possible, with the analysts only getting to see the communications of their legitimate suspects. In that way, an ethical test must be applied even to the design of the intelligence operation (just as weapons design must conform with international humanitarian law). Such an ethical test would undoubtedly rule out placing a camera in every bedroom as grossly disproportionate to any possible gain in any conceivable circumstance, even a Churchillian "supreme emergency," and thus as comprehensively unlawful.

Mark Phythian: So you are not maintaining the view that a privacy violation can be held to have occurred in reality only when a human being reads, listens to, or watches the material without legal authority. A violation could occur if the system design itself fails to meet privacy rights standards of discrimination or of proportionality, as in the example of the camera in every bedroom. That then means that the potentially chilling effect of bulk access operations (through interception, equipment interference, or using bulk personal databases) authorized via legislation must be kept under review by the overseers of intelligence operations to ensure that over time mission creep does not occur, particularly as technology advances.

David Omand: In assessing the extent of privacy intrusion, one of the factors is whether potential (or actual) harm results. In the case of intelligence operations, we should not be unduly concerned by the computers' "knowledge" of our communications, including the reasonable retention of data for analysis. Instead, what is likely to be done in the real world as a result should most influence the harm calculation. We need to be especially careful over the design of any system that incorporates (through the construction of a computer algorithm) the selection of material on which direct action may be taken. Another example would be the design of a system that allows the analyst to set selectors and criteria for selecting data that the analyst would examine during an investigation.

We already allow private sector telecommunications and Internet companies to access and store vast quantities of personal data about us as their computers process and transmit our communications. We need not fret unduly over that since machines are not conscious and do not of their own accord have volition; only people do. What we need to be most concerned about in assessing potential harms is when human agency allows the direct or indirect unauthorized access to all that digital information for some purpose. An example from the private sector would be if an Internet company, without our consent, sells our data for marketing purposes or even draws inferences from it of commercial interest to insurance companies or credit agencies.

In addition to the working of the system, UK law requires, therefore, the individual analyst to justify the actual questions asked of the material as being necessary and proportionate. Proportionality is an essential Just War–derived test. For example, the Israeli Supreme Court looked in detail at the lawfulness of Israeli attacks in Judea, Samaria, and the Gaza Strip: "In other words, attack is proportionate if the benefit stemming from the attainment of the proper military objective is proportionate to the damage caused to innocent civilians harmed by it. That is a values based test. It is based upon a balancing between conflicting values and interests."[61] Substitute "interception" for "attack" and "intelligence" for "military," and the statement applies.

Mark Phythian: The Israeli example well illustrates the points I made earlier about "us" and "them." Who exactly is undertaking the utilitarian calculation of proportionality, and what metric are they using in doing this? It also raises the question of how "combatant" and "noncombatant" are defined. Given sufficient latitude in the definition, many more people can be held to legitimately fall within the target group than on a stricter definition, which inevitably tips the proportionality scales in the desired direction. To illustrate with a reference to Gaza, in its 2008 annual report, Amnesty International found in that year's conflict that "actions in Gaza have demonstrated that Israeli forces consider all individuals and institutions associated with Hamas to be legitimate targets. The consequences of applying such an overly broad definition, which undermines the principle of distinction, are evident in the growing numbers of civilians killed and injured in Gaza."[62] This approach to identifying who is a legitimate target and who, as a consequence, is an innocent civilian would allow the Israeli

Supreme Court to consider it as having passed the proportionality test. The point is that proportionality, whether in a military or an intelligence context, is judged following a process of categorization that can be undertaken subjectively with a view to a desired outcome.

In light of this discussion, let's return to the case of historian Christopher Hill used in chapter 2. Would you consider appropriate discrimination and proportionality were applied there?

David Omand: The Hill case of the 1950s of course long predated the legislation that governs both the activity of the Security Service and the intrusive investigatory surveillance powers, all of which explicitly require consideration of necessity and proportionality. We can only judge the actions of those approving such operations by the standards of the day and the knowledge available to them, not by what we know of how history unfolded. We do know today, in fact, much more about how Soviet intelligence officers had indeed recruited young idealists at British universities as agents, encouraging them to follow careers that would give them access to classified information; so the justification of the 1951 Security Service in the Hill case has some point. And even if we might now assess that Hill was not directly involved in pointing out potential targets to communist recruiters, we know other communist academics were, so he would have fallen into my category of "legitimate suspects worth investigating." By today's standards of acceptance of diversity, we would no doubt find some of the reports lacking objectivity and even of being small minded. But we also need to read the language used in the reports in the MI5 files through the eyes of the 1950s that would be accustomed to seeing such opinionated, even crude, personal views of character and manners (pen portraits, as they were called) in routine personnel files and performance assessments.

Mark Phythian: In one way your point takes me back to my earlier one about cultural relativism. You mentioned totalitarian states and their habit of conducting surveillance on the general population to check whether the people posed a danger to the regime through their thoughts, writings, and actions. Now clearly significant differences emerged from the respective political cultures of the United Kingdom and, say, the German Democratic Republic. There were no dungeons or cells (as far as I know) in the basement of MI5 headquarters, but I have seen them in the basement of the former Stasi headquarters in Berlin. Suspected communists in the United Kingdom were not subject to arbitrary arrest at night, leaving relatives searching for the disappeared. Moreover, MI5 did not have to police potential escapees who sought to leave a walled-in state. But the principle of discrimination, with clear limits to state surveillance, should constitute the most fundamental difference in approach between the two political and intelligence cultures, whose intelligence agencies ultimately shared the same aim—namely, state security, or the defense of the realm.

But let me make two essentially contradictory points about discrimination in the case of Christopher Hill that, taken together, I think encapsulate the liberal democratic intelligence-ethics dilemma. First, I don't think that discrimination was properly applied in his case, or in many comparable ones, because the framework for its application was essentially absent. If the twentieth century can be read as a story of the generally progressive, though not linear, professionalization of intelligence in the United Kingdom, the 1950s remained the era of the gentleman amateur supported by the former policeman, whether domestic or colonial. One guiding light that these people lacked was a formal definition of subversion. In 1971 Director General of MI5 Sir Martin Furnival Jones conceded that he had "always refrained from trying to define subversion."[63] The following year John Jones, the head of MI5's F Branch, finally defined it in the context of an upsurge in trade union militancy: *subversion* involved "activities threatening the safety or well-being of the State and intended to undermine or overthrow Parliamentary democracy by political, industrial or violent means."[64] Under this definition I do not think that Hill was a legitimate target in terms of counter-subversion.

Second, though, this is, as you point out, an ex post facto judgment and one that I could not make today with any great confidence had that surveillance not taken place, leaving behind a detailed record. As noted previously, intelligence takes place in a preventive mode, which involves casting nets widely, and these nets caught individuals then, as they do today, based on the company they kept and what such connections might, or might not, reveal.

Given this, and returning to the handling of your third category of those intercepted—that is, the innocent who just happen to be in the way— at what point do you think surveillance of a particular target legitimizes the extension of surveillance to others ("the lives of others") and in what contexts?

David Omand: The Security Service of the 1950s had therefore to expend much time on counterintelligence as well as on counter-subversion, and both involved keeping an eye on communist academics at leading universities. Today's British intelligence officers are under a legal as well as an ethical obligation to take all reasonable steps to avoid dragging others unnecessarily into the intelligence net. And they have a very strong incentive to avoid wasting effort, especially as there are very many more serious terrorist suspects deserving of surveillance than there is capacity available. Quite possibly, nevertheless, collateral intrusion may occur; as noted, the suspect's computer may be used by family members, and that is also likely to be the case with old-fashioned, fixed-line home telephones (although much less so with mobile phones). That needs to be considered before a surveillance operation is authorized, and at the least measures should be put in place to minimize the examination and retention of such material, as well as the means of discarding it altogether.

Rather different considerations apply when finding new suspects. That a police or intelligence agency investigates the contacts of a suspect to see if others are involved in a criminal conspiracy is accepted as a legitimate practice. This "chaining" of communications data (for example, examining those with whom known terrorists have communicated, as found on mobile phone records after an attack) is a very powerful tool to that end and is often more useful than accessing the content of the communication itself. Often it is possible to eliminate the contact quickly as being of no interest, and that is one advantage of using communications data to avoid long-term intrusive surveillance. A different example would be the deliberate covert interception of the telephone of person A (such as the family of B, a terrorist on the run) because A's contact with B might reveal B's whereabouts. Those determining the ethical acceptability of such a stratagem need to have in mind both that the target is B, not A, and the likely consequences of not locating B if, for example, B was a violent extremist planning an attack. A harsh case of this chaining logic is found in French law, adopted after the terrorist attacks of the 1990s, making it an offense to associate with a terrorist even if the association is peripheral and the interaction would otherwise be lawful (such as lending a car without knowing about the attack for which it would be used).[65] The law's intention is to make obtaining support from the population hard for the terrorist. That goes further than what the United Kingdom and the United States have so far considered reasonable in their counterterrorism legislation.

Mark Phythian: Another striking difference that I have referred to emerges when we compare intelligence collection with the use of lethal force in warfare. It is important to bear in mind that here we are focusing on intelligence collection rather than intelligence action, which is the focus of chapter 6 and where "last resort" has an important place in ethical thinking. However, in terms of collection, intelligence should be the first, not the last, resort. Intelligence needs to be engaged earlier if the last resort in security terms is to be identified. Given this, we need to ask what last resort means in terms of intelligence collection. My view is that its meaning is so far removed from what we understand by the Just War concept, and its purpose in relation to Just War thinking, that we must face this and look for a different, more accurate concept.

David Omand: I think you are right to question the most appropriate translation of the Just War principle of last resort in the realm of intelligence gathering. An indirect interpretation of last resort that I have used in my writing on the subject is that, for example, a police officer considering using lethal force can use a Taser to subdue a suspect rather than opening fire. In other words, intrusive intelligence gathering should not be resorted to if a viable alternative likely carries lesser ethical risk.[66] This idea fits the Just War–international humanitarian law requirement of having to demonstrate necessity.

I agree nevertheless that it would perhaps be better to avoid the term "last resort" and encourage instead the application of the concept of necessity. Running agents or intercepting communications might well have been the only ways of accessing what was going on in a closed society like the Soviet Union in the early Cold War. Today the Internet provides ready access to open source information in a way that was inconceivable before the digital revolution. If, as I have argued, all secret intelligence activity carries ethical risk, including some unavoidable invasion of the privacy of the innocent, then nations should exercise restraint in its use. In the words of the 2015 Independent Surveillance Review panel, what is needed is a "democratic licence to operate" for the intelligence services, and "it should never become routine for the state to intrude into the lives of its citizens. It must be reluctant to do so, restrained in the powers it chooses to use, and properly authorised when it deems it necessary to intrude."[67] I take comfort too that Alan Rusbridger, when serving as editor of *The Guardian* newspaper and publishing the Snowden allegations, read my account of the Just War–derived ethical principles and said he was adopting them as principles to govern investigative journalism![68]

Mark Phythian: I think we agree, then, that given the problems involved in relating judgments of last resort to intelligence practice, this is the wrong test to apply to intelligence. Given this, it may be beneficial to collapse this consideration into thinking about the nature of necessity. However, I think there are important qualifiers here—one relating to the domestic polity, the other to the impact on the international system. First, in broad terms, if the two concepts were merged in an intelligence context, there needs to be a robust and clear definition of necessity that only permits actions meeting the literal test of the term itself and that would not undermine domestic values. In doing this we cannot, of course, fully escape some of the problems that attempts to identify the last resort generate—they still exist in determining necessity in preventive contexts—but this does offer a more appropriate framework for considering possible solutions to them. Second, we need to be aware that the international roles and actions of national intelligence agencies contribute to low levels of trust in the international system, so we must seek to avoid as far as possible actions that accentuate this problem. One commentator has referred to this issue as an intelligence version of the security dilemma: intelligence arising from collection may reassure the host state and so raise its confidence, but at the same time the means of, or knowledge of, collection may cause concern on the part of the target state, thus undermining its confidence and generating its own further intelligence requirements and interventions.[69] It is difficult to see a way out of this spiral, which is rooted in the nature of the international system. Just as there is no intelligence equivalent of going to war, so there is no intelligence equivalent of an end to war.

International trust is also affected by a related issue. While the intelligence systems of a number of Western states might be regarded, particularly in their own countries, as paragons of efficacy combined with responsibility, in the global South—where past actions of these services have passed into popular memory—the perspective can be far less positive. "Intelligence's most powerful worldwide associations are still with covert collection, covert action, repressive regimes and American imperialism. It is still often seen as an instrument of power and ideology, inherently threatening."[70] There are no easy answers to the question of how this can be addressed other than through the considered and consistent application of guiding principles such as necessity and discrimination.

Mark Phythian and David Omand: We can agree in conclusion that the reasoning that has come down to us from the Just War tradition teaches that ethically problematic behavior is sometimes the lesser evil to secure peace and justice. But when that is understood to be the case represents a subjective judgment made in relation to a specific time, place, and political culture. The Just War–derived concepts—just cause, right intention, pro-portionality, right authority, a reasonable prospect of success, discrimina-tion, and necessity—can be useful in separating the ethical considerations to take into account at a strategic level and should have a role at the opera-tional and tactical levels, since they can help intelligence officers and over-seers alike balance the different components of ethical thinking that need to be applied. These concepts must however be regarded as general tools for clear thinking and not be reduced to a set of moral tick boxes. Clearly work still needs to be done to clarify how these terms from the Just War tradition are best understood in the world of secret intelligence.

4

Secret Agents and Covert Human Sources

Mark Phythian: Focusing on intelligence at the level of the state encourages us to consider the questions it raises in impersonal terms. However, as soon as we mine down and focus on human intelligence collection, the personal dimension unavoidably comes to the fore, and the ethical dilemmas at the heart of intelligence are brought into sharp relief. If intelligence is about collecting information that can inform the decisions of civilian and military leaders to maximize their advantage and provide security, and if the most valuable information that others hold is that they guard most closely and so is the most difficult to acquire, then to what lengths is it permissible to go to acquire it? In particular, if people are gateways to, or keepers of, that information—a potentially weak link in the protective shield behind which the information sits—what are the limits to the means that can be used? How far, and at what risk, can agents be used in a target group to provide information? To what extent should they participate in actions of the group that are ethically contentious simply to maintain access to information?

In many ways, this focus takes us back to espionage as it was practiced prior to the rise of the modern industrial state and the evolution of espionage into modern intelligence.[1] For as long as people have been writing about war and statecraft, the value of secret agents and undercover sources has been recognized. For example, in *The Histories* Herodotus recounts the story of Zopyrus and his part in Persia's conquest of Babylon. Zopyrus decided to infiltrate Babylon, gain the trust of the Babylonians, and use it to bring about the city's downfall. To do so, we are told, Zopyrus "coolly gave himself crippling permanent injuries: he cut off his own nose and ears, roughly shaved his head, and flogged himself."[2] Having discussed his plan with the Persian king Darius, Zopyrus presented himself to the Babylonians as someone who had been punished by Darius, had defected as a result, and was now prepared to share his plans with the Babylonians. As Herodotus explains: "The sight of one of the most distinguished Persians without his nose and ears and covered with blood and welts from being flogged inclined the Babylonians to believe that he was telling the truth and had come as their ally."[3] But to secure the victory for Darius over the Babylonians, Zopyrus first led his Babylonian comrades against lightly armed Persians and massacred them as a means of building trust. After two successful massacres of Persians, "praise of Zopyrus could constantly be heard throughout Babylon on everyone's lips."[4] After leading a third massacre, he was made commander in chief of the army and placed in charge of the city's defenses. When Darius's forces attacked Babylon, Zopyrus opened two of its gates, thereby facilitating the Persians' victory.

This story focuses our attention on at least three things. First, deception is at the heart of the use of covert human sources. Second, the quality of the cover story, or legend, is a key factor in the mission's success. Third, there may be a need to willingly sacrifice or harm others in developing this legend in pursuit of the broader strategic aim. On this basis, using human sources to gather secret information is inherently problematic in ethical terms.

We can also see something of this issue in Sun Tzu's characterization of the five types of spy in *The Art of War*. As well as native, inside, and doubled spies, Sun Tzu also lists *expendable agents*, or "those of our own spies who are deliberately given fabricated information" to pass on to the enemy, in contrast to *living spies* who "return with information."[5] As Tu Yu, one of Sun Tzu's commentators, explained: "We leak information which is actually false and allow our own agents to learn it. When these agents operating in enemy territory are taken by him they are certain to report this false information. The enemy will believe it and make preparations accordingly. But our actions will of course not accord with this, and the enemy will put the spies to death."[6] Another of his commentators Tu Mu tells us of the qualities required of living agents, who "observe the enemy's movements and learn of his doings and plans."[7] These men must be "intelligent but appear to be stupid; who seem to be dull but are strong in heart; men who are agile, vigorous, hardy, and brave; well-versed in lowly matters and able to endure hunger, cold, filth, and humiliation."[8] Thus, similar ethical issues arise from this account: recruiting an agent (whether to gather intelligence or to be a covert channel of influence); infiltrating the agent, thus deceiving and manipulating the target; raising the possibility of potential harm to third parties to maintain the agent's cover; and determining the duty of care owed to those involved in the infiltration.

In light of this, how the practice of human intelligence collection can be reconciled with the most stringent ethical standards, such as those established by Immanuel Kant via his notion of the categorical imperative, is difficult to see. Outlined in his *Groundwork of the Metaphysics of Morals* (1785), Kant wrote all judgments about ethical conduct, or right actions, were intended to flow from this principle: "Act always so that you treat humanity whether in your person or in that of another always as an end, but never as a means only."[9] In his 1797 work *The Metaphysics of Morals*, Kant went on to outline his Universal Principle of Right: "Every action which by itself or by its maxim enables the freedom of each individual's will to co-exist with the freedom of everyone else in accordance with a universal law is *right*."[10] From this principle, it followed that "if my action or my situation in general can co-exist with the freedom of everyone in accordance with a universal law, anyone who hinders me in either does me an injustice; for this hindrance or resistance cannot co-exist with freedom in accordance with universal laws."[11] It further followed that "each individual can be free so long as I do not interfere with his freedom by my *external actions*, even although his freedom may be a matter of total indifference to me or although I may wish in my heart to deprive him of it. That I should make it my maxim to *act* in accordance with right is a requirement laid down for me by ethics."[12] This, in turn, gave rise to the "universal law of right": "Let your external actions be such that the free application of your will can co-exist with the freedom of everyone in accordance with a universal law."[13]

But as we have already discussed, inevitably circumstances will arise from the nature of the international system and the nature of the state itself under which the state deems it necessary to depart from the strictest ethical standards regarding the freedom of an individual in pursuing its obligations relating to security. In *The Metaphysics of Morals* Kant himself made it clear that "Right entails the Authority to use Coercion."[14] How, then, do we recognize situations where diversions from the high road of deontological reasoning may be considered justified, and how far is it permissible to stray from it and for how long?

It is worth noting here that Kant was not blind to the realities of espionage and the use of spies. In his *Perpetual Peace* (1795) he set out six "preliminary articles of a perpetual peace." The final one states: "No state at war with another shall permit such acts of hostility as would make mutual confidence impossible during a future time of peace. Such acts would include the employment of assassins or poisoners, breach of agreements, the instigation of treason within the enemy state, etc."[15] Kant also suggested that "the employment of spies," something that "exploits only the dishonesty of others," should be added to this list of what he called the "diabolical arts." Kant regarded spying as "intrinsically despicable" in part because such "practices will be carried over into peacetime and will thus vitiate its purpose"; that is, spies risked undermining the very political culture in the service of which they were employed.[16] Hence, while alert to their existence, Kant did not suggest that intelligence personnel acting on behalf of a state should enjoy any degree of latitude in their ethical conduct because of the roles they may be required to play. On the contrary, he seems to have had a low opinion of them.

We are often invited to draw this same understanding when we encounter undercover spies in literature. In George Orwell's *Nineteen Eighty-Four*, Mr. Charrington, the apparently kindly junk shop owner ("a man perhaps sixty, frail and bowed . . . eyes distorted by thick spectacles"[17]) who rents the room above his shop to Winston Smith as somewhere to meet his lover Julia, is revealed as an undercover officer of the Thought Police and arrests them both. We don't applaud the thoroughness of his disguise: "His hair, which had been almost white, had turned black. And he was not wearing his spectacles. . . . The black eyebrows were less bushy, the wrinkles were gone," and he had the "cold face of a man of about five-and-thirty."[18] Nor do we admire the way his cover had enabled him to deceive Smith, even though we know that Smith was committing a crime. Instead, we see Charrington's efforts as underhanded and contrary to liberal norms.

It is unlikely that Kant would have recognized the distinction between domestic and foreign intelligence as being of ethical significance in terms of the duty we owe to other human beings. Yet developing our discussion of the ethics of intelligence as constituting a distinctly liberal problem, we inevitably draw distinctions between the acceptability of some of these actions and their consequences in domestic and overseas contexts. The distinction is clearly relevant because the state in liberal theory has a particular responsibility toward its citizens, and that is the essence of the state's side of the social contract. Without wanting to lose sight of the universal claims made by Kant, I want here to focus on the liberal dilemmas that can arise from the state's use of intelligence to keep its side of the social contract bargain.

In doing so I use case studies that are each extreme in their own ways. I do this because with the study of intelligence, lessons are often drawn from analyzing failure—that is, what was not done and could have been done, or done differently, to avoid failure. Similarly, in discussing intelligence ethics, we are drawn to exceptional cases to understand what might have been done differently and whether key requirements such as necessity were met. The clearest lessons are often found in the more extreme cases, where clear ethical lines can most easily be recognized.

Running agents inside target organizations to collect intelligence can involve considerable risk to the agents' safety. Groups that employ violence as part of their modus operandi—for example, terrorist and other criminal groups—can be expected to use violence to protect their secrets. The suspicion that agents are being run in target organizations may lead those organizations to root out and eliminate people they suspect of spying or at the least to engage in highly intrusive surveillance. Infiltrating targets such as terrorist or other criminal groups, then, clearly places agents at high levels of risk. Moreover, maintaining their cover is likely to involve such agents participating or acquiescing in crimes. The history of British intelligence gathering on paramilitary organizations operating in Northern Ireland from the 1970s to the 1990s features examples of this particular, and acute, ethical dilemma of whether to collude in an agent's participating in a crime to preserve the access to intelligence.

In the 1980s the British Army was tasked with combating a wave of random murders of Catholics by Loyalist paramilitary groups. The army had set up the Force Research Unit (FRU), a highly secret intelligence-gathering unit, to run agents against both the Provisional Irish Republican Army (PIRA) and the Loyalist groups. The Special Branch of the Royal Ulster Constabulary (RUC) and the British Security Service also had agents in Northern Ireland, but cooperation between them at that point was poor to nonexistent, and cases were jealously guarded. The FRU succeeded in infiltrating Brian Nelson, a former soldier with a previous conviction for a serious sectarian offense, into the Loyalist group the Ulster Defence Association (UDA), where he was soon appointed its intelligence officer. Like Darius with Zopyrus, Nelson's position must have seemed a golden opportunity for the FRU to penetrate the heart of the enemy, but as the intelligence officer, Nelson was responsible for identifying and developing intelligence on potential targets for murder. To maintain his cover, he would have had to appear to be acting no differently from anyone else occupying that role while secretly promising to report when he could to his army handlers on the targets he had identified. The idea was that the army could take covert action to frustrate the FRU's attacks and to identify the killers. But the UDA continued its activities, with murders still taking place, including of individuals whose names Nelson had not passed on to the FRU (or where the FRU had not wanted to intercede for fear of exposing Nelson), along with punishment shootings, beatings, and extortion. Acting with little or no supervision from the chain of command (and completely outside the knowledge of ministers, government lawyers, and senior officials), the FRU thus let themselves be sucked into a legal and ethical tangle of guilty knowledge.

One particularly notorious case involving Brian Nelson was the killing of the lawyer Patrick Finucane in 1989. The 2012 report of the independent review by Sir Desmond de Silva into the killing concluded that the FRU did not have foreknowledge of the UDA conspiracy to murder Finucane.[19] However, in seeking to embed an agent within a Loyalist paramilitary group, the FRU had clearly exposed itself to serious risks of collusion with the worst forms of criminality, where *collusion* involves "deliberately turning a blind eye or deliberately ignoring improper or unlawful activity" and not just "agreements, arrangements or actions intended to achieve unlawful, improper, fraudulent or underhand objectives."[20] Indeed, while determining that the FRU did not have foreknowledge of the UDA plot to kill Finucane, de Silva did find that the FRU bore a clear ethical responsibility for his death. De Silva concluded:

> In being tasked by the FRU to target "PIRA activists" for the UDA, Nelson would, to all intents and purposes, properly be considered to be acting in a position equivalent to an employee of the Ministry of Defence. It follows, therefore, that the Army must bear a degree of responsibility for Brian Nelson's targeting activity during 1987–89, including that of Patrick Finucane. This must be so irrespective of the nature of the information that he failed to impart to his FRU handlers in that case and some others.[21]

Nelson's activities on behalf of the FRU were uncovered during subsequent investigations into allegations of collusion between members of the locally recruited Ulster Defence Regiment and Loyalist paramilitaries. The investigation was carried out by John Stevens (later Sir John, commissioner of the London Metropolitan Police Service [MPS], and now Lord Stevens).

Stevens reported that in conducting his investigations he had, in his own words, "uncovered the criminality of the Army's agent, Brian Nelson."[22] In his final report Stevens heavily criticized the FRU over its "failure to keep records, the absence of accountability, the withholding of intelligence and evidence, through to the extreme of agents being involved in murder."[23] An independent inquiry by the Canadian judge Peter Cory, conducted as part of the process that led to the Northern Ireland peace settlement, confirmed that in that period there was "strong evidence that collusive acts were committed by the Army (Force Research Unit), the Royal Ulster Constabulary Special Branch and the Security Service."[24]

Agent running within the PIRA was also a key means by which the British state sought to neutralize the terrorist campaign and its associated risks to life and challenges to the state in Northern Ireland. For example, a highly placed agent in the PIRA is considered to have provided the intelligence that led to the 1987 interception of the freighter *Eksund*, which contained Libyan arms destined for the PIRA that were intended to facilitate an expansion of violence modeled on the Vietnamese Tet Offensive.[25] Prior to this, compromised operations had generated a pronounced suspicion among the leadership that informers were active inside the PIRA, along with concern that any member detained and questioned by the authorities could have been persuaded to become an informer. This concern led directly to the creation of the PIRA's Internal Security Unit, also known as the Nutting Squad. Members would interrogate and determine the fate of suspected informers, many of whom were killed.

Logic suggested that the squad's members were also the guardians of some of the PIRA's most keenly kept secrets. Having an agent inside would therefore be of immense value. A series of accusations in the early 2000s suggested that the FRU had achieved precisely this over the previous decade, when an agent code-named Stakeknife volunteered his services. According to one source, Stakeknife's intelligence was "high-grade," with "much of it read at the highest levels of the political and security establishments."[26] The running of agents inside both Loyalist and Republican paramilitary groups collided when, in 1987, Brian Nelson reported to his handlers that one potential UDA target was Frederick Scappaticci, who was said to have been the deputy head of the PIRA Nutting Squad and, (as the story goes) unknown to Nelson, the British agent Stakeknife. As in Nelson's case, Stakeknife "could only shine if he immersed himself in the activities of those he was reporting upon, including murder and other illegal acts."[27]

It has been alleged that to protect Scappaticci and to divert attention from him, the FRU provided Nelson with the profile of someone with a similar background, a pensioner and veteran Irish Republican called Francisco Notorantonio, that deliberately but inaccurately portrayed him as the "godfather" of the IRA in Ballymurphy.[28] Notorantonio was killed shortly afterward. Early one morning in October 1987, two masked men forced their way into his house and shot him in his bedroom.

In any context, the recruitment and deployment of covert human intelligence sources can entail varying types and degrees of deception. Even where they are absent or minimal, such recruitment is inherently exploitative. In discussing agent recruitment and motivation in the context of the Northern Ireland conflict, FRU agent handler "Martin Ingram" has written that some people "became agents for the 'buzz'. It gave them a status, a sense of being important. They enjoyed the secrecy, the sense of danger and the feeling of belonging to the intelligence 'family.'"[29] Some were motivated by financial reward, while a desire for revenge—for example, following a punishment beating—was "probably the best motivation for any potential recruit."[30] Coercion—for instance, after an arrest—could also be used in recruiting agents in Northern Ireland. A similar range of motivations could be identified among Palestinians in Gaza acting as informers on behalf of the state of Israel.[31] These relationships are exploitative precisely because, in Kant's terms, they treat humans as means rather than ends. Moreover, they place people in a situation with demands and stresses that they may not fully anticipate but that the recruiter will better understand, and from which it can be difficult to withdraw, leaving them susceptible to demands for greater involvement. Depending on the nature of the target group, if they are exposed or decide to give themselves up as the only route out of the relationship, then the human agents could face a range of possible consequences, from ostracism, through prosecution and imprisonment, to death.[32]

Even apparently noncoercive relationships between intelligence officers and human sources can be considered exploitative. Writing in the wake of the 1970s' Church Committee investigations in the United States, E. Drexel Godfrey Jr.—a former director of current intelligence in the CIA—described covert intelligence collection in terms of an ethos "rooted in a concept as old as human society: the weak or the vulnerable can be manipulated by the strong or the shrewd." Human intelligence collection, he wrote, "is the process of extracting from others information or national assets they would not willingly part with under normal circumstances."[33] Moreover, he noted,

The highest art in tradecraft is to develop a source that you "own lock, stock and barrel." According to the clandestine ethos, a "controlled" source provides the most reliable intelligence. "Controlled" means, of course, bought or otherwise obligated. Traditionally it has been the aim of the professional in the clandestine service to weave a psychological web around any potentially fruitful contact and to tighten the web whenever possible. . . . The modus operandi required, however, is the very antithesis of ethical interpersonal relationships.[34]

In discussing the qualities he looked for in a domestic informer (*inoffizieller mitarbeiter*, "unofficial collaborator"), former East German Ministry of State Security (Stasi) recruiter Herr Bock told journalist Anna Funder that mostly, "people we approached would inform for us. It was very rare that they would not. However, sometimes we felt that we might need to know where their weak points were, just in case. For instance, if we wanted a pastor, we'd find out if he'd had an affair, or had a drinking problem—things that we could use as leverage."[35]

In recruiting informers overseas, East German foreign intelligence was likely to engage in deception and came to be particularly associated with the use of so-called Romeo agents, who targeted and exploited vulnerable women, usually West German secretaries, in a position to access useful information. The former head of the Foreign Intelligence Service Markus Wolf felt that if he were to "go down in espionage history, it may well be for perfecting the use of sex in spying."[36] Once a threshold level of attraction or dependence had been established, the Romeo would explain the help he needed from the target, who could receive training in how to collect the information required. If exposed, the female target carried the risk, and many served prison sentences after being uncovered.[37]

While it proved a useful tool for foreign intelligence gathering during the Cold War, the use of sex as a means of facilitating covert human intelligence collection was not restricted to communist states, to that era, or to foreign intelligence gathering, as revelations concerning the conduct of undercover police officers working for the United Kingdom's Metropolitan Police Special Demonstration Squad (SDS) prove. Concerns about a lack of intelligence from within left-wing groups in the United Kingdom, heightened after the police failed to anticipate the extent of the March 1968 anti–Vietnam War demonstrations in London (where there were an estimated ten thousand protestors and some two hundred arrests), led Scotland Yard's Special Branch to set up what became the SDS. Its officers, known as the "hairies," would "go native" by growing long hair and beards and equipping themselves with a solid grasp of the Marxist or appropriate vernacular. The officers would assume new identities and infiltrate fringe political groups on behalf of the state, reporting any planned demonstrations or other activities deemed of interest.[38] As with all undercover intelligence work, this infiltration rested on deception. When the existence and activities of the SDS were revealed, former "comrades" of the undercover police officers felt betrayed.[39] As one of those involved, Special Branch Officer Tony Robinson reflected: "The whole business . . . in many instances of being a Special Branch Officer is based on lies. . . . And deception, otherwise you can't do your job."[40]

Over recent years it has emerged that infiltrating environmental and other protest groups in the twenty-first century, and maintaining a long-term cover within them, involved undercover police officers forming sexual relationships with other group members. Moreover, in a small number of cases, the undercover officers fathered children with activists who, of course, had been deceived as to the officers' true identities. This also meant that they had also been misled as to the future prospects for their relationship, not least because these police officers were married with children already.[41] More than ten women discovered that their relationships were actually with undercover police officers. Some had lasted several years, meaning the officers did not merely deceive these women but also denied them genuine relationships around which they could build their lives. Lisa Jones, who had a seven-year relationship with undercover police officer Mark Kennedy (posing as environmentalist Mark Stone), spoke of how "no amount of money or 'sorry' will make up for the lack of answers about the extent to which I was spied upon in my most personal and intimate moments."[42] This was in response to an unreserved apology from the Metropolitan Police and payment in 2015 of substantial damages to seven of the women involved. Martin Hewitt, an assistant commissioner with the force, conceded that the relationships were "abusive, deceitful, manipulative and wrong" and that they amounted to "a violation of the women's human rights, an abuse of police power and caused significant trauma." He added that "relationships like these should never have happened."[43]

His apology came in the wake of the announcement of a public inquiry and criticism from UN special rapporteur Maina Kiai, who termed the

Kennedy case "shocking as the groups in question were not engaged in criminal activities." Kiai also criticized the "duration of this infiltration, and resultant trauma and suspicion it caused" as being "unacceptable in a democracy."[44] In 2014 an official inquiry into the SDS was clear that there had never been "any circumstances where it would be appropriate for such covertly deployed officers to engage in intimate sexual relationships with those they are employed to infiltrate and target. Such an activity can only be seen as an abject failure of the deployment, a gross abuse of their role and their position as a police officer, and an individual and organizational failing."[45]

There was a further ethical dimension to this: it was publicly revealed that dead children's identities were used as the basis of the officers' cover, generating a public backlash. Consistent with general record-keeping, management, and oversight standards relating to the SDS, an official inquiry did not find out who introduced the tactic or when it was first used, although the report did suggest that the inspiration might have been the 1943 Operation Mincemeat deception used against Nazi Germany and described in Ewen Montagu's book *The Man Who Never Was*.[46] Discussion of ethics was notably absent from the report, except in the following paragraph:

> The deployment of properly trained and managed under cover officers to both disrupt and investigate crime is an approved vital policing tactic and has the full support of the courts, the wider public, Parliament and the Home Office. The issue of the historical use of covert identities based on the details of deceased children, however morally repugnant, should not detract from the importance of this tactic and the bravery of officers who have previously and still choose to volunteer to work in this field.[47]

A subsequent official report into these issues (by the same author) noted that the tactic of using the dead babies' identities

> was officially sanctioned and was seen at the time as the most appropriate means of securing and maintaining the covert identity. The ... tactic largely ceased towards the end of the 1990's and despite being seen by many as distasteful, it was not actually in contravention of any laws of the land nor any MPS or national policy guidance at the time.

The Commissioner has publicly apologised for distress the practice may have caused and has confirmed that deceased identities are
no longer used by undercover officers.[48]

This section conflated legality and ethicality, but it was also a tacit
acknowledgment that the practice was ethically dubious. However, it is
worth noting that the practice was protected by a secrecy justified in terms
of operational effectiveness. As the public was never supposed to find out
any of this, it was not in a position to offer the "full support" that Mick
Creedon claimed in his Operation Herne report.

All infiltration of target groups to gather secret intelligence raises a
more general ethical issue. Although their purpose is to gather secret intelligence, those infiltrating these groups cannot be neutral *observers*; by definition they have to become *participants*. Therefore, they have an impact
on the environment while they observe it. As with the common practice
of sting operations, we cannot assume that what the group does once the
agent is in place is what it would have done had the agent not been in place.
In July 2011 the appeal court accepted that undercover police officer Mark
Kennedy's participation had affected the course taken by the group he had
infiltrated and quashed the convictions of twenty environmental activists,
judging that Kennedy's deployment amounted to entrapment and that he
had acted as an agent provocateur.[49]

This discussion has highlighted the fundamental ethical dilemmas generated by using secret agents and covert human sources. The Kantian standard of moral imperative to treat people as an end and never as only a means
is a highly demanding one. If applied strictly to human intelligence collection and allowing only those instances where Kantian standards are met,
it seems likely that little, if any, human intelligence collection could take
place. We should not lose sight of the reality that the world is an uncertain
and insecure place, where national boundaries are highly permeable, the
politics of identity complex, and the challenges to state authority numerous.
In this context, decisions taken in relation to security may generate controversy, and some may even be found offensive in ethical terms, but intelligence interventions may well spare us from harder decisions with even
greater ethical costs further down the line. In other words, perhaps inherent
within intelligence interventions is an element of what we might call *ethical
risk transfer*, which accepts that an intelligence intervention will inevitably
have an impact on the surrounding environment and entail ethical costs,

so failing to meet the highest ethical standards. However, these costs are acceptable because they are more limited than the greater costs that would ensue if the intervention occurred later—for example, when fully blown threat situations arise or, absent early intelligence intervention, the threat is actualized, and at that point intelligence would be considered to have failed.

Nevertheless, in a liberal democratic context, the key issues are where risk is thought to exist and what kind of risk constitutes a legitimate target for intelligence intervention. In these contexts, revelations of intelligence interventions (and suspected interventions) that might impact the political process—extending to civil society, protest groups, and industrial disputes—have been highly controversial, suggesting that there are clear spaces in liberal democratic contexts where, at the very least, significant sections of the population regard intelligence intervention as illegitimate.[50] More generally the lessons of the past should inform future thinking about how necessity is understood with regard to undercover deployment, given the inevitable impact it has on other human beings, and once deployments occur, what can be done to reduce the risk of individuals being treated as means rather than ends. Moreover, we should examine who should be clearly responsible for identifying and mitigating the risks and to whom, in turn, they should themselves be responsible.

David Omand: In chapter 3 we established a set of concepts that can be used to tease out the ethical implications of intelligence activity, such as right authority, necessity, proportionality, and sufficient discrimination to manage the risk of harm to the innocent. We saw how such ideas, once incorporated into the fabric of international humanitarian law, not least through the Geneva Conventions, has helped tame some of the worst excesses of violence to which state-on-state conflict has given rise in the past.

We also emphasized that going through a set of ethical tick boxes as part of operational decision-making is not enough. There must be a genuine will to apply these ideas with sufficient imagination to reduce as far as possible the inevitable harms that conflict can bring. The same injunction rightly applies to the intelligence world. So let us apply the Just War ideas to assess the rightness of the actions taken in your examples from the army's agent running in the 1970s and 1980s in Northern Ireland and from the more recent Metropolitan Police infiltration of environmental protestors. As we do so, let us recognize that when it comes to human intelligence, the case officer concerned will have to make some decisions on the spot and in possibly dangerous circumstances. So not only does the structure of ethically sound processes for obtaining the right authority and for making management decisions on proportionality and necessity have to be in place but also—through the selection, training, and reinforcement of good management—the integrity of the personal values and ethics of the officers concerned in the field must be reliable.

In our discussion of the ethics of intelligence activity, so far we have stopped short of adopting a full-blown utilitarian view of always acting to seek the greatest good of the greatest number, preferring the ethical boundary condition of minimizing harm to the innocent as the state pursues legitimate national security and public protection goals. We recognize that what you have termed ethical risk transfer may exist where, if we refrain for ethical reasons from taking steps now that an act of omission may carry greater hidden ethical costs for the future, a situation you were trying to manage worsens. In those terms, the situation in Northern Ireland in the late 1970s and early 1980s does meet a stringent jus ad intelligentiam criterion to justify the use of national intelligence capabilities in managing the severe risks to public security and the need to help with the detection and prevention of crime. The civil rights protests of 1969 had provided the spur for mob violence between deeply divided communities, spilling over into serious threats to life. The British government was obliged to deploy the British Army onto the streets to relieve an exhausted and discredited police service. As the level of intercommunal violence escalated into a form of civil war and even threatened to draw in the Republic of Ireland, the UK government suspended Stormont, the Northern Ireland Parliament, and imposed direct rule from London.

What law and order remained became the army's responsibility to sustain, operating in support of a civil power that was absent (or, in the shape of the RUC and the RUC Special Branch, not trusted to be impartial) and that was confronting growing terrorism and gangsterism from both Republican and Loyalist extremists. Operational intelligence on the situation on the ground was largely missing, with the British intelligence agencies having to try to build a capability from a low or nonexistent base. Quickly the army recognized that it was not enough just to hope that the troublemakers could be identified through stop and search, roadblocks, and house-to-house searches while maintaining a deterrent presence through patrolling. Without high-grade intelligence on the identities, locations, and intentions of the leaders on both sides, army operations on the streets were bound to end in further polarizing the conflict and with the British Army as the common enemy.

That in a nutshell explains the British Army's need to create from scratch a unit capable of recruiting and running its own agents within both Republican and Loyalist extremist circles. The first such organization, the Military Reconnaissance Force, suffered significant casualties from the PIRA and was reformed as the better-resourced Force Research Unit as part of the Intelligence Corps. It trained volunteers from all three armed services, under conditions of great secrecy, in agent running and in how to pass unnoticed within either the Republican or Loyalist community. The extreme difficulty of the task must be borne in mind given the tightly knit nature of the urban housing estates and rural communities involved and the risks of almost subliminal telltale signs that an individual or a vehicle was "not from 'round here." The FRU personnel were brave beyond the call of duty, operated in extremely exposed conditions, and, as the Nelson case showed, achieved results, although at a cost. In this vicious campaign in which many lives were lost through terrorist action and the public remained in constant danger from sectarian violence, the general commanding officer and the commander of the land forces, who were both based in Headquarters Northern Ireland in Lisburn just outside Belfast, saw the FRU as a vital strategic asset. Certainly in creating the FRU they would have been right to argue that a jus ad intelligentiam criterion was met.

Turning to jus in intelligentia, however, any ethical assessment is bound to be far more critical of the FRU's conduct of agent running. The first Just War principle we derived in chapter 3 was right intention, or acting with integrity and no hidden political or other agendas behind the authorization of intelligence activity. Here is the nub of the accusation against the British Army in that period in Northern Ireland. While the military doctrine was to operate in support of the domestic civil power, absent an effective civil administration the army operations rapidly morphed without conscious political choice not only into a form of undeclared counterinsurgency campaign aimed principally at the Provisional IRA but also into a way to contain the Loyalist paramilitary groups responsible for extreme violence against the Catholic community, which the Loyalists held responsible for abetting the PIRA's terrorism. Leadership of the security effort was left to the army, which saw comprehensive intelligence gathering as an essential component and therefore was prepared to let the secret FRU operate on a very loose rein.

The majority of commanders, under armed attack from the terrorist gangs, would have wished for a legal framework appropriate to armed combat, not to domestic peacetime law. At the time they would certainly have found otherworldly and idealistic the rejection by John Stevens as a professional civilian police officer, and by Peter Cory as a Canadian judge, of the practice of collusive agent running into violent criminal organizations. It is striking that in the report of the most authoritative inquiry into the matter, Sir Desmond de Silva wrote:

> I have not concluded that the running of agents within terrorist groups is an illegitimate or unnecessary activity. On the contrary, it is clear that the proper use of such agents goes to the very heart of tackling terrorism. The principal lesson to be learned from my Report, however, is that agent-running must be carried out within a rigorous framework. The system itself must be so structured as to ensure adequate oversight and accountability. Structures to ensure accountability are essential in cases where one organisation passes its intelligence to another organisation which then becomes responsible for its exploitation.
>
> It is essential that the involvement of agents in serious criminal offences can always be reviewed and investigated and that allegations of collusion with terrorist groups are rigorously pursued.[51]

The principle of proportionality of course implies that the means chosen for an intelligence operation should reflect the seriousness of the harm that the activity seeks to counter. When the very existence of the state is in danger, governments will feel justified in taking extreme measures. Nevertheless, onto such a teleological calculation we argued in chapter 3 that it is necessary to add the deontological limits embodied in the universal human rights movement, notably the absolute prohibition of torture in the 1948 UN Declaration on Human Rights and extrajudicial killing outside the narrow limits allowed by international human rights law (that since 1998 have been incorporated into UK law). When it comes to the human dimension of intelligence gathering, therefore, we should not countenance operating outside that framework of human rights even if, at times of great danger, we are forced to its edges.

The principle of right authority is that decisions are taken within a legal framework at the level appropriate to the ethical risks that may be run and that can then allow for accountability for decisions and oversight of the process. As the de Silva inquiry found, that principle appears to have been comprehensively ignored throughout the FRU's existence. It is not clear what, if any, form of exercising right authority from the political level was obtained for delicate army intelligence operations early in the campaign (although we should bear in mind that in this period the very existence of the civilian British intelligence agencies was itself regarded as secret and no legislation governed their activity; knowledge of the FRU, the bases from which it operated, and the identity of its personnel was very tightly held; and there was no external scrutiny of British intelligence agencies' working processes from within the Ministry of Defence or the British intelligence community). Part of the explanation may also be that some in the British Army command in Northern Ireland behaved as if the campaign necessarily had to be conducted under different rules (for example, regarding intelligence operations that crossed the border with the Republic of Ireland) than would apply to the military's being used to provide aid to the civil power under peacetime conditions. If so, that represents a failure on the part of the ministers in London as much as on the military to establish sufficient strategic direction to meet a right intention criterion.[52]

The Nelson case is nevertheless capable of passing the "reasonable prospect of success" test, given Nelson's knowledge of the Loyalist paramilitaries and their campaign of randomly killing Catholics. Only high-grade intelligence would be likely to allow the perpetrators to be identified and the evidence gathered. We should be careful not to sit in judgment from comfortable armchairs without taking account of the conditions of the time, even as we conclude that as the campaign went on and the pace of operations stabilized, there should have been the opportunity to introduce sounder practices. No doubt distrust between the army and the RUC (whose relationship was never defined by the ministers), and even the security service MI5, hindered exploitation of Nelson's reporting to protect innocent civilians. It does seem also to have prevented the transfer of the best practice in agent running that might have mitigated the ethical risks the FRU took and that led in the end to its disbandment.

Similarly, in relation to the principle of discrimination, the assessment and management of the risk of collateral harm appear to have been inadequate. An operation such as running Nelson while he continued to be the intelligence officer of a terrorist group carried large risks to innocent members of the community. The case therefore can be seen as a flawed success, a case that with hindsight should have been better handled; but it should not be described as an agent recruitment that should never have happened on the ethical grounds of collateral risk, as the Stevens and Cory reports can be read as implying.

Finally, was the Nelson recruitment necessary, with no reasonable way to achieve the authorized mission (combating the murderous attacks by the Loyalist paramilitaries) at lesser ethical risk? Without having access to all the intelligence records for the period, it is not possible to answer this definitively. But in the given situation, with the potential offered by Nelson, the necessity test is probably passed. To satisfy even a minimal ethical assessment, however, the case would have had to be run very differently, with a shorter timescale and with intensive evidence gathering to ensure that most of the gang could be put behind bars in short order. That was not how the FRU was set up to work.

It can be argued therefore that at least some moral responsibility for the deaths of those innocents killed by the paramilitaries while Nelson was being run passes to the British Army commanders and to the British ministers. On their commanders' shoulders rested the weighing of the public good in continuing to run their criminal agent, even if they had a sound utilitarian argument on their side, and in turn the ministers should have provided sufficient strategic direction and legal guidance to the generals running the campaign.

The Northern Irish case of Stakeknife is also cited in the previous section and raises some of the same issues. Obtaining high-grade intelligence from within the Provisional movement would legitimately have been a top UK intelligence priority, endorsed by the Joint Intelligence Committee and the ministers. According to media accounts, Stakeknife, imprisoned in the early 1970s, joined the Provisional IRA and became the deputy head of an internal security unit tasked with counterintelligence, or finding and dealing with informers within the ranks. He had volunteered his services first to RUC Special Branch and then to the FRU, which is said to have accepted him as a highly paid agent. Sources on the case have to be treated with caution, and his role is murky given Scappaticci's subsequent use of the media's claim that he was Stakeknife to try to discredit Sinn Féin's Martin McGuinness. Scappaticci's initial media denials that he was Stakeknife and the PIRA's denials that he was a double agent add to the mystery. The sensationalist allegations from the FRU whistleblower Martin Ingram also have to be treated with circumspection.

Nevertheless, the strategic significance of the senior sources who undoubtedly were within the PIRA was probably considerable. As mentioned earlier, high stakes were being played by Prime Ministers Margaret Thatcher, John Major, and Tony Blair in allowing covert contacts throughout the period between the joint MI5-MI6 unit in Belfast with the PIRA and then in authorizing the delicate back-channel discussions that underpinned the peace process.[53] It is hard to imagine that they would have sanctioned such talking to terrorists without having corroborative secret intelligence from the highest levels of the PIRA that key figures in the leadership were genuinely seeking a settlement and not deceiving the British. It was indeed through this covert channel in February 1993 that a message came from the PIRA:

> The conflict is over but we need your advice on how to bring it to an end. We wish to have an unannounced ceasefire in order to hold a dialogue leading to peace. We cannot announce such a move as it will lead to confusion for the volunteers because the press will interpret it as surrender. We cannot meet the secretary of state's public renunciation of violence, but it would be given privately as long as we were sure that we were not being tricked.[54]

Stakeknife therefore (at least as represented in the media) is another example of the contemporary dilemma of agent recruiting in a violent criminal or terrorist organization. To find someone with sufficient access to justify the operation almost certainly means working with someone with blood on his or her hands from previous criminality and quite possibly with every intention of continuing the activity either for personal gain or simply to maintain his or her cover in the criminal enterprise. Nor would it be unusual for the authorities to be offered information in return for the criminal's seeking a "get out of jail card" should the need arise. In forming an ethical judgment about necessity and proportionality, such circumstances have to be taken into account. Operations that would certainly be ruled out in pursuing a conventional criminal gang might have to be considered in the case of a very serious terrorist threat or a war of survival. It becomes all the more important, therefore, that those involved work through the ethical principles that we are suggesting, take careful legal advice, obtain the right authority, and think about any impact on the strategic objective should the operation become public. There are no easy choices when facing serious threats.

The most striking intelligence example I know of that illustrates what you termed ethical risk transfer—that is, assessing actions to protect one section of the population at the expense of another and where the greatest good is in reducing the risk to the greatest number—was the use in 1944 of MI5's double agents to deceive the German high command as to the accuracy of the V-1 flying bombs being fired at London (Operation Crossbow).[55] False information was to be fed through the double agent network that more rockets were falling north of London and thus lead the Germans to alter their aiming point, resulting in more of the weapons falling to the south, where the population density was less. The saving from this deception was estimated at twelve thousand casualties. Prime Minister Churchill, Minister of Home Security Herbert Morrison, and Minister of Production Oliver Lyttelton, however, after discussing the proposal, refused to accept responsibility for deliberately directing the attack against any part of London. The moral responsibility for killing British civilians had to rest with the enemy, and the ministers were not prepared to sanction a situation where some citizens would have to be sacrificed even in order that many more might live. Undeterred, the British chiefs of staff resubmitted a slightly amended proposal to Deputy Prime Minister Clement Attlee, a Christian socialist who was no doubt more inclined to accept a utilitarian argument of the greater good. Attlee approved the continuation of the operation, which was then extended to the V-2 campaign. Analysis after the war estimated that about thirteen hundred more people would have been killed, ten thousand injured, and twenty-three thousand houses damaged had the Germans not been deceived into altering their V-2 aiming point. For the British Army in Belfast in the 1970s and 1980s, there must have been times when it did feel like being engaged in full-blown armed conflict. Nor is the possibility of having to make such cold-blooded ethical judgments confined to wartime: consider the position of a president or prime minister today who might be asked in light of 9/11 whether a hijacked airliner heading for a busy city center should be shot down while still over the outer suburbs.

Today in the United Kingdom, running covert human intelligence sources is governed by law and published codes of practice and by judicial oversight through the intelligence services commissioner for the intelligence agencies and the chief surveillance commissioner for the police.[56] In the case of domestic covert human sources, the police have published their ethical code following the scandals of the Metropolitan Police Special Demonstration Squad.[57] It is therefore instructive to review the SDS cases from the preceding section and examine why some fell far short of the standards that might be expected and what lessons should thereby be drawn.

The Special Demonstration Squad dates back to 1968 when the police wished to control the violent protests against the Vietnam War. Having established its covert successor, the National Public Order Intelligence Unit capable of infiltrating undercover police officers into target organizations (not just the standard police practice of recruiting paid informers), Scotland Yard had equipped itself with a powerful tool of influencing as well as reporting on events. As the independent Ellison inquiry reported,

> We acknowledge that for decades the SDS provided effective warning to enable the parts of the MPS dealing with the policing of public disorder to plan and allocate appropriate resources to meet the risks. Intelligence provided by the SDS thereby enabled a tighter management of the MPS resources. Valuable intelligence was also provided to the Security Service. There were also many examples of SDS undercover officers running great risks to themselves in order to gain very valuable intelligence. The potential for substantial public benefit to accrue from the squad's work was accordingly both real and substantial.[58]

That seems a suitable jus ad intelligentiam justification for the capability.

In terms of jus in intelligentia, however, Scotland Yard's investigations of protest movements exhibit many of the same failings as in the early days of army intelligence in Northern Ireland. It gave too much license to a covert unit, inadequately supervised frontline operatives, and lacked clear accountability and record keeping (an observation that itself raises the issue of inadequate oversight mechanisms that should have ensured the lessons painfully learned in the world of secret intelligence were transferred to law enforcement).

As the Ellison report concluded,

> The potential for "collateral damage" to result from the work of an SDS undercover officer was accordingly both real and obvious. Whether the damage resulted from:
>
> - the deceitful human interaction the work entailed;
> - the commission of crimes by officers sworn to uphold the law;

- the deception of other police officers and the courts when the undercover officers were arrested and prosecuted; or
- the long-term effects of the work on the officers themselves;

the potential for such collateral damage should have been carefully assessed by the MPS. It should have acted as a constant check against which the initiation and continuation of particular undercover deployments should have been balanced.[59]

The Metropolitan Police senior management instead appear to have authorized the setting up of the unit and then largely left it to its own devices, with inadequate procedures and safeguards that certainly fall short of the enhanced authorization arrangements in the current statutory code of practice for covert human operatives for handling what are called relevant sources that have a position within the police service.[60] The MPS commissioner gave an unreserved public apology.[61]

Any police officer deployed in this way in the United Kingdom today is required to comply with and uphold the principles and standards of professional behavior set out in the College of Policing Code of Ethics, with the following injunction:

What is expected is that you apply the intent of the Code to your decisions and ask yourself questions such as:

- Is my decision in line with the principles and expected behaviours outlined in the Code of Ethics?
- Will this action or decision reflect well on my professionalism and policing generally?
- Would I be comfortable explaining this action or decision to my supervisor?
- Would I be prepared to defend this action or decision in public?[62]

Above all, the cases cited demonstrate a failure to recognize that covert operatives struggling to maintain their cover in a suspicious environment will be liable at times to lose their internal ethical bearings. In these exact circumstances, having supervision is essential, in the same way that psychoanalysts and psychotherapists take their difficult or dangerous cases and seek the supervision of an experienced peer as a check on their handling of the cases.

Mark Phythian: I agree that the core dilemmas that we have discussed regarding the use of covert human sources could be mitigated by more effective management and oversight. As de Silva found in the case of the FRU in Northern Ireland, there is a responsibility (at the level of the state, as well as in the specific organization) to provide it, as without supervision there is no way the state can satisfy itself that, in the Just War terms we used in chapter 3, the obligations around jus in intelligentia are being considered, let alone met. As I suggested earlier, an additional requirement is using greater discrimination in deployment. Covert human sources tend to be deployed where advance notice of a target group's planning is required, but what makes a target group a legitimate target for such intrusive operations? In making these decisions, the guidance of Herbert Scoville Jr. in the wake of the Church Committee hearings in the United States remains relevant: "In each case . . . the place to start is with a serious evaluation of the importance of the activity to our total national security and foreign policies. How much does covert intelligence matter as compared with other forms of intelligence collection?"[63] These are questions of necessity and such assessments are becoming more formalized and common, but the bases on which these assessments are made require regular reflection to guard against the risk of slippage.

The cases we have discussed not only raise the ethical question of when to go in but also highlight the importance of regular reviews of the necessity of the deployment, as well as the question of when it is time to get out. The resources required to prepare the ground for an undercover deployment or to cultivate an agent, together with often exaggerated concerns about the likely impact of a withdrawal, function as strong bureaucratic disincentives to curtail such deployments once under way, even if ethical problems arise. There is scope to reflect on the questions of when to end an operation and of how reviews are conducted when thinking about bright clear lines guiding conduct.

The two cases I focused on earlier in this chapter—the use of intelligence agents in the context of the Northern Ireland conflict and the SDS infiltration of environmental protest groups—have their origins in a pre-oversight era. Not only was a culture of external oversight absent in the 1970s and 1980s but also both cases involved organizational cultures insulated by high levels of secrecy that accorded a low priority to formal ethical consideration while, at the same time, rewarding risk taking. In tight organizational cultures characterized by low levels of staff mobility, limited contact with other professional groups, and a strong sense of the necessity of their work (again reflecting the importance of the official narrative, as we discussed in chapter 1), external oversight and investigation can be not simply unwelcome but actively resisted.

We can identify an ethical gap rooted in the absence of effective oversight at the organizational level in both cases. A Scotland Yard review of the SDS completed in 2009, but only revealed to the public as the result of a Freedom of Information Act request in 2015, noted how a "number of ethical/moral dilemmas arose from the activity of SDS operatives and the management of them" but that in the "vast majority of cases" they were dealt with "internally and on occasions informally."[64] It also found "in some instances apparent ethical/moral dilemmas were simply not addressed as they formed part of the 'accepted consequences' of such operational deployments."[65] Similarly, the Ellison review found that the SDS "adopted an ad hoc approach towards assessing the benefit potential to its customers, rather than conducting a detailed 'cost-benefit analysis' weighing up the collateral damage that might be caused against the true value of the intelligence being obtained."[66]

As you rightly say, we are now in an era of greater regulation and closer oversight of these activities than what prevailed in the 1960s and 1970s, when the SDS was in its formative phase. However, in the case of the SDS we only now know what we know because of the actions of a whistleblower. The ethically dubious behavior that was revealed would not otherwise have been exposed to the public. When it was, it clearly failed a form of what we referred to earlier as the Stansfield Turner test.

Regarding the example of Northern Ireland, Sir Desmond de Silva's inquiry into the murder of Patrick Finucane provides a particularly rich seam of evidence on official thinking at the time about whether the FRU's former agent inside the UDA, Brian Nelson, should be tried for murder and/or conspiracy to murder in light of John Stevens's findings and the question of whether there was a public interest in avoiding a trial.[67] This reveals the construction of a complex ethical balance sheet and provides an insight into what we might term the bureaucratic politics of ethical thinking in an intelligence and national security context at that time. In a letter of May 30, 1990, to the director of public prosecutions, an assistant chief constable of the RUC explained:

Nelson's role as an Intelligence Officer for the UDA/UFF [Ulster Free-dom Fighters] meant that to preserve his position within the terrorist group, he would commit crime unless very closely supervised. The control of Nelson in such an important role was impossible for he had the latitude to carry out criminal acts without the Military being made aware until after the event. Notwithstanding this the Military allowed him to continue his work even though he had clearly reached a point of involvement which was undoubtedly criminal.[68]

The letter went on to say that Nelson's "participation in criminal activity is without question. He clearly went beyond what was expected of him as an agent."[69]

Nelson certainly contributed to state goals in Northern Ireland while working undercover. In 1984 and 1985 he had provided information on Protestant paramilitary membership and training, and photographs of people involved. He gave advance notice of a proposed arms shipment from South Africa destined for the UDA (something he was able to do because he had negotiated the weapons deal himself). As a result the shipment was never made, and lives were potentially saved. In May 1987 he alerted security forces to a paramilitary effort to murder Sinn Féin's Gerry Adams by attaching a limpet mine to his car.

This ethical balance sheet had a further dimension. The FRU claimed that the purpose of running Nelson as an intelligence officer in the UDA was to give greater focus to UDA targeting—that is, to direct it from randomly killing Catholic members of the public toward targeting IRA activists.[70] This, it was argued, brought two benefits. First, attacks on innocent victims would be reduced or cease completely. Second, because IRA activists were understood to represent harder targets, any attempt to kill them required a longer period of reconnaissance and planning, giving greater opportunity for the RUC to prepare countermeasures. As a memo of March 11, 1991, from the attorney general explained: "The purpose was to *save* lives."[71] But as the attorney general—and later de Silva—recognized, that stratagem created a further ethical obligation on the British Army to check that the RUC was indeed acting on the targeting intelligence that the FRU passed to it, and the army should have realized that the RUC's response was far from adequate.[72]

To compound the problem, Nelson had his own agenda. In some instances of murder and conspiracy to murder, Nelson did not inform his handlers or did not provide key information in advance, thus denying the possibility of a preventive intervention.[73] Moreover, claims regarding the number of lives potentially saved by Nelson's intelligence—put at seven hundred threat warnings involving 217 individuals by the military—were wildly exaggerated. The Stevens inquiry could identify just two instances where information from Nelson was used to protect potential victims of Loyalist paramilitaries (one being the case of Gerry Adams). In other cases, Stevens found, "information received from Nelson was so old that it was used for record purposes (in some cases three or four days after the event) or of such low quality as to be not worthy of special consideration."[74] Chief Constable of the RUC Hugh Annesley agreed with Stevens's assessment, which was endorsed by Attorney General Sir Patrick Mayhew. In conducting his review into the Finucane case, de Silva considered whether at Nelson's trial the court had been misled by evidence about the number of lives Nelson's activities had saved. He found that it was not the case, because the evidence given in mitigation had referred only to the "potential" value of Nelson's evidence. Nevertheless, de Silva concluded that "the Army were fully aware of the fact that Nelson's intelligence had not generally saved lives and that the initial claims made by the MoD [Ministry of Defence] to the Attorney General were utterly wrong."[75]

Nelson's undercover role, of course, provided no immunity from the law, but the letter of the law proved not to be the only consideration in deciding whether to go ahead with a prosecution. As summed up by Charles Powell, private secretary to Prime Minister Major, one consideration was that "grave damage will be done to the capability of the security forces and to our intelligence-gathering activity if the prosecution is mounted."[76] Powell reported that the secretary of state for defense "argues strongly indeed ferociously that prosecution would be against the public interest." The essence of the defense secretary's argument was as follows:

> I accept that it is a grave step to decide as an act of policy not to proceed with serious criminal charges but in this case I believe the damage which we risk to our capability to combat terrorism is sufficient to warrant it. I do not accept that such action would represent a greater challenge to the rule of law than that which comes from the terrorist evils we continue to face. . . . Many people in Northern Ireland owe their lives to Brian Nelson. In balancing the need to combat terrorism against the impartial administration of justice, I

believe that in this difficult case the public interest justifies a decision not to prosecute.[77]

Two points about this argument are worth highlighting. First, this utilitarian calculation was based on inaccurate information regarding the number of lives Nelson had saved. Given Sir Desmond de Silva's conclusion, it would seem that the secretary of state was misled on this point. Second, there was no obvious way to calculate the cost in utilitarian terms of a decision to proceed with a prosecution. As John Stevens pointed out, the rate of taking life in Northern Ireland depended on a range of factors, not simply the actions of a single individual, while statistical evidence did not point to a sharp rise in Loyalist paramilitary killings after Nelson's arrest.[78] Nevertheless, in considering whether to prosecute Nelson, the Northern Ireland secretary agreed with the secretary of state for defense on the grounds of the public interest in defeating terrorism and that "the preservation of life from terrorist action has to be of first importance."[79] The view of MI5 was that the damage to intelligence work would be "very grave indeed," and the cabinet secretary supported this view.[80]

Hence, in the application of the law, a parallel set of ethical considerations had to be weighed: on the one hand was the rule of law; on the other hand were the number of lives Nelson was held to have saved, the potential damage to future intelligence work, and the possible loss of life. Moreover, much bureaucratic weight argued for a decision not to prosecute. As Charles Powell noted, "This is a very murky world we are dealing with," and in it, he suggested, the old adage "it takes a thief to catch a thief" applied.[81] This case, then, is interesting in considering the important role of operational oversight in monitoring and ensuring ethical standards where covert human sources are involved, and it returns us to the question of the relationship between law and ethics. In this case, the argument was that there was an ethical case for not applying the law, despite the gravity of the offenses.

David Omand: With hindsight and with today's eyes, we can certainly criticize the processes in place then to manage human agents in Northern Ireland. That should not lead us to conclude that the ethical case for the practice of agent running was flawed. As the de Silva report concluded:

I believe that the intelligence-led security response to the Troubles did play a significant role in constraining all terrorist organisations, to the extent that they were forced to realise that their aims were not achievable by violence.

In the context of this Report, it is important to acknowledge, in particular, that the work of the Royal Ulster Constabulary's Special Branch (RUC SB) and the Security Service had a significant impact in thwarting and constraining loyalist terrorist groups. Many intelligence-led operations against republican paramilitary groups were also notably successful during this period.[82]

In light of the obligations flowing from both domestic and international law, the security authorities were presented with a fundamental dilemma during the campaign in Northern Ireland. They were required on the one hand to have regard for the state's paramount duty to protect the life of its citizens, including its own military and law enforcement personnel, and on the other hand to have minimum resort to the use of lethal force, save in lawful self-defense, in dealing with paramilitary terrorists of any creed as terrorists were essentially categorized as ordinary criminals.[83] In chapter 2 I suggested that in this period intelligence officers commonly saw themselves as the necessarily secret and thus publicly unappreciated "secret guardians" of civilized society who were expected to do what they believed was necessary to keep the public safe yet knowing that they were on the front line without legal or political protection if later they were judged to have made mistakes. As the de Silva report concluded: "Intelligence officers were, in effect, being asked to perform a task that, in some cases, could not be achieved effectively in ways that were lawful. It is my view that those charged with upholding the law should never be put in the position of potentially having to break the law in order to discharge their official duties."[84] The actions of the FRU have to be seen in that context.

Returning to the general subject of intelligence ethics, another important conclusion was reported by Sir Desmond de Silva in the report you cite into the murder of Patrick Finucane:

In my view, the running of effective agents in Northern Ireland was such a fraught and difficult task that it manifestly required the support of a clear legal and policy framework. . . . It was apparent that successive Governments knew that agents were being run by the intelligence agencies in Northern Ireland without recourse to any effective guidance or a proper legal framework. I found that repeated attempts were made by senior RUC, Security Service and (latterly) Army officers to raise this very issue with Government Ministers at Cabinet level. Yet it was not until 1993 that some Cabinet Ministers belatedly came to support the creation of a legislative framework. Even then, it was not until seven years later, when the Regulation of Investigatory Powers Act 2000 (RIPA) was passed, that any description of a statutory regime was created.[85]

Today we have assurances from British ministers that all intelligence activity is now conducted in full accord with domestic law. As chapter 2 explains, the legal basis of intelligence activity has evolved from the direct use of royal prerogative powers through compliance with laws such as RIPA to the present state of being placed fully under the modern rule of law with its requirement for transparency in how the law might affect the citizen.

We have examined in some detail the very hard issues that arise when human intelligence activity is directed against hostile non-state terrorist groups. We should conclude this discussion of the ethical issues involved in human intelligence work by looking at a different set of circumstances, the acquisition of intelligence from inside state targets to guide policy in defense and foreign affairs.

This chapter began by reminding us that the value of human intelligence is spoken for by its antiquity and by its ubiquitousness. Any intelligence agency will maintain a network of contacts—or, to use the French term, "honorable correspondents"—who from time to time can be approached to provide local knowledge, introductions to key personalities, and practical help such as the loan of a safe house, boat, or vehicle. Although not strictly covert human intelligence sources, a duty of care extends clearly to such individuals, who may come to pay a price for their patriotism.[86] British businessman Greville Wynne did, spending eighteen months in the Lubyanka prison after being caught couriering messages to GRU colonel Oleg Penkovsky, who was being run jointly in Moscow by the Secret Intelligence Service and the CIA in the early 1960s.

The Penkovsky case demonstrates the strategic value of covert human intelligence at its best. Penkovsky was a volunteer agent who provided technical details of Soviet strategic and theater nuclear weapons systems that provided essential data when it came to assessing the Soviet nuclear arsenal, information that also proved highly useful in the run-up to the Cuban missile crisis of 1962. Such a willing agent with access who is prepared to take the risks of being run long term is a huge asset, in which the personal chemistry between intelligence case officers and an agent will make or break the case. In such circumstances the professional tradecraft must be flawless and the case run with great patience. Tragically the urgent need for Penkovsky's intelligence led his case officers to arrange short-notice use of dead drops that may have in the end helped harden the suspicions the Soviet authorities already had of him. Penkovsky was accused of treason and paid for his beliefs with his life. According to some accounts he was cremated alive as a warning to others.

Another example of how a well-placed agent can be a strategic asset is the case of Oleg Gordievsky, a colonel in the KGB who became disenchanted with the Soviet Union after the invasion of Czechoslovakia in 1968. He volunteered to work for SIS while serving in Copenhagen in 1974 and ended his career as the KGB rezident (station chief)–designate in the London embassy in 1985. He was able to inform the British intelligence community of past and current attempts to penetrate the agencies. His knowledge of Soviet leadership thinking directly influenced the assessment of the potentially dangerous Able Archer nuclear war scare of 1983. He identified Mikhail Gorbachev as a future Soviet leader in a new mold that influenced Prime Minister Thatcher to see him as a man with whom she could do business. He also briefed US president Ronald Reagan and is credited with helping convince him that opening a constructive dialogue with the new Soviet leaders was possible.[87] Gordievsky subsequently survived a possible Russian attempt to assassinate him with thallium, and at the time of this writing he lives peacefully in retirement in the United Kingdom, surfacing from time to time to give talks about the future of Russia, for whose current leadership he has only scorn.

The carefully choreographed professional human intelligence activity in such cases as Penkovsky and Gordievsky certainly stands in sharp contrast to the improvised British Army's efforts to gather intelligence in the early days of the Northern Ireland emergency. Nevertheless, human intelligence gathering in any context is an activity that inevitably involves an intimate relationship between the intelligence officer and the covert agent and is thus vulnerable to human failings. For that reason, a professional human intelligence agency will insist on scrutinizing the recruitment and the subsequent handling of agents by experienced officers outside the operational management line. To avoid the obvious danger that an intelligence officer will see all their geese as swans, and to minimize the risk of deception by sources or sub-sources, reporting from human agents should likewise be examined closely from outside the operational chain of command. An example of the dangers that can arise if this practice weakens is seen in the failures of human intelligence in the run-up to the 2003 Iraq War. As one of the SIS witnesses to the Robin Butler–led inquiry explained, an earlier reorganization had weakened the service's quality assurance process whereby the "requirements" function, which was responsible for quality assurance of agents' reporting, was independent of the "production" function responsible for producing reports.[88]

A professional intelligence officer will seek to manage the possibility of harm to the agent, his or her family, and others involved by maintaining constant awareness of ethical risks. Picking up your earlier references to Kant, the intelligence officer must be able in that way to acknowledge the humanity of those for whom they accept a moral responsibility. To them the officers owe a duty of care to avoid treating them ruthlessly, or as simply means to the end of acquiring desired intelligence. In the process, nevertheless, some manipulation of the human source—through motivations, ambitions, desires, and fears—seems inevitable.

Are those remarks a counsel of perfection? We can identify several good reasons why a professional human intelligence agency might be well advised to train its officers to follow such an ethical approach based on its purely practical advantages. Seeking out those who have genuine motives and want to provide information rather than attempting to coerce unwilling recruits (at the extreme by entrapment and blackmail) is likely to result in more, and more reliable, information being garnered. Agents who are the subject of blackmail are likely to spend their waking hours trying to think of how to get out of the headlock the intelligence officer has on them and may very well take resentful satisfaction in passing on partial or even misleading intelligence reporting. Having a reputation for looking after one's agents will be an asset to a professional intelligence agency (and the opposite, revelations of deception and betrayal, will seriously tarnish a reputation). A track record for maintaining high levels of secrecy and tradecraft, essential if the duty of care is to be respected, will also help when recruiting. The promise that an agent's identity will forever remain a deep secret is a standard to which the British Secret Intelligence Service holds strictly, with the only exceptions being the few individuals who positively wanted their contribution celebrated after completing their period of service, such as some agents from the Second World War, and notably the former Soviet

KGB archivist Vasili Mitrokhin. Smuggled out of the Soviet Union by SIS, Mitrokhin then worked with British intelligence and Professor Christopher Andrew of Cambridge University to chronicle the Cold War secret activities of the KGB.[89]

The KGB itself had benefited from ideological recruitments in the 1930s and 1940s, such as the Cambridge Five, as many British intellectuals looked to support international communism to halt the rise of fascism.[90] Similarly, the Soviet sources inside the Manhattan Project to build the first atom bomb were largely motivated by the idealistic belief that such a weapon should not be the postwar monopoly of the United States. With subsequent Soviet behavior in colonizing Eastern Europe, in brutally suppressing the Hungarian uprising in 1956, and in quelling the Prague Spring of 1968, the supply of willing agents dried up. Later cases, ranging from Geoffrey Prime at the GCHQ to Ronald Pelton at the NSA, rested on amoral Soviet recruiters manipulating a combination of personal greed, character weakness, and hubris on the part of their victims. Allegedly the KGB then "burned" Pelton, who had betrayed hugely sensitive signals intelligence operations, when his usefulness had expired to divert US counterespionage from the KGB's well-placed spy within the CIA Aldrich Ames, whom they had recruited through his greed.[91]

The well-placed human agent, for as long as records have been kept, has provided invaluable insights into the thinking and actions of the leaders and military commanders of potentially, and sometimes actually, hostile states. There is no reason to imagine that will ever change, although in the future the value of key agents may well rest on the help they can provide with technical collection, ranging from the planting of listening devices to facilitating access to computer networks. In chapter 5 as we explore that world of digital intelligence, we should remember that behind its successes often stand the human intelligence officers and their agents in the shadow of Immanuel Kant and his categorical imperative with the planning of a recruitment, the moment of truth when a proposition is made, and the subsequent operational life of an agent and the aftercare that may be necessary.

5

Digital Intelligence and Cyberspace

David Omand: In this chapter we consider the ethical issues raised by the widespread practice of obtaining intelligence from digital data. These issues largely concern personal intrusions into privacy but also involve concerns over freedom of expression when authorities attempt to restrict material on digital social media, such as that put out by terrorist organizations or their sympathizers. The nature of digital information also lends itself to rapid exploitation and use, for example, when the location of a terrorist suspect overseas is revealed by a telephone or other mobile device, a topic we explore in chapter 6.

We are living through the beginning of a revolution in human affairs enabled by the digitization of information and the means of communication through the Internet, the World Wide Web, and mobile devices (with the Internet of Things rapidly growing[1]). We are now dependent on this technology for economic and social progress, for international economic development, and for national security and public safety. Trust has to be built both in the open Internet as a safe place to innovate, to do business, to shop, and to interact socially, and in the ability of the authorities to be able to uphold the law in cyberspace. That trust cannot be taken for granted. The Internet, and the World Wide Web that it carries, were not originally designed with security in mind, and many seek to exploit this weakness for their own antisocial, criminal, or aggressive ends.[2]

A global coincidence over the last fifteen years has shaped the rapid development of digital intelligence and heightened ethical concerns: the post–Cold War growth in demand for information about individuals to manage the threats from terrorists (especially after 9/11), international criminals, and other individuals of concern has coincided with the ability of the Internet and Web-based technologies, developed for commercial

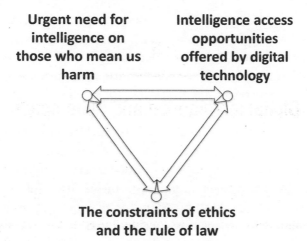

Figure 5.1   A Global Coincidence.

purposes, to supply detailed data about individuals in ways never before possible. Demand for and supply of such data have been interacting dynamically, and the process continues. The question posed for the democracies that we aim to address, at least in outline, in this chapter is the extent to which that dynamic interaction between supply and demand for digital intelligence should be modulated by considerations of law and of ethics, including the possibility of international norms on right behavior in cyberspace.[3] The exposure of many of these digital intelligence capabilities using the material stolen by Edward Snowden from the NSA and its UK partner GCHQ has heightened the concerns over privacy and has placed in the public domain information about these capabilities that was previously regarded as deep national security secrets.[4]

Conflicting priorities arise at three levels. Civil liberties organizations report increasing ethical concerns by *individuals* for their right to privacy and for the protection of their personal information from hackers, from carelessness on the part of corporations, from unrestrained government surveillance, from new techniques such as predictive analytics, and from the very business model of the Internet that rests on the monetization of personal data. As a result demand is increasing for end-to-end encryption, for anonymization software, for secure apps and mobile devices, and for stronger data protection law and stronger enforcement of it. Some governments are therefore seeking to restrict where their citizens' data may be processed or stored, creating the risk of fragmentation of the Internet.

At the same time, *law enforcement* expresses growing concern over the way that serious criminals are able to exploit the vulnerabilities of digital technology (and human behavior when using it) to conduct their crimes at scale. ISIS terrorists have been able to use the Web to publicize their atrocities, to direct attacks, and to recruit new followers while hiding their communications from the authorities. Criminal activity using the Internet (including the Dark Net) includes terrorist facilitation and sale of cyber attack exploits, global fraud and money laundering, narcotics trafficking, proliferation, human trafficking, child sexual abuse, and intellectual property theft.[5] Law enforcement is finding it increasingly difficult to counter these threats, to establish the identities of those responsible, and to secure the evidence they need to bring the criminals to justice, especially when they are hiding overseas or the evidence is in corporate databases in another jurisdiction.

Meanwhile, *national intelligence agencies* have been able to exploit digital technology to gather information for the protection of public and national security (the fundamental duties of government), including generating intelligence for military operations and force protection around the world; to support diplomacy and national security policy making; and to safeguard the critical national infrastructure from destructive cyber attacks. At the same time, many intelligence agencies have been trying to use their advanced capabilities to assist law enforcement in their mission to keep the public safe, to uncover global criminal networks, and especially to track terrorists across frontiers. The legal framework for such activity, however, has been shown to be defective or missing altogether in many nations.

As with all hard public policy issues, there is no easy way of reconciling conflicting ethical concerns. Place the security of personal data and one's anonymity on the Internet above all else and law enforcement is shut out, the rule of law is undermined, and crime, terrorism, and cyber attacks flourish. Insist on a right of access to all encrypted data for law enforcement and intelligence agencies—for example, through controlling or weakening encryption standards—and confidence in the Internet as a secure medium will be lost, and fragmentation of the Internet will spread.

Satisficing is a decision-making strategy that aims at finding solutions that are adequate for the purpose in hand when searching for the optimum may take too long and in the end be unachievable.[6] A set of sufficient satisficing measures, as discussed in this chapter, is needed to ensure respect for *all* our fundamental rights: the right to life, to the rule of law, to freedom of speech and assembly, to enjoyment of property, and to privacy. In particular, the right to live in security needs to be recognized as a human requirement along with the right to enjoy privacy for personal and family life. They should not be traded one for the other; a sufficiency of both is necessary in a civilized society.

The leading global intelligence and law enforcement agencies (foremost those of the United States and its Five Eyes partners and those of Russia, China, and Israel) were quick to realize the potential represented by the digitization of communications carried by packet-switched networks around the globe.[7] Access to such Internet traffic can be obtained via fiber-optic cables, satellite links, or microwave links. The packets that compose a communication may travel along different paths, resulting in some domestic communications being on paths intercepted overseas and vice versa. Detecting, classifying, attributing, and responding to advanced cyber attacks also benefit greatly from bulk access to the Internet.[8]

A direct consequence of the business model of the Internet is that it involves the provision of services such as search engines that is free at the point of use but is paid for by the monetization of personal data for marketing purposes. The big Internet companies have thus come to a position where they can know much more about us and our personal habits and tastes than any intelligence agency ever could (or should). The commercial value of personal information has also driven the development of apps used on mobile devices (more than a million of which are available at little or no charge to the consumer), again generating new opportunities for gathering intelligence.

It is thus now very hard to live without leaving a digital trace as the private sector can widely capture personal data through, for example, our debit and credit card purchases, loyalty cards, and airline and hotel bookings, as well as the records kept by the government through border controls, vehicle licensing, and passports. Intelligence agencies realized that by mining data and overlaying data sets, it would be possible to answer questions—for example, about the patterns of life, the identities, and the locations of suspects—that would have been infeasible using analog (shoe leather) methods of detective investigation.

Essential for the development of the World Wide Web was strong, public key encryption, which allowed secure online shopping and financial transactions. The same cryptography, of course, enabled high levels of security for personal communications. Early in the digital age, very strong commercial encryption such as PGP (pretty good privacy) was freely available to download for any user, but few bothered. For those who did, they often made mistakes, and their encrypted communications thus made them stand out to the searching computers of the intelligence agencies. Today such strong encryption comes seamlessly as standard with most communication applications.[9]

Intelligence agencies and law enforcement have therefore increasingly relied for their investigations on data about the facts of a communication rather than on being able to access its content. Furthermore, they realized that if they could retain and store communications data (an increasingly viable option over the period as the cost and complexity of bulk data storage fell), then given a trigger event such as a terrorist attack or a sighting of a suspect, the records could be specifically searched using a targeted selector (for example, to find any calls from a precise location at a given time) and could uncover new leads for investigation.

The methods of obtaining digital data for intelligence purposes can be broadly categorized as:

- *Intercepting data about an individual's communications that is carried in the "header" of each data packet.* This information enables the servers operating the networks of the Internet to route the packet to its ultimate destination, where the communication (text, pictures, video, data) is reassembled for the recipient. Essentially this data is the "who is calling whom, where, when, how, and for how long" of the communication and is analogous to the information in an old-fashioned itemized telephone bill. The difference is that for communications such as a voice call over the Internet this data is in the form of a so-called Internet connection record, showing which device communicated with which server and the details of how, when, where, and for how long.
- *Intercepting the actual content of a communication.* Defined in UK law, *content* is considered any element of the communication, or any data attached to or logically associated with the communication, that reveals anything that might reasonably be considered the meaning (if any) of the communication but excludes any meaning arising from the *fact* of the communication. Content could therefore include the title of an email or the full browsing record from an Internet session by a user. In the latter case, the communications data would show that an individual accessed a server from a laptop but not which pages were then sought or which places were examined with Google Earth or Google Street View (a known method for

terrorist reconnaissance of potential targets); such detail would count as content. The term "metadata" is often used loosely to refer to such associated information.

- *Hacking into a suspect's computer or mobile device or a target network by equipment interference to access the data directly or to facilitate access.* This hacking may be accomplished by *physical* interference (e.g., covertly downloading data from a device to which physical access has been gained), *remote* interference (e.g., installing a piece of software on a device over a wired or wireless network to remotely extract information from the device), or *equipment* interfering (e.g., planting malware on the relevant communications system to enable access).

- *Applying advanced data-mining techniques to databases.* This effort targets databases containing personal information relating to numerous individuals that comes from either government sources (passport records, vehicle licenses, etc.) or the private sector (e.g., airline passenger information) to derive information about a suspect. Because these datasets are very large, they cannot be processed manually.

For the first few years of the twenty-first century, it looked as if the advantage would lie with the intelligence agencies that were able to exploit these new, digitally available sources of supply. Spurred on by the 9/11 terrorist attacks, former national security adviser to President Reagan Adm. John Poindexter proposed what became in 2002 the Total Information Awareness (TIA) initiative, a five-year Defense Advanced Research Projects Agency program aimed at revolutionizing the ability of the United States to detect, classify, and identify foreign terrorists. By integrating intelligence and surveillance programs and information from the Internet itself and by applying advanced data mining and pattern detection algorithms, TIA would have provided federal agencies with focused warnings of unusual events inferred from patterns of data and thus enable preventive action to be taken. Although the Pentagon had rapidly renamed TIA in late 2003 as the Terrorist Information Awareness initiative, media criticism of the domestic surveillance implications alleged that American citizens would be included in the total awareness program. Congress defunded the program, which was suspended.[10] The US National Security Agency took up individual components of the TIA, such as advanced translation software and data-mining techniques, for its own foreign intelligence programs under its own legal authorities.

As the NSA and other advanced signals intelligence organizations were grappling with the dynamic interaction of urgent demands for and copious supply of digital information, the individuals of concern to the authorities—dictators, terrorists, pirates, weapons proliferators, cyber criminals, narcotics and people traffickers, child abusers, and so on—recognized that the Internet and the Web offered new opportunities. In a world in which communications are broken into packets that may take different routes to their destinations, interception is not straightforward in any case, even for the US NSA, the most advanced digital intelligence player. As new social media applications, chat rooms, drop boxes, and other applications were introduced, the choice of platform for an exchange of communications or an Internet voice call increased. Accelerated by the Snowden material, the Internet companies then took rapid steps to offer their customers greater security from government interception, adding end-to-end encryption to their services and stronger protection for mobile devices. The advantage was increasingly shifting to those seeking to hide from the authorities.[11]

There is no *absolute* right to privacy in any nation's law. The fundamental 1948 UN Declaration of Human Rights, the European Convention on Human Rights, and the US Constitution—all embody the principle that where privacy itself risks harm to others, a balance must be struck. Prohibitions must be complied with against arbitrary or unreasonable searches, but, in some circumstances, lawful intrusion can be justified. In a well-known passage the ECHR declares, "There shall be no interference by a public authority with the exercise of this right [privacy] except such as is in accordance with the law and is necessary in a democratic society in the interests of national security, public safety or the economic well-being of the country, for the prevention of disorder or crime, for the protection of health or morals, or for the protection of the rights and freedoms of others."[12]

What, therefore, might count as an *un*reasonable search and seizure on the Internet? As we did for human intelligence in chapter 4, we can apply the "just intelligence" principles of chapter 3 to the privacy issue. We can start the search for an answer by recognizing the law provides for general categories of just cause for interfering with personal privacy, when necessary and proportionate in individual cases, as described in the preceding paragraph.

Another ethical principle, right intention, shows integrity of motive. If powerful surveillance tools are to be in the hands of state authorities, then the public must have confidence in independent mechanisms (e.g., for the United States, involving the Foreign Intelligence Surveillance Court and congressional oversight; and in the British case, involving very senior retired judges and senior parliamentarians) to detect and expose any misuse by those seeking intelligence and by those providing it.

Proper authority as a principle is already built into the US Constitution and the ECHR and thus into the requirements that should apply to those authorizing a warrant or other access to digital material, as well as to analysts querying digital data. As we discussed in chapter 3, a necessary (but not sufficient) condition for authority to be granted should be that the information sought relates to a legitimate intelligence requirement, within the just causes for which intelligence activity is sanctioned by law, and that the request comes from a sufficiently senior level within the agency as prescribed in law. For the most intrusive forms of surveillance, it is now common practice in democracies to have an independent judicial officer or court approve or review warrants.

Similarly, proportionality must be demonstrated in a request for authorization, meaning that the possibility of causing unintentional harm to the subject or to others through an invasion of privacy must have been specifically considered and judged to be reasonable when set against the harm that it is intended to mitigate or prevent by the intrusion.

Where this proportionality principle requires fine judgment in application is in the case of seeking bulk access to large quantities of digital data—for example, when an intelligence agency intercepts a bearer on a fiber-optic cable. The bearer carries a large volume of data packets of all types. Much of it—such as computerized market trading, streamed films, or online pornography (these three categories do represent a large part of Internet traffic)—will be of no intelligence interest, and computerized filtering can be expected to remove such material. The remaining streams of packets representing emails, messaging, and voice and video calls will also mostly be of no intelligence interest; therefore, further computer algorithms, filters, and selectors must be applied to the data stream to reduce it closer to the information actually being sought by the intelligence analyst. Whether the proportionality test is passed will depend crucially on how effective such discriminators are.

Another example where care is needed is when a government requires a communications company to turn over all telephony metadata (a frequent occurrence for mobile phone companies around the world[13]). A specific example exposed by Snowden in 2013 that generated considerable political attention was the approval, originally in 2006, by the US Foreign Intelligence

Surveillance Court of such an FBI application to Verizon and other major US communications providers.[14] Almost all the information naturally related to innocent users who were not the subject of any investigation. In response to criticism, the Obama administration released a white paper arguing that the program was for counterterrorism purposes and was both legal and constitutional because the bulk data set could only be interrogated using a discriminating identifier, or "seed," where there is a "reasonable articulable suspicion" that the seed is linked to a foreign terrorist organization.[15]

As we argued in chapter 3, what seems the right ethical approach is to accept from the outset of an intelligence operation that the privacy rights are being engaged of those whose communications are *potentially* able to be accessed (even if only by a computerized system and never seen by a human analyst due to efficient filtering and selection). The question therefore becomes the empirical one: How significant is the interference, and when does it become so significant that it constitutes an unlawful violation? This approach recognizes that an important part of privacy is "the right to be let alone" and the chilling impact of the knowledge that such digital surveillance may be possible.[16] The extent of actual *harm* possible to an individual does nevertheless depend on whether a computer only scanned and discarded the relevant material or whether a human analyst saw and logged it for future action. That logic is why a bulk access intelligence operation to find specific information is a quite different concept from mass surveillance, which involves persistent observation of the population or a significant section of it.

Civil liberties organizations have been greatly concerned about bulk capabilities following the accusations of mass surveillance laid against American and British authorities based on the Snowden material. A study by David Anderson, the independent reviewer of counterterrorism legislation in the United Kingdom who was given full access to the classified work of the GCHQ and the Security Service, concluded that bulk access methods were essential to combating terrorism, cybercrime, and other harms.[17] He reported evidence from the agencies themselves that digital bulk accesses are among the most important tools that they can use to do the following:

- obtain intelligence on overseas subjects of interest, including threats to the domestic population and to the armed forces;
- identify domestic threats, which sometimes come from fragments of intelligence;

- establish and investigate links between known subjects of interest, at pace, in complex investigations;
- understand known suspects' behavior and communications methods to identify potential attack planning;
- verify information obtained about subjects of interest through other sources (e.g., agents) and resolve sometimes anonymous online personae to real-world identities; and
- detect, classify, manage, and attribute cyber attacks against national infrastructure and economic life.

As argued in chapter 1, public confidence is needed in the ethics of intelligence activity as practiced by the authorities. Domestic law needs to reflect a general consensus about what those ethical principles should be. It should include placing such activity fully under the modern rule of law, which, as we explained in chapter 2, involves a level of transparency about the existence and regulation of intelligence capabilities that marks a distinct break with habits of the past. A cautionary tale comes from the 2014 and 2016 UK court judgments on the cases brought against the GCHQ by Liberty and other civil rights organizations.[18] The court found that all the digital intelligence activity in the complaints had been properly authorized on legal advice under the relevant statute, and the GCHQ was not evading the constraints of UK law by getting the United States to conduct the activity and pass on the results. Nevertheless, the court concluded that the UK government had failed to uphold the rule of law since it had not explained how the (very complex) set of laws involved and the safeguards that did actually exist in law for the citizen were being applied. The importance of the transparency needed under the rule of law was emphasized in several reports in 2015: March, *Privacy and Security* by the parliamentary Intelligence and Security Committee (ISC); June, *A Question of Trust* by David Anderson; and in July, *A Democratic Licence to Operate* by the Independent Surveillance Review (ISR), which was set up at the instigation of then deputy prime minister Nick Clegg, a leader of the Liberal Democrat Party and the junior partner in the coalition government between 2010 and 2015.[19] In the end the UK government had no alternative but to rewrite the legislation from scratch (now the Investigatory Powers Act 2016) to place all forms of digital intelligence fully under the rule of law and to explain in much greater detail than ever before what is involved and what safeguards will apply not only to the acquisition of digital data but also about the rules for its retention for future use. The same case for greater transparency applies to the US administration before President Obama took steps once the Snowden material began to be published.

After the UK government had introduced the Investigatory Powers Act in Parliament, demands arose for even more information that would allow a fuller assessment of the need for these powers. The result was another lengthy but illuminating report from David Anderson that examined the value in both terrorism and serious crime investigations of the authorities being able to interrogate databases they have kept of communications data with specific queries to test hypotheses or to try to establish common identities of suspects operating with different devices and aliases.[20] As noted earlier, when a trigger event such as a suicide attack occurs, the identity of a terrorist may suddenly become known and lead, if the data has been retained, to discovering others who may have been part of the support network or who may have engaged in planning further attacks. Some selection may be possible at the time of interception, or very shortly thereafter, although the material may have to be buffered and thus retained for a time to allow for the filtering and selection processes. The key task of identifying both new suspects for investigation and potential attack planning from an understanding of known suspects' behaviors and communications methods, however, does require the retention of bulk data. The period of retention, and thus the potential for analysts' access, also must be part of the proportionality judgment since it is obviously germane to the ethical acceptability of the overall digital intelligence regime.

Mark Phythian: On the surface, intelligence collection may appear to be a straightforward principle, but in practice it is beset by dilemmas relating to what to collect, how much to collect, and from where and from whom it should be collected. Is the relevance of a piece of information necessarily obvious at the point of collection? Its significance may only become clear in the future—that is, three months, six months, or a year after collection. Perhaps the collection of a further piece of information sometime in the future will help reveal the full meaning of something collected months earlier. Individual pieces are fragments, but they are fragments of a larger picture for which the dimensions, features, and focus remain unknown while the collected evidence remains fragmentary. Ultimately, no picture at all may be made from the fragments, because the picture that analysts and machines seek to construct is a security picture, and the vast majority of the fragments collected will have no security relevance.

This dilemma helps explain Mark Lowenthal's rejection of the simplicity of the 9/11 Commission's finding that the 9/11 attacks occurred because US intelligence failed to "connect the dots" warning of impending attack. "The flaws in the epithet are overwhelming," Lowenthal points out. "When a child attempts to connect the dots, he or she has only as many dots as needed, not one dot more or less. And they are numbered, sequentially. . . . Finally, the typical connect-the-dots page has hints, sketches—eyes, faces, surroundings—to give the child a sense of what the final picture should be."[21] Lowenthal's objection to the 9/11 Commission's conclusion takes us back to Ray Cline's observation that "there is no way to get at the nuggets without taking the whole ore-bearing compound."[22] Collection needs to be undertaken broadly if it is to minimize the risk of missing anything that turns out to be significant.

The surveillance potential provided by developments in digital technologies has offered a means of satisfying this collection impulse, holding out the prospect of former NSA head general Keith Alexander's motto "Collect everything" as being realizable, at least in relation to the targets.[23] To be clear, nothing is new about this impulse, which in a US context can be traced to the lessons drawn from the 1941 Japanese attack on Pearl Harbor.[24] By the end of the Second World War, Rear Adm. Joseph R. Redman, the head of US naval communications, was advising that the aim of US signals intelligence, "whether or not it actually can be done in practice," was to come "as close as is humanly possible [to reading] every enemy and clandestine transmission."[25] What was new, post-9/11, was the sense that technology was making this aim increasingly feasible.

The ways in which the United States and its partners used the possibilities offered by new technologies to collect and store information that could be useful in intelligence analysis, and the extent of this work, were the subjects of the Snowden leaks in 2013. The Snowden revelations raised various ethical dilemmas in a liberal democratic context, with the most important ones concerning the scale of the democratic deficit. In a US context, this was well illustrated by Director of National Intelligence James Clapper's testimony to the Senate Select Committee on Intelligence on March 12, 2013, only three months before the publication of the material from Snowden. "Does the NSA collect any type of data at all on millions or hundreds of millions of Americans?" asked Sen. Ron Wyden (D-OR). Clapper replied, "No, sir." In explaining his answer subsequently, Clapper sought to frame it in terms of what constituted surveillance and what amounted to actions short of it. As he told NBC interviewer Andrea Mitchell: "I responded in what I thought was the most truthful or least most untruthful manner, by saying, 'No.' And again, going back to my metaphor, what I was thinking of is looking at the Dewey Decimal numbers of those books in the metaphorical library. To me collection of U.S. Persons data would mean taking the books off the shelf, opening it up and reading it."[26]

At the same time, Clapper conceded that "while transparency is good for our system, others less ideally motivated are taking advantage of that." On this basis, when faced with Wyden's question, it seems he did not feel able to engage in any open discussion of bulk access for security reasons. As Clapper elaborated, "From the Intelligence Community perspective, [we] preserve and protect the secrecy because by exposing the tactics, techniques and procedures we use, our adversaries go to school on that and they make it even harder for us."[27] That intelligence professionals have a preference for secrecy on these grounds should come as no surprise. If a target is unaware of the methods by which an agency will attempt to obtain its secrets, then the chances of success will be higher. However, the issue is less whether there should be secrecy and more to what the extent of it should be. In liberal democratic contexts, who should know, and how much need they know, about the kind of measures revealed via the Snowden leaks? How should these questions be resolved if very few outside the relevant intelligence organizations understand that a basis exists for posing them in the first place? How can citizens understand and consent to the scale of secrecy that surrounds a practice if that practice is entirely secret? Should state expectations around trust extend to matters about which citizens are permitted to know nothing?

We focus on the role of intelligence oversight in chapter 7. For now we need only recognize that in the United States the most powerful intelligence oversight system in the world, whether deliberately or not, was misled on this issue. Was the situation any better in the United Kingdom? The parliamentary oversight body, the ISC, was placed in an awkward situation over the details of the NSA-GCHQ relationship revealed via the Snowden leaks, for example, in relation to the Tempora program.[28] The committee was certainly aware of the nature and extent of the NSA-GCHQ relationship, but its members seem not to have fully understood the implications of such digital activity for privacy. Not having access to the technical expertise that would have allowed them to pose the kind of questions that emerged in the wake of the Snowden leaks clearly contributed to this state of affairs. To admit these things publicly would have been to concede a failure on their part. Beyond the ISC, one former cabinet minister wrote that the cabinet "was told nothing about GCHQ's Tempora or the NSA's Prism, or about their extraordinary capability to vacuum up and store personal emails, voice contact, social networking activity and even internet searches."[29] He revealed that even as a member of the UK National Security Council he was not made aware of this information. Former deputy prime minister Clegg told of how "only a tiny handful" of cabinet ministers were made aware of the detail and extent of the interception capabilities and practices of state communications, something that was only formally revealed to Parliament in 2015 in the context of reviewing the government's Investigatory Powers Act. This disclosure again suggests the existence of a democratic deficit, one that there is little reason to suppose government would have moved to correct had the Snowden intervention not occurred.[30]

Further ethical dilemmas arise from the implications of the preventive mode in which intelligence essentially operates. In the Internet age the ability to gather large volumes of electronic communications data offers intelligence agencies an opportunity to anticipate threats that other methods cannot match. Of course, intelligence agencies use the interception of Internet and other electronic communications data as an investigative tool in cases where the agencies have specific information about a threat or potential threat and can use it to undertake "targeted interception" of named individuals' communications. However, the later a threat or potential threat is uncovered, the greater the risk that it will not be preventable because it will not be fully understood in time. Moreover, threats may develop and be actualized because they were undetected. Hence, the primary advantage that the interception of Internet communications offers over the past interception of letters and phone calls is its ability to allow the agencies to intervene much further "upstream" and piece together potential risks and threats at the earliest feasible point, from within the realm of uncertainty.[31]

This, then, is a second important way in which intelligence agencies use bulk digital data interception (whether intercept, communications data, or personal databases); as a means for "discovery," or as an intelligence-gathering tool through which they seek to uncover the potential threats that will form the basis of subsequent targeted interception and other forms of investigation. The ISC has explained:

Bulk interception capability is used primarily to find patterns in, or characteristics of, online communications which indicate involvement in threats to national security. The people involved in these communications are sometimes already known, in which case valuable extra intelligence may be obtained (e.g. a new person in a terrorist network, a new location to be monitored, or a new selector to be targeted). In other cases, it exposes previously unknown individuals or plots that threaten our security which would not otherwise be detected.[32]

The Snowden leaks created the possibility of an informed discussion of these practices, and of their costs and benefits, for the first time. In the UK context, the situation transformed from one in which the practices were officially unacknowledged and largely unknown to one where informed public debate was facilitated by the publication of the three detailed reports you cited earlier from the ISC, from David Anderson, and from the ISR, of which you were a member. It is worth considering a couple of cases that Anderson cited in his report to give a sense of how this bulk interception capacity has proved effective. Anderson's examples were particularly useful to the debate in the context of the conclusion of the US President's Review Group on Intelligence and Communications Technologies that, contrary to the NSA's view, its expansive approach to collection "was not essential to preventing [terrorist] attacks."[33] Among the cases cited by Anderson are the following:

In 2010 GCHQ analysts identified an airline worker in the UK with links to al-Qaida. Working with the police, agencies investigated the man, who it transpired had offered to use his access to the airport to launch a terrorist attack from the UK, and pieced together the evidence needed to successfully convict him. This individual had taken great care to ensure that his extremist views and plans were totally concealed in his offline behaviour, meaning that this investigation and conviction would have been highly unlikely without access to bulk data.[34]

... In 2010 an intelligence operation identified a plot which came right from the top of al-Qaida: to send out waves of operatives to Europe to act as sleeper cells and prepare waves of attacks. The intelligence specified unique and distinctive communications

methods that would be used by these operatives. GCHQ, in partnership with many other countries, was able to identify operatives
by querying bulk data collection for these distinctive patterns. This
international effort led, over a period of months, to the arrest of
operatives in several European countries at various stages of attack
preparation—including one group literally *en route* to conducting a
murderous attack.[35]

In such ways, then, bulk interception has been used to reduce the potential of an identified risk developing into a threat and then for a threat to reach
a stage where it can be realized. Hence, intelligence agencies emphasize the
indispensability of bulk collection in being able to counter contemporary
security threats. The ISC went so far as to claim that "bulk interception has
exposed previously unknown threats or plots which threatened our security that would not otherwise have been detected."[36]

Following this logic, we can agree that identifying potential threats at the
earliest feasible stage is preferable; however, it seems doubtful that it allows
a conclusion that in every case the (ultimate) threat would "not otherwise
have been detected." After considering a range of evidence, including some
sixty detailed case studies provided by MI5, MI6, and the GCHQ, David
Anderson therefore concluded that bulk powers "play an important part in
identifying, understanding and averting threats in Great Britain, Northern
Ireland and further afield." He added, "Where alternative methods exist,
they are often less effective, more dangerous, more resource-intensive,
more intrusive or slower."[37] The ISC accepted that, alongside the capacity to
provide improved security, the ethical issue in the bulk interception of data
constitutes an "intrusive capability," and because of this it is "essential that it
is for a legal purpose, but also that it is necessary and proportionate."[38] The
committee also recognized that while interception of data was intrusive,
"this remains considerably less intrusive than [interception of] content."[39]

Each of these inquiries emphasized, as you do and in line with the
ECHR, that privacy is a qualified right, one that is qualified by the state's
responsibility as a security provider. Anderson's *A Question of Trust* nevertheless discussed the importance of privacy at some length, recognizing that
to secure personal privacy was to assert and maintain a sphere of individual
freedom from state power. Anderson also recognized the key differences
between the state and other organizations that collect data on individuals, such as supermarkets and other commercial organizations: individuals

consent (at least in theory) to the latter form of surveillance as part of an explicit bargain from which they are free to withdraw if the costs outweigh the anticipated benefits, and none of these organizations have the coercive capacity of the state and so are not in the same position to compromise or deny the liberty of the individuals.

Ultimately, resolutions of the kind of ethical issues considered in these reports are rooted in national political and intelligence cultures.[40] For example, the extent to which people are willing to contemplate intrusions into their privacy in return for promises of security—the illusory "liberty-security trade-off"—is likely to differ in accordance with the political culture. History, geography, and current understandings of threat, as mediated by politicians, intelligence and security managers, and the media—all play a part in determining this culture. In this respect, US citizens and media have seemed at times bemused by the United Kingdom's appetite for different forms of surveillance, such as the closed-circuit television cameras that are ubiquitous across Britain.

The liberty-security trade-off may well be illusory, but public opinion polling on attitudes toward security at times tends to suggest it is an actual choice that has to be made. Differences rooted in the respective US and UK political cultures concerning authorization and oversight of electronic communications interception in the Internet era have been reflected in such public opinion polling in the United States and the United Kingdom. Polls in the former have shown a majority are opposed to collecting data from telephone and Internet communications. In contrast, in the United Kingdom a 2014 poll found that 71 percent agreed that the government "should prioritise reducing the threat posed by terrorists and serious criminals even if this erodes people's right to privacy."[41] A January 2015 poll revealed 52 percent offered the view that the security services needed greater access to communications to fight terrorism effectively, as opposed to 31 percent who disagreed.[42]

The Snowden leaks have encouraged reflection on the nature of concepts, such as privacy and surveillance, that are central to this debate. One question that has arisen is whether bulk collection of data constitutes surveillance or, as some have suggested (as with James Clapper's library analogy, cited earlier), whether surveillance begins only when a human analyzes a selection of collected data. In its *Privacy and Security* report, the ISC's proposal of a third category of information, "Communications Data Plus," implicitly accepts that valuable personal information can be harvested from metadata and so casts doubt on the feasibility of making clear distinctions here. For its part, the ISR panel concluded that "privacy is engaged at point of collection," suggesting that surveillance occurs from this point.[43] In conducting a review of the operational case for the four bulk powers proposed in the UK government's investigatory powers bill—bulk interception, bulk equipment interference, bulk acquisition, and bulk personal datasets—David Anderson judged that "the exercise of each of the powers under review is liable to interfere with the right to privacy guaranteed by the Human Rights Act 1998 (which gives effect to Article 8 of the ECHR) and the equivalent provisions of EU law. That is because *in law, there is an interference not only when material is read, analysed and shared with other authorities, but also when it is collected, stored and filtered, even without human intervention.*"[44]

If we can assume that interference must be a consequence of surveillance—without it, after all, no state interference takes place—then we would conclude that collection and storage of personal data can be considered forms of surveillance. As noted earlier, bulk data collection represents an early form of intervention in potential threat development and leads to targeted surveillance of some subsequently. Hence, rather than represent two separate processes, they might be more usefully considered in terms of a continuum. In this respect, it may be useful to think in terms of "macro" and "micro" surveillance, with the former involving analysis of metadata and mining of bulk data sets, and the latter involving the application of surveillance to known individuals and/or premises. Such debates about what we understand surveillance to mean and about its impact are set to continue.

One irony of the Snowden leaks is that despite the vilification of Edward Snowden in many quarters, the governmental responses and public discussions about intelligence that have followed in their wake, and would have been unthinkable had the leaks not occurred, are likely to provide a legitimacy for intelligence collection practices that they previously lacked when they were not only unquestioned but also, in effect, concealed from the public. In a very real sense in the past, the law was part of the problem rather than the solution. To return to a point I made in chapter 2, assertions of legality were used as a form of de-contestation, in an area where the law was not well understood and where its complexity did nothing to assist public understanding or even effective oversight and accountability.[45]

Post-Snowden, by contrast, in the United States, the United Kingdom, and elsewhere, public debate has improved understanding. In the UK context, the reports by the ISC, Anderson, and the ISR, and detailed discussions of the government's Investigatory Powers Bill, have facilitated public engagement with issues that impact fundamental rights but have up to now been poorly understood. This engagement suggests that the idea that privacy is no longer a social norm is too simplistic and that, while notions of privacy may have evolved, issues of control and consent remain of importance to individuals.[46] This point was recognized in the ISR report, which concluded that the debate arising from the Snowden leaks has "made it imperative that what was previously an essentially implicit bargain between government and citizens over the rights of intrusion into private life should be made explicit."[47] That is, it recognized the need for a "democratic licence to operate" and even adopted the notion as the title of the report. Hence, the idea that public consent cannot be assumed from governmental arguments about legality but must be explicit—and renewed at reasonable intervals (a key liberal requirement)—might be considered one dimension of what we can term the "Snowden effect."[48]

Perhaps, in light of this and given that the sky didn't fall after the leaks, Snowden's actions will be assessed differently in historical perspective, as has happened with the leaks by Daniel Ellsberg, with whom Snowden is often compared, regarding how the United States was conducting its war in Vietnam.[49] There are, however, related questions regarding the ethics of whistleblowing here—in particular, of when it is justified to leak information of perceived wrongdoing, of what to leak, and to whom. This begs a series of ethical sub-questions, such as whether whistleblowers are competent in accurately assessing the risk of unintended consequences in leaking classified information. For now, though, Snowden's own cost-benefit analysis of the leaks does not seem unreasonable: "I think that when people look at the calculations of benefit, it is clear that in the wake of [the leaks of] 2013 the laws of our nation changed. The Congress, the courts and the president all changed their policies as a result of these disclosures. At the same time there has never been any public evidence that any individual came to harm as a result."[50]

David Omand: I have to disagree with that self-serving cost-benefit analysis that Snowden makes of his actions, not least for the ethical reason that the benefit of stimulating greater transparency (which I accept) could have been achieved at much lesser cost. Exposing only a handful of documents would have been all that was necessary to create a political firestorm around the Bush administration's practices of domestic surveillance and to force President Obama to take the actions he did. And the backwash given the GCHQ's role would have still prompted the court cases in the United Kingdom and the subsequent critical judgments on the modern interpretation of the rule of law. That exposure could have been to the chairs of the congressional oversight committees and, if necessary, to the editors of the major news outlets directly. Snowden's defense of public interest then would have been persuasive. Instead, he changed jobs to get access to even more highly classified material. And fleeing first to Hong Kong and then to Russia inevitably made him a wanted fugitive. The scale of Snowden's theft of classified information meant that, as he conceded, he had not examined it all himself before handing it over to the journalists, leaving the ethical judgments to them of what to make publicly available. As a result direct damage has been caused by his exposure of intelligence-gathering operations unrelated to his stated concerns about mass surveillance (such as the operations in support of coalition military operations against the Taliban and the joint US-UK operation to intercept data feeds from Iranian reconnaissance drones flown by Bashar al-Assad's regime over combat zones in Syria).

Mark Phythian: Snowden's own cost-benefit analysis of the leaks might not seem unreasonable now, but it is important to acknowledge that there is also a futures dimension to concerns about the damage they may do. We have stressed from the outset that the purpose of intelligence—whether framed as stealing secrets or overcoming the will of the person with the secret who does not want others to know it—by definition marks it as a distinct ethical area. As you have pointed out, one consequence of the Snowden leaks was to raise awareness of state practices both in terms of their nature and extent. This may well have acted as a catalyst for targets and potential targets to undertake more effective measures aimed at resistance in the future. This possibility was, of course, the substance of the concern expressed by James Clapper in his NBC interview.

It is important to emphasize again that not all targets are criminals. While it is unlikely that German chancellor Angela Merkel's mobile phone would have revealed anything in the way of planned criminal activity, for example, its data could have revealed other kinds of plans, advance knowledge of which could have handed the United States a relative advantage.

Nevertheless, those planning or contemplating criminal behavior may well have altered their behavior as a consequence of the Snowden leaks, making it more challenging for the state to steal their secrets or even to identify them as people with secrets worth stealing in the first place. For example, alerted by the Snowden leaks, those wishing to hide from the authorities are greatly aided by the availability of specific software (of which the most popular is Tor) that renders its users anonymous by hiding their real Internet protocol (IP) address. The Dark Net—the collection of websites that can be visible only when such anonymity is assured and many of which cannot be entered without a secure password—thus assumes a potentially greater significance and represents a potentially increased risk. Do you think that, in this context, the Snowden leaks will come to be seen as contributing to the erosion of the advantage some states enjoyed in exploiting digital sources of information up to that point? If so, how will, and how far can, states seek to reverse this process while remaining faithful to the liberal-democratic Queensberry rules of state surveillance that they have signed up to post-Snowden?

David Omand: We know from their own Internet postings how members of ISIS, other terrorists, and serious criminals have learned how intelligence and law enforcement were seeking to track them down (something they have shared with their supporters). And predictably the net effect of Snowden's exposure of the effectiveness of digital intelligence methods has not resulted in nations shunning these techniques. Indeed, quite the reverse has occurred, as we see them scrambling to catch up with the United States and the United Kingdom and promoting the commercial export of capabilities such as social media monitoring and analysis to regimes that are anxious to keep a close eye on their populations. And since responsible Internet companies do not want to be portrayed as helping terrorists and have an interest in upholding the law against hackers and cyber criminals, resumed cooperation with democratic governments is already replacing the standoff they felt obliged to take when the Snowden stories first broke.

The difficulty that James Clapper found himself in, giving public evidence on a (then) highly classified program, was almost certainly mirrored in the United Kingdom's parliamentary Intelligence and Security Committee, which would have had impressed on its members the need for complete secrecy over the GCHQ's development with the US NSA of powerful digital techniques. The many redactions on grounds of security from the ISC's annual reports is mute testimony to the power of classification. This was changing, however, even before Snowden, as a result of the investigative reports from journalists such as Matthew Aid and James Bamford, who studied the NSA in detail, and even more so by the development of the applied academic discipline of cryptography complete with textbooks.[51] The waking up to the issues around digital intelligence would have happened eventually, but Snowden certainly provided an accelerant. What has emerged is a new inner boundary around what is considered genuinely secret.

Traditionally the reason for absolute secrecy around signals intelligence was entirely rational. Any stray public reference, however general, especially as sadly did happen from time to time even by prime ministers, was liable to be noticed abroad and led to questions being asked about security. In turn, nations changed ciphers simply as a precaution, undoing what could be years of cryptanalytical effort. That argument is no longer so compelling in the Internet age, as cyber security has become a mainstream subject. So given the decisions today to acknowledge the existence of digital intelligence–gathering methods including hacking, there can be a public debate about legal limits and safeguards while leaving intact the inner secret boundary to protect the knowledge of which sources and methods are actually being deployed against individual targets and how—information the adversary must not know. In the digital age, that represents a more defensible boundary for genuine secrecy.

We also need to remain alert to the semantics of the subject. *Surveillance*, defined as the close observation of a person, especially a spy or criminal, is not the same as *intelligence gathering*, which has much wider objectives, including counter-surprise with indicators and warnings, and involves a broader category of activities including military and diplomatic intelligence. When almost all information can be digitized and thus accessed, stored, and searched, digital intelligence will increasingly be seen as central to many of the traditional national security tasks supporting the indicators and warning function, military operations and planning, counter-proliferation, arms control, and diplomacy, as well as to understanding the behavior of adversaries in cyberspace such as Russia's cyber attacks on Ukraine and Syria.[52]

Mark Phythian: There is also the question of how bulk data capabilities could be used in the future. An implicit assumption seems to be that future governments will have the same commitment to liberal democratic values and not have a reason to use the capacities that have been developed for reasons that negatively impact liberal democratic freedoms. Yet much depends on national context and the impact of the international on the national. We have already agreed that privacy must be regarded as a qualified right, notwithstanding its centrality to liberalism as an ideology. We have seen how a state of emergency can be used to suspend or qualify rights via new legislation or assertions of legality. The fear that the future may not necessarily resemble the past is clear, for example, both in objections to the British government's Investigatory Powers Bill, unveiled in the wake of the Snowden leaks, and in reactions to the 2016 election of Donald Trump to the US presidency.[53] Indicative of this, in late 2016 the outgoing Obama administration moved to dismantle the remnants of the George W. Bush–era National Security Entry-Exit Registration System, seemingly as a way of placing an obstacle in the path of the incoming Trump administration's intention of either preventing Muslims from entering the United States or placing them under surveillance once there.[54]

The specific question that arises is how does today's liberal state ensure that the powers and capabilities it acquires do not adversely affect the liberties of future generations, or at least sections thereof? There is an interesting parallel here with the international environment that gives rise to the need for national intelligence capabilities in the first place. One reason for this is that states do not fully trust other states in an international system where "alliances are only temporary marriages of convenience: today's alliance partner might be tomorrow's enemy, and today's enemy might be tomorrow's alliance partner."[55] Hence, states are inherently apprehensive about the future intentions of other states. At the domestic level, though, citizens are required to be relaxed about the future of their domestic polity and place levels of trust in their state that their state does not place in its own neighbors. "In the end," suggests legal commentator Joshua Rozenberg, "it all comes down to trust. Can we rely on those who work in the secret world and those who oversee them? Do they come across as honest, decent people?"[56] This is true so far as it goes, but it neglects an important dimension: liberal concerns also focus on possible futures.

David Omand: What becomes increasingly important for nations that value personal freedom is that the surveillance use of the digital capabilities is regulated, overseen, and conducted proportionately with an independent judiciary that can force debate if, under any future government, attempts are made to smuggle in more repressive measures. At the heart of confidence in such digital surveillance regulation is the technical ability to discriminate adequately so that a focus is targeted on authorized missions that are not only necessary but also proportionate to the dangers being countered. To take terrorism as an example, a bulk access operation is likely to touch personal data relating to three categories of persons. The intention is first to identify, among the subjects whose data is present, those believed to be responsible for terrorist offenses that have happened or are being planned. I know no one who would challenge the right of the authorities to intrude on those subjects' privacy. They cannot claim privacy protection given their own actions just as lawyers cannot claim legal professional privilege protecting their communications when they engage in a criminal conspiracy with their clients and as civilians lose their noncombatant protection under international humanitarian law when they engage in combat on one side of a conflict.

Next are those who must be regarded as legitimate suspects for further investigation (as readers of detective novels know, rarely is the identity of the murderer evident to the police at the start of the case), including those who may later be cleared by a court of the suspected offense. Often those individuals' communication with or association with a known terrorist suspect triggers the search for their information. Then there are those against whom there is no suspicion. These innocent citizens are of no interest to the authorities (indeed, the demands of intelligence efficiency are that time and effort are not wasted on their communications), but their data is inevitably mixed up with what the intelligence or law enforcement agency initially accessed. The ethical objective, as far as is reasonably possible, must be to minimize engaging their privacy rights and intruding into their privacy. There is a whole intelligence science to selecting communications for examination that maximizes the chance of finding relevant data packets of sought-for communications, involving sampling of the global communications networks.

What we are discussing is a targeted process of selection for overseas communications (as specified in the UK Investigatory Powers Act 2016). I agree therefore that an opportunity for greater clarification was lost when the act continued to use the old terminology of "targeted warrants" to refer to domestic interception only and kept the "bulk" descriptor, a term that naturally brings fears of mass surveillance to mind. Your suggestion of micro and macro warrants is much closer to the spirit of the act.

Mark Phythian: An important part of an ethically acceptable bulk collection regime has to be clear guidelines and adequate arrangements for the destruction of unwanted material, for a strict necessity test for the retention of material, and for factoring in any time needed for the actual filtering and selection processes. Material that has been selected for examination and judged relevant to a case will have to be retained, but it should be only a very small fraction of what is accessed.

David Omand: Security and intelligence agencies live by their files. The Security Service's official history of the early period during the Second

World War recounts the near disaster when the antiquated filing system broke down under the strain of war. It was then modernized with Hollerith punched cards, and today, of course, digital databases are the norm.[57] The present level of terrorist threat in Europe has promoted digital data sharing on suspects, with arrangements under the Counter Terrorism Group of the Berne Group and the European Commission's Schengen Information System.[58] Reducing the overall volume of unexamined digital material retained is also a matter of efficiency for the agencies (or at least for the UK and European agencies whose budgets are very much smaller than those in the United States). Costs of digital storage and processing have reduced over the years, but the total of global CO_2 emissions from the data centers that support the modern Internet is greater than that of all of global aviation![59]

You are right to point both to the difficulty of "connecting the dots" and the risk of creating links where none in reality exist, as conspiracy theorists conspicuously fail to recognize. The late professor R. V. Jones, the originator of scientific intelligence during the Second World War, once coined the following aphorism (Crabtree's bludgeon) to warn intelligence analysts of the danger: "No set of mutually consistent observations can exist for which some human intellect cannot conceive a coherent explanation, however complicated."[60] Connecting dots irresponsibly could result in harm to an innocent individual, ranging from wrongly being placed on a no-fly list to being subjected to intensive surveillance, detention, or arrest. But as a former director of the GCHQ has suggested, the mining of big data today can reveal unexpected associations that can trigger more conventional investigation:

Post 9/11 US and British agencies have found themselves dragged from the shadows into the front line of national defence. . . .

One technique they have used is the linking of things which, while innocent in themselves, together might constitute a profile which demanded investigation. There is nothing wrong with living in a small flat. And there is nothing wrong with buying a hundred tons of chemical fertiliser. Flying regularly to Somalia or to Pakistan is in itself also innocent enough. But if a man living in a small flat and flying regularly to Somalia starts buying large quantities of fertiliser that certainly deserves investigation. Making such links without scrutinising the daily lives of hundreds of thousands of innocent people is only possible if you can task your computers to drag their net through very large quantities of data.[61]

Data analytics has advanced very rapidly. For example, it can find insights from dirty and even inaccurate data on a "good enough" basis provided that data is not systematically biased, thus overtaking the previous necessity to clean data sets before they can be compared. But without the data, the hypothesis could not be formulated in the first place. In fact, one of the most frequent uses of communications data by the police is to eliminate suspects from their inquiries, thus reducing the ethical risks that arise from unnecessarily keeping individuals under observation.

Mark Phythian: One problem here, of course, is that not only criminals have a need to conceal their interactions from states. Journalists, for example, may need to communicate via encrypted means to protect themselves and their sources in producing public interest stories, just as those working on the Snowden leaks themselves did. Moreover, the risk to people who contest state power in such ways can be very different depending on the nature of the state in question. In certain contexts, political opponents of a government or state may feel they have a legitimate need to hide their meetings and communications from regimes that have a track record of eliminating opponents, such as Russia, while in others they can face imprisonment for their dissenting role, as in China. Banning software that enables anonymity might inhibit criminals who have exploited the Dark Net websites, but that gain would be offset by the harm likely to those seeking a better future in nondemocratic contexts, where intelligence surveillance could well end in arrest or elimination. That is certainly the conclusion of the United Nations rapporteur on freedom of speech in his report to the UN General Assembly.[62]

David Omand: As you suggest the very existence of the Dark Net poses an ethical dilemma. It is a largely unpoliced part of the Internet only a few mouse clicks away from the everyday Web, which is well lit by the search engines of the browser companies such as Google, Safari, and Firefox. If the Web were a city, a small percentage might be public buildings—the town hall, museums, libraries—parks, and recreation (the open Web, mapped by Google, etc.). Ninety-plus percent might be private dwellings, research labs, offices, and embassies—all quite legitimate—but you need to arrange permission to enter (often referred to as the Deep Web). But the Dark Net, to develop that cityscape analogy, can be thought of as the city's red light district with a small number of establishments (sometimes very hard to find) whose access is controlled because the operators want what is going on inside to remain deeply private. They house the illegal speakeasies, gambling and strip clubs, brothels, criminal dives, and places to fence stolen property.

Traditionally, those who wished to disguise illegal purchases could simply pay cash, making them untraceable. Bank transactions on the Internet, however, leave a trail to the account holder, so Bitcoin (using blockchain technology) has become the anonymous payment system of choice. It thus became possible to create online exchanges and marketplaces for drugs, weapons, stolen credit cards and other personal information, cyber exploit kits and cyber attacks for rent, and child pornography in which not only are transactions secure and authenticated but also the sellers themselves are hidden both from the buyer and from any other third party such as tax authorities and the police. The most notorious was the Silk Road. In its two years of existence, until the FBI took it down, the Silk Road netted $1.2 billion of sales between four thousand vendors and 150,000 customers. The so-called Islamic State, or Daesh, launched its first Dark Net hidden site in 2015.

We would not accept today such no-go zones for policing in our cities. But is the rule of law to be different in cyberspace? We agreed that digital privacy was not an absolute right, so then digital anonymity should not be either. Important related ethical issues are whether law enforcement should have the right, with a legal warrant, to seek the cooperation of private sector Internet companies holding evidence on suspects and whether such companies are exercising ethically responsible behavior if they deliberately design devices and systems from which they cannot extract data even when presented with a valid warrant.

There is no settled view on the matter, but perhaps the most convincing line of argument runs on the following lines. Cyberspace is a useful shorthand term, but it does not exist as a separate dimension. When cyber criminals conduct fraud, for example, they steal real money. When terrorists or hostile states hack into critical infrastructure, real lights go out, and real people are hurt.

So we should expect the rule of law that applies in real life to apply in cyberspace. (An example is that it is unlawful under the Geneva Convention to bomb a hospital; therefore, it should be equally unlawful to achieve the same effect by a cyber attack.)[63]

And just as lawful warrants should allow evidence to be obtained (for example, bank account records), so warrants should be equally applicable to records held in digital form (for example, in a cloud).

Finally, we would also expect a reasonableness test to be applied to the amount of effort that could be expected in a search for physical evidence. Thus, the same should apply to the search for digital intelligence, for example, in asking a company that made a device seized by the authorities to devise ways of unlocking it to reveal its contents. While the device might contain necessary evidence, the search might be regarded as unreasonable if the security of material on all the similar devices used by the general population is put at risk.

6

The Ethics of Using Intelligence

David Omand: If knowledge can be regarded as power, then secret knowledge must be thought of as turbocharged power. It can be used by governments to spring surprises on adversaries and to bypass the slower processes of overt diplomacy. Being able to see through the backs of the cards in an opponent's hand helps negotiations even if it carries the everyday connotation of cheating. It can also tempt governments into trying to take shortcuts and do in the dark what they would shrink from being seen by their publics to be doing in the light. Using secret intelligence carries therefore its own ethical issues, which we address in this chapter.

Mark Phythian: Questions concerning the ethics of using secret intelligence have always had the potential to generate acute controversy, which is often linked to wider arguments about whether an ethical foreign policy is possible and, if possible, actually to be desired. We can draw a convenient distinction here to parallel that made in cyber security between *cyber-dependent* crimes, which can be committed only through using cyber technology, and *cyber-enabled* crimes, which are traditional crimes that can be made more potent by cyber means. We wish to examine intelligence-dependent actions rather than intelligence-enabled activity such as the exercise of traditional military strategy or foreign policy that is almost always supported by intelligence assessments and reporting. The ethical issues around the latter are best considered as part of international relations, and so are outside the scope of this book, while the ethical issues around the former take us directly into the new possibilities generated by technological developments in intelligence access. Taken together with the development of international human rights law and the prominent role of intelligence in post-9/11 counterterrorism strategies, they have resulted in more ethical scrutiny for intelligence-led operations than ever before, despite the high levels of secrecy that governments seek to maintain over such activities.

We see the tension that results when national intelligence agencies with an international reach act in ways that are understood to defend or advance the interests of their own nationals but at the same time do not protect the rights of other people to the same standard. We encounter again in this chapter Just War theory principles; however, the one key difference from our previous consideration of them is that in chapter 3 we were concerned with the extent to which these principles might be adapted to the conduct of intelligence, focusing essentially on intelligence collection. In considering the use of intelligence, for example, in military or counterterrorism contexts ("action-on"), there is no need to think in terms of possible adaptation; in these war contexts, intelligence plays a frontline role, so we can apply Just War principles directly.

Indeed, in a sense this frontline role has impacted the very nature of intelligence, which has seen a shift in emphasis as it has adapted to a "find, fix, and finish" approach. As a result, a significant part of the intelligence function has come to focus on target location, which then results in a military or violent response (albeit one often carried out by intelligence personnel). As Director of National Intelligence James Clapper explained, "Many aspects of the [US] intelligence community today, including some investments and practices, are legacies of the Cold War era and anachronistic. . . . Today's targets are very elusive and therefore quite hard to find, yet once they are found, they are very easy to finish. This reality has a very profound effect on the way intelligence is done today."[1]

David Omand: The ethical actors we wish therefore to focus on are those who decide how and where to authorize action based on intelligence, be they policy makers, military commanders, or police officers. In this chapter we see the ethical baton passing from the intelligence analyst who issues the reporting—with, we hope, adequate caveats about reliability—to the decision maker who receives it and decides whether to act on it. "Originator control" is, of course, a fundamental principle of intelligence work, and those wishing to take action will first have to refer to the agency originating the material to establish that it is safe to use it in the way desired without compromising sources or at least without having to make the argument that the value of the action is expected to outweigh the risk of compromise. The nature of the ethical issues that might accordingly arise for the originating intelligence agency has already been touched on in chapters 4 and 5.

To illuminate the ethical dilemmas associated with the desire to take action that rests on secret intelligence, we discuss four different examples. The first and last examples should remind us not to lose sight of the fact that intelligence-dependent covert operations, and the ethical issues they raise, have a history that long predates those of the post-9/11 war on terror that have dominated the discussion of intelligence-led action in recent years. We start therefore with an example that illustrates where intelligence both reveals a domestic threat of radicalization in the service of a hostile ideology—not the current jihadist threat but that from international communism during the early Cold War—and provides covert means to counter it but involves deceiving the domestic population. The second example is very different, as today's intelligence technology provides an unparalleled capability to identify and locate targets of interest, whether inside or outside of armed conflict. It is clearly seen in the US use of remotely piloted aircraft, a term that reminds us that a pilot is still in control—albeit on the ground, not in the air—but for simplicity we use the popularized but pejorative term "drones." The third example involves very highly skilled human tradecraft on the part of intelligence officers to conduct covert operations in hostile environments, as demonstrated in the (presumed Israeli) assassination in 2010 of leading scientists supporting the Iranian nuclear weapons program. The final and more traditional example, in that it relates to diplomacy and statecraft, is where intelligence gives a government access to a deep secret that can be used to strategic effect, thus illustrating the deceptions that may be necessary to disguise the secret source. One historic instance is clearly seen in the decryption of the Zimmermann telegram that precipitated the United States' entry into the First World War.

Covert operations by intelligence agencies during the Cold War were a way of expressing the East-West competition, in many ways acting as a surrogate for the armed conflict that would have broken out were both sides not mutually deterred by the fear of all-out nuclear war. The game was understood to be zero-sum in nature, and the governing principles were rooted in deniability rather than ethicality. Often the motive for deniability on the part of Western agencies was to avoid domestic controversy. To illustrate the point, after the Second World War, MI5 and MI6 covertly countered the appeal of the Soviet-backed World Federation of Democratic Youth to British students by secretly funding the setting up of the International Youth Congress as a liberal democratic alternative and by covertly promoting student movements that were judged favorable to facilitate the breakaway of the National Union of Students from communist control by 1948. Another ploy was the covert provision of anti-communist propaganda and support to prevent a communist government being elected in Iceland in the late 1940s.[2] Other, now well-documented, cases include the CIA's secretly funding the monthly *Encounter* magazine as a liberal forum for leading intellectual and political writers on both sides of the Atlantic and the promotion of George Orwell as a leftist but anti-totalitarian writer, with his books including *Animal Farm* being translated and distributed worldwide. The Information Research Department (IRD) of the UK Foreign Office, the successor to the wartime Political Warfare Executive, orchestrated this secret counter-subversion campaign. Most of the work was overseas, but there were domestic activities that, given their evident sensitivity, were superintended by a committee of the permanent secretaries of the key departments and agency heads that was chaired personally by the secretary to the cabinet.

Mark Phythian: In the West, such covert activities represented a clear departure from core liberal values, since they involved actions such as interfering with democratic elections overseas and deceiving one's own population. Such interventions were understood as being part of an action-reaction cycle. They were justified by the idea that the United States and its allies would be at a significant disadvantage if they did not adopt similar methods to those of their Cold War adversaries. As the CIA's Ray Cline put it: "The United States is faced with a situation in which the major world power opposing our system of government is trying to expand its power by using covert methods of warfare. Must the United States respond like a man in a barroom brawl who will fight only according to the Marquis of Queensberry rules?"[3] Nevertheless, it is useful to remind ourselves that in the emerging Cold War period of the late 1940s, senior British government ministers approved of the framework within which this took place. In particular, Foreign Secretary Ernest Bevin was extremely concerned to see postwar communist subversion effectively handled. On this basis, Christopher Mayhew, a junior Foreign Office minister in the Attlee government, established the IRD within the Foreign Office. Its explicit aim was countering Soviet propaganda. Unfortunately, for a time it counted Soviet spy Guy Burgess among its employees.[4]

The operations you cite would not have seemed so morally doubtful to those involved at the time as they do today, given the high degrees of moral certainty they exhibited (noting the importance of the sense of organizational mission again). By the standards of the day the ethical risks should have been obvious, especially the long-term erosion of trust in democratic government to be expected when, as is inevitable, such activity finally begins to surface. Hence, it is useful as well to consider that the IRD's semisecret existence is not regarded as a particularly glorious chapter in the history of the Foreign Office and that another Labour foreign secretary, David Owen, closed it in 1977 as a result of his concerns.[5] The kind of ethical dilemmas its existence raised can be seen in the response to the revelation that George Orwell—as you point out, a beneficiary of Western intelligence support in some ways—passed on to IRD employee and friend Celia Kirwan a list of some thirty-eight public intellectuals he considered "crypto-communists, fellow-travellers or inclined that way and [who] should not be trusted as propagandists."[6] In a general sense Orwell was felt to have acted as an "informer" for the state (the *Daily Telegraph* newspaper headline announcing the story was "Socialist Icon Who Became an Informer") and to have engaged in a form of blacklisting, even though the consequences of inclusion on the list were relatively minor. Moreover, the list probably revealed more about Orwell than those included on it.

David Omand: Honesty about threats is a key part of demonstrating just cause. The expansion of the Soviets' reach over Eastern Europe was real, as were the subversive actions of their intelligence agencies. The North Atlantic Treaty Organization (NATO) was created in what was seen as an existential moment for the survival of the democracies of Western Europe. I imagine that much of the overseas IRD activity was justified by the idea that the United States and its fledgling NATO allies would be at a significant disadvantage if they did not recognize the subversive methods of their Soviet adversary, noting the Eastern European experience that once communists were elected to positions of power, whether in trade unions or national and local legislatures, the democratic process would then be manipulated to maintain what would become a one-faction-dominated body. It is easy, nevertheless, to imagine the media firestorm that would be created today if the UK government was suspected of comparable *covert* (there are, of course, plenty of overt) attempts to manipulate public opinion within the country itself, for example, on the highly contentious subject of the country's future relationship with Europe, the subject of the 2016 referendum.

Yet a crucial part of the intelligence war in the late 1940s and early 1950s was the covert funding by the CIA, encouraged by UK ministers, of political movements such as European federalism as a bulwark against the spread of communism. As a leading historian of that era concluded, "By the early 1950s promoting European unity was the largest CIA operation in Western Europe." The covert CIA contribution to the European Movement (that counted Winston Churchill and Paul-Henri Spaak as honorary presidents) "never formed less than half the European Movement's budget and, after 1952, it was probably two-thirds. Simultaneously this programme sought to undermine the staunch resistance of the British Labour Party, and then of the Conservatives, to federalist ideas."[7] It appears that leading British politicians, including Churchill, knew and encouraged this foreign interference in domestic politics that continued to fund pro-European Labour members of Parliament even after the Labour Party had cooled on Europe. Even if we accept their view of the just cause they were fighting for, in contemplating domestic interventions, the strictest application of the principle of necessity, as well as care over proportionality in the choice of means, is essential. It should not therefore be a surprise that when in 1964 Harold Wilson's Labour Party won the UK general election, the secretary to the cabinet quickly wrapped up his domestic counter-communist committee and ceased the very few of its ongoing activities, leaving the field of counter-subversion monitoring to the Security Service.

Mark Phythian: The case of the IRD and other counter-propaganda efforts illustrate intelligence-led covert actions at the lower end of what can usefully be thought of in terms of an ethical "ladder of escalation."[8] The lowest rungs involve routine options such as benign propaganda and climb up to modest interventions such as low-level funding of political groups, such as you describe. But from there we can see the attraction of higher-risk options such as black propaganda disinformation campaigns smearing adversaries and opponents or covert arms transfers to insurgent groups. At the upper end of the scale lie extreme options such as assassinations and orchestrating coups d'état and major secret wars, where arms are covertly provided to the chosen side and where Special Forces may be deployed secretly to provide training or even to accompany local forces into action and conduct reconnaissance and target identification on their behalf. Such higher-end extreme options can be tempting to governments since they offer the illusory prospect of shortcutting the long and frustrating processes of diplomacy or having to endure the antics of hostile leaders. Generally, however, actions at the top end of the scale have been characterized by the use of force and violence and have been employed less frequently than lower-end options. Such high-end interventions are much more difficult to keep secret and so maintain deniability for them. The existence of a hidden hand has too often been all too obvious. Moreover, in the contemporary world, the problem of maintaining secrecy for covert operations has been exacerbated by the advent of the Internet and a globalized media, whose operations can attract the attention of international opposition led by human rights nongovernmental organizations such as Human Rights Watch and Amnesty International.

David Omand: A useful legal distinction introduced in 1991 in US legislation distinguishes between clandestine and covert actions. The former are simply actions conducted in secret (for example, routine operations by the military and by law enforcement, as well as by intelligence agencies in their investigations, so as not to alert the target to their interest). Covert, or deniable, actions are designed directly to influence events. Today the US rules for what Ray Cline called the brawl with the adversary are set by the mechanism of a presidential finding, which requires the president to sign off on covert operations by the CIA and thus establishes his accountability, but at the same time it ensures important legal safeguards. A finding cannot authorize any action that violates the rights of US citizens, that violates the Constitution or any statutes, or that influences US political processes, public opinion, policies, or the media; but, of course, it does not protect non-US entities and persons. The House and Senate Oversight Committees must be notified about the finding within forty-eight hours of the president's signature, giving Congress control through the opportunity to veto the action by cutting off funds for it. No comparable ex ante mechanism is in the UK oversight system (which we discuss in chapter 7), but the foreign secretary would have to sign off on any overseas covert operation and be satisfied first of its legality and with the ethical justification put forward.

In the contemporary world, secrecy can certainly be maintained by tight security controls for short periods, such as that exercised by the White House before the Osama bin Laden raid. But the globalized media has indeed reduced the possibility of running major deniable covert operations (and long-term clandestine activity of all kinds).

Mark Phythian: Historically, however, deniability has been important for the obvious reason that much covert action has been conducted secretly precisely because of its relationship to ethical standards and international law. As Richard A. Falk argued:

The international law case is, in a sense, self-evident and is partially conceded by the CIA's insistence upon secrecy and the related practice of defending itself against allegations by cover stories (i.e., lies). The secrecy/deception pattern arises in part because the behavior is inherently objectionable to a segment of domestic and, even more so, world public opinion. There is also an implicit awareness that CIA covert activities in foreign societies violate their fundamental international law rights as sovereign states.[9]

Falk was commenting in the era of the Church Committee's inquiry into the CIA's involvement in plots to assassinate foreign leaders such as Fidel Castro. In its wake President Gerald Ford issued an executive order banning political assassinations, and his successors have renewed it in slightly different form. For example, the Reagan version (Executive Order #12333) dropped the term "political" and stated: "No person employed by or acting on behalf of the United States Government shall engage in, or conspire to engage in, assassination."[10]

David Omand: The UK government elected in 2015 set out principles to the effect that its actions and policies will be in accordance with national and international law and that it expects others to do the same (espionage, remember, is not considered to be prohibited by international law as we discussed in chapter 2).[11] Such a public commitment makes the risk to the government of authorizing a covert deniable operation that transgresses those principles very great. Were the circumstances to arise, for example, derogation from the government's international human rights obligations would be needed. That is not to say that the British government will refuse either to authorize clandestine operations in the future or to allow intelligence-led covert operations (or at least operations covered by the standard "neither confirm nor deny" [NCND] formula as used for Special Forces activity). But ministers will have to be satisfied first that national and international legal tests, including international human rights obligations, are met. An example might be considering the provision of intelligence training and equipment to a friendly foreign government at its request, but the government concerned wants the United Kingdom's involvement kept under wraps for domestic political reasons.

Mark Phythian: That example takes us back to the point we made in chapter 2: not everything that may be lawful may be considered right or may satisfy an ethical test. In the example of intelligence support, we must hope that there would have been a check on the uses to which the support would be put so as not to collude, for example, in the suppression of legitimate opposition or in the use of torture. Assuming that there are no human rights implications to providing such support—a big assumption, I suspect, in such cases—the test would then be whether the United Kingdom is right to act covertly and thus encourage a culture of intelligence secrecy at odds with its own approach to the rule of law as we outlined in chapter 2.

A much more testing case today comes from our second example, the CIA's armed drone program targeting terrorists outside areas where US forces are legitimately engaged in operations. As we noted in chapter 5 a significant part of the tactical intelligence function has come to focus on target identification and location, which can then enable taking direct action, including attack by armed drones. Initially focusing on the targeting of specific terrorist leaders (personality strikes), armed drone strikes evolved to also include signature strikes, where targets are identified not by name but by intelligence "signatures," or "patterns of behavior that are detected through signals intercepts, human sources and aerial surveillance, and that indicate the presence of an important operative or a plot against US interests."[12] A senior counterterrorism official has explained, "We might not always have their names, but . . . these are people whose actions over time have made it obvious they are a threat."[13] The CIA drone program has highlighted its paramilitary operational function, controlling and directing a program of selective strikes by armed drones that are believed to be flown by US Air Force personnel but under the targeting direction of the CIA.

Concerns about international law and ethical acceptability (both domestically and internationally) over the drone program were evident in the CIA's response to a January 2010 American Civil Liberties Union Freedom of Information Act request for records relating to the CIA's use of armed drones. The response argued that "by admitting that it possessed responsive records, it would indicate that the CIA was involved in drone strikes or at least had an intelligence interest in drone strikes. . . . In either case, such a response would reveal a specific clandestine intelligence activity or interest in the CIA, and it would provide confirmation that the CIA had the capability and resources to be involved in these specific activities."[14] The declaration went on to hint at the tension between clandestine action and international law in arguing that to even confirm or deny the existence of records relating to drones could have a negative impact on US foreign relations.

In carrying out its legally authorized intelligence activities, the CIA engages in activities that, if known by foreign nations, reasonably could be expected to cause damage to US relations with affected or interested nations. Although it is generally known that the CIA conducts clandestine intelligence operations, identifying an interest in a particular matter or publicly disclosing a particular intelligence activity could cause the affected or interested foreign government to respond in ways that would damage US national interests. An official acknowledgement that the CIA possesses the requested information could be construed by a foreign government, whether friend or foe, to mean that the CIA has operated undetected within that country's borders or has undertaken certain intelligence operations against its residents. Such a perception could adversely affect US foreign relations with that nation.[15]

David Omand: That argument just quoted is of course applicable to any and all foreign intelligence collection activities as well as covert action and is at the heart of the "neither confirm nor deny" approach to government responses when intelligence operations are disclosed. This approach can be intensely frustrating where what could be revealed is a past success. But the media will quickly home in, should a denial or confirmation be issued in one case, and assert that silence on other alleged operations must imply confirmation of the story, thus putting live cases at risk.

Mark Phythian: It is particularly interesting in the case of armed drones in that it highlights a problem arising from the covert/overt nature of that campaign. The CIA's role was not openly or fully acknowledged at first but became too obvious to be denied. US drone use itself could never be entirely covert because the United States held a near monopoly on armed drone operation, and a death toll that was otherwise inexplicable was mounting from aerial attacks inside Pakistan, Yemen, and Somalia. Hence, it became necessary to articulate a legal defense to demonstrate their legitimacy. This defense was aimed not only at international opinion but also at domestic opinion. The process began with Legal Adviser to the US State Department Harold Koh in a March 2010 speech. Further speeches followed by Obama administration officials, notably by John Brennan, then assistant to the president for homeland security and counterterrorism; Jeh Johnson, general counsel of the Department of Defense; Eric Holder, attorney general; and Stephen Preston, general counsel of the

CIA. All were made in the context of an additional pressure for publicly discussing targeting criteria. The acknowledgment by Obama administration officials that Anwar al-Awlaki, a US citizen, had been added to a drone "kill list" and was subsequently killed by a drone strike in Yemen in September 2011 raised specific legal questions about the due process guaranteed to American citizens by the Fifth Amendment to the US Constitution.[16]

David Omand: The British government too has had to defend publicly the use of a Royal Air Force (RAF) Reaper drone strike in Syria to kill Reyaad Khan and Ruhul Amin, two ISIS members and British citizens who were actively plotting on behalf of ISIS imminent attacks by supporters in the United Kingdom.[17] The justification given to the United Nations Security Council was that the strike was a necessary and proportionate exercise of the United Kingdom's individual right of self-defense against ISIS, an organization that at the time was engaged in an ongoing armed attack against Iraq from Syria and against which UK forces were contributing airpower at the request of the Iraqi government. The UK government has insisted that RAF armed drones are used in accordance with the international humanitarian law of armed conflict and thus have to be operated as part of a lawful UK military involvement in a theater of operations (today Iraq and Syria). That restrictive policy cannot legally exclude their use elsewhere (as with any use of lethal force) in circumstances where the inalienable right of self-defense is invoked, but that brings with it the need to interpret the imminence of the threat in the case of terrorists in Syria and elsewhere who control operatives in the United Kingdom.[18]

The UK attorney general has drawn attention to a series of tests that Sir Daniel Bethlehem, a former Foreign Office legal adviser, devised in 2012 to assess the military intervention required to prevent an attack.[19] The factors Bethlehem advocates include the nature and immediacy of the threat; the probability of an attack; the determination of whether it is part of a concerted pattern of continuing activity; the likely scale of any threat and the injury, loss, or damage that may result; and the probability of other opportunities to undertake effective action in self-defense that may be expected to cause less serious collateral injury, loss, or damage.

We should take care not to focus exclusively on drones in such cases. They are only one of several weapons systems available to a military commander, and in the UK case, they are subject to the same ministerially approved rules of engagement as a manned aircraft.[20]

The United Kingdom does not accept the US strategy of using armed drones to kill those identified as terrorists but outside armed conflict. That is not the first, and is unlikely to be the last, occasion on which US and UK methods of achieving a common objective differ. The United Kingdom's legal position is that (despite 9/11 resulting in the largest ever loss of British lives to a terrorist attack) it is not in a state of armed conflict with al-Qaeda and associated groups, but it was lawfully engaged in an armed conflict with the Taliban in Afghanistan, where the RAF drones proved their worth in the armed mode for protecting British forces.

The legal position of the United States is clearly different. In the first of the speeches you cite, Koh linked his justification for the armed drone policy to what he termed the law of 9/11.[21] Key to this was the assertion that the United States was engaged in an armed conflict as a consequence of the 9/11 attacks. Hence, "as a matter of international law, the United States is in an armed conflict with al-Qaeda, as well as the Taliban and associated forces, in response to the horrific 9/11 attacks, and may use force consistent with its inherent right to self-defense under international law."[22] Koh also addressed the question of whether the armed drone policy constituted assassination and as such violated the domestic US ban on assassinations when he argued that the use of drones "for precision targeting of *specific high-level belligerent leaders* when acting in self-defense or during an armed conflict is not unlawful" and hence does not constitute "assassination." He went on to explain that drone targeting policy operated on a case-by-case basis and was predicated on considerations "related to the imminence of the threat, the sovereignty of the other states involved, and the willingness and ability of those states to suppress the threat the target poses." Once a target had been identified, he maintained that the killing of the target would conform to the law of war principles of distinction and proportionality, that "civilians or civilian objects shall not be the object of the attack," and that any attack that might be expected to cause loss of civilian life, injury, or damage to civilian objects was prohibited where they "would be excessive in relation to the concrete and direct military advantage anticipated."[23]

Mark Phythian: To consider armed drones as simply one of several weapons system options may risk overlooking the fact that the advent of the armed drone option has made feasible a greater number of attacks than would have been possible absent this option for a combination of technological and political reasons. For one, the Obama administration's assertions of accuracy gained traction through regular repetition. Notwithstanding

the framework provided by Koh that was fleshed out by subsequent interventions from other Obama administration figures, the legality of a policy
of planned killing by drone outside armed conflicts remains highly contested in terms of whether the United States could really be said, according
to international law, to be in a state of armed conflict with al-Qaeda; of
whether the right to self-defense in Article 51 of the UN Charter can be
invoked against a non-state actor; and of the applicability of the concept of
preemptive self-defense and, in particular, the degree of elasticity that the
concept of imminence, which is central to understandings of the permissibility of preemptive action, could bear.[24] Key questions about how concepts
such as threat, imminence, distinction, and proportionality are understood
in practice remain unclear. Moreover, the logic of such preventive defense is
that states must themselves be the arbiters of when a nascent threat requires
preventive intervention. To stretch that to situations (absent specific knowledge of an imminent threat) where a suspect has been tracked over a long
period and is then killed is surely to violate the meaning of imminence.
As UN special rapporteur on extrajudicial, summary, or arbitrary executions Philip Alston observed, "If invoked by other States, in pursuit of those
they deem to be terrorists and to have attacked them, the application of this
principle would cause chaos."[25]

   David Omand: I share that view. But I have to observe the ethical paradox that the United Kingdom and other European nations have benefited
greatly from the US campaign that has killed many of the al-Qaeda leadership and disrupted their movements, so removing their ability to mount
complex operations on the lines of 9/11 and the frustrated plot in 2004
to down multiple airliners over the Atlantic. The CIA-led campaign has
used methods that the United Kingdom would not for legal reasons allow
their own authorities to pursue. It has high levels of US public support:
according to a February 2012 Washington Post / ABC poll, 83 percent of
Americans approved of armed drone use against terrorist suspects overseas,
making it the most popular aspect of Obama administration policy and
scoring considerably higher than the president's overall approval rating.[26]
Had the administration not launched this campaign to assert the legality of
the program, but instead continued to attempt to implement the plausible
deniability–led approach that characterized the earlier years of the war on
terror's armed drone use, this outcome would have unlikely been possible.
In short, the articulation of a legal defense was not insignificant in this process, regardless of the legal and ethical questions it has begged.

Mark Phythian: I agree with this, but repeated assertions of legality and of the achievement of standards that cannot be independently verified should not be equated with ethical acceptability. Nevertheless, this draws our attention to the ways in which powerful actors in the international system are able to revise conventions that have become inconvenient. This conclusion is important for future ethical considerations of covert operations. As Alexandra H. Perina, a legal adviser to the US State Department, argued: "In areas where international law is particularly ambiguous or contentious, state practice and publicly articulated interpretations are critical in defining the substantive content of the rules."[27] The same applies to norms in emerging areas of ethical concern such as the permissibility of killing by drone or killing outside of conventional war zones in what are deemed to be conditions that meet the test of imminence, especially when accompanied by arguments that developments in the nature of the threat have necessitated a revised approach to understanding imminence. In a sense, Michael Walzer captures the essence of this problem well when he argues that Special Forces operations (a category that would cover frontline operational intelligence roles) exist "somewhere between the police and the army" in the war on terror; however, while it is accepted that "the rules for the police are not the same as the rules for soldiers . . . I am not sure that anyone knows what the rules are or should be for Special Forces."[28]

Both international laws and norms are weakened when the legitimacy that derives from universal or near-universal acceptance is eroded by violation. As one legal scholar has put it: "When the benefits of violation are broadly distributed, early violations of legal rules are quickly emulated. Changes within the system then become self-amplifying."[29] In this context, the greater "the number of observable incidents of noncompliance, the lower the psychological threshold confronting future violators, and the greater the likelihood of future noncompliance."[30] And as Richard Falk recognized with regard to the CIA and international law in the mid-1970s, a country such as the United States "is especially important; its noncompliance influences the whole climate within international society and undermines any effort to take international law seriously as a restraint on others."[31]

David Omand: On the contrary, a legal expert in the law of war notes that the law of armed conflict does not prohibit the targeted killing of individual enemy combatants if certain rules are complied with, such as the proportionality rule and the rule prohibiting treacherous or perfidious killing.[32] Another scholar identifies five requirements for his view of targeted killing: an international or non-international armed conflict must be in progress, the victim must be a specified individual targeted by reason of his activities in relation to the armed conflict, the individual must be beyond a reasonable possibility of arrest, only a senior military commander or senior domestic government official representing the targeting state may authorize the targeted killing, and the targeted individual must be directly participating in the hostilities either as a continuous combat function or as a spontaneous unorganized act.[33]

Mark Phythian: For a number of international lawyers, it is not at all clear that the US case is able to meet the first of these requirements, given which those that follow it do not become active.[34] Nevertheless, it is important to recognize that by articulating a legal defense and so asserting a legitimacy for such armed drone use, the Obama administration nevertheless benefited from the following logic: covert behavior by states, such as that involving intelligence activity, may not of itself be inherently wrong, but there is a sense in which "because covert behavior remains normatively illegitimate, effectively disowned by the responsible state, it cannot become a legitimizing reference point."[35] It follows that if a state chooses to keep quiet about an exposed covert operation rather than seek to mount a defense, then this constitutes an implicit recognition that the action cannot be defended convincingly in terms of international norms or law. The state in question will choose to brazen it out until the international opprobrium dissipates. It therefore follows that when a state chooses to acknowledge a covert practice and mount a legitimating defense, the state does so not because it considers the action to be indefensible but because it considers the action legal and ethically just.

The US homeland's being attacked on 9/11 clearly marked a turning point in US policy. Prior to 9/11 the United States had led international condemnation of targeted killings. Just a couple of weeks prior to the 9/11 attacks, for example, State Department spokesman Richard Boucher had responded to Israel's targeted killing of a Popular Front for the Liberation of Palestine leader by reiterating that "we remain opposed to targeted killings. We think Israel needs to understand that targeted killings of Palestinians don't end the violence, but are only inflaming an already volatile situation and making it much harder to restore calm."[36]

David Omand: Nevertheless, post-9/11, the United States has maintained an important formal distinction between the counterterrorist operations it has engaged in after 9/11—referred to as targeted killings in self-defense—and assassination, perhaps reflecting the legacy of the Church Committee and the political experience of having American political leaders assassinated in the United States.[37] US administrations continue to condemn the 1976 killing in Washington of the Chilean opposition leader Orlando Letelier by Augusto Pinochet's secret service. The CIA described it to President Reagan as a blatant example of a chief of state's direct involvement in an act of state terrorism.[38] However, in pursuing Osama bin Laden in 1998, the George W. Bush administration sidestepped the prohibition on assassination by adopting a line of reasoning that said that it was a "capture or kill" operation where "under the law of armed conflict, killing a person who posed an imminent threat to the United States would be an act of self-defense, not an assassination."[39] This formed a basis for Koh's articulation of the "law of 9/11" as well as the legal opinions on the legality of killing bin Laden in the Abbottabad raid of May 2011 and the killing of US citizen Anwar al-Awlaki in September of that year.[40] That specific US legal argument is also important to prevent other states seizing on the CIA drone program to justify their own assassinations, such as the Russian authorities' murder of the exile Alexander Litvinenko in London.

Mark Phythian: The level of confidence in the intelligence used for targeting represents another ethical issue. Clearly, this problem is accentuated in the case of signature strikes. Michael Hayden, former director of the NSA and the CIA, once boasted, "We kill people based on metadata."[41] However, metadata can be an unreliable guide in the world of targeted killing. For example, a target may be engaged because a mobile phone he or she is linked to by metadata is found in a vehicle traveling from A to B, perhaps via the geo-location system attached to drones (find). At this point visual contact is established via the drone camera (fix), leading to a missile being launched from the drone (finish). Yet, the phone, or its SIM (subscriber identity module) card, may have been traveling not with its owner but with a third party.

The lack of human intelligence sources in areas where armed drones regularly operate has generated a heavy reliance on signals intelligence as a source of information in target identification. As former National Security Council spokesperson Caitlin Hayden has explained, "After any use of targeted lethal force, where there are indications that civilian deaths may have occurred, intelligence analysts draw on a large body of information—including human intelligence, signals intelligence, media reports, and surveillance footage—to help us make informed determinations about whether civilians were in fact killed or injured."[42] This level of care, seemingly evident in postmortem inquiries, should instead precede drone strikes. Still, the Obama administration proved reluctant to admit to civilian casualties, despite mounting evidence that it was not always clear who was being killed, for such an acknowledgment would undermine the discrimination criteria it had set out and the level of certainty claimed to underpin it.[43]

David Omand: I agree about the level of care needed, and having talked to members of the RAF squadrons operating their Reaper aircraft, I have no doubt that such care is part of their operational ethos.[44] That is one reason why it is ethically sensible to have drone operations directed within a chain of command subject to military discipline and not as a covert intelligence agency operation. (President Obama was quoted in 2015 in the same sense, although transferring US control from the CIA to the military was not fully completed before he left office.[45]) But we have to accept that moral dilemmas can nevertheless occur in the conduct of all branches of warfare. Painful choices may have to be made between minimizing losses to one's own side and avoiding collateral casualties.

The accuracy of armed drone strikes can also create what amounts to an ethical obligation to use them rather than any other form of military strike. For example, in December 2009, with some intelligence pointing to suicide bombers from Yemen's tribal areas preparing to launch an attack in the capital, Sanaa, but with Djibouti's government not permitting armed drones to fly from the base established there, the Obama administration authorized cruise missile strikes on two targets, including an apparent al-Qaeda training camp in Abyan. Just days after these attacks, having visited Yemen to meet with Anwar al-Awlaki and a bomb maker, Umar Farouk Abdulmutallab boarded a flight from Amsterdam to Detroit while wearing an explosive device and was intent on blowing it up over the United States. The cruise missile strike appears justified and killed fourteen suspected militants, but a Yemeni parliamentary committee concluded that it had also killed some forty-one civilians.[46] Would therefore the use of an armed drone have been preferable in this case, in the sense of being capable of more accurate targeting and so reducing the number of innocent people killed? This is the logic of the case.

When we come to the choice of whether to use manned aircraft, thereby exposing service personnel to the risks of combat, or to use drones piloted from the ground, governments and military commanders have a moral as well as a legal duty to afford their personnel as much protection as possible.

The UK Supreme Court reinforced this duty when in 2013 it applied Article 2's right to life provision of the Human Rights Act of 1998 (and the ECHR) to the duty of care owed to British soldiers serving in Iraq. Thus, the substantive obligation requires the state not to take life without justification, and by implication, it must establish a framework of laws, precautions, procedures, and means of enforcement that, to the greatest extent reasonably practicable, will protect life.[47]

Mark Phythian: Another ethical dimension relating to the use of armed drones in a find, fix, and finish context concerns the consequences of the drone operators being so physically remote from their targets. This is significant in that the distance and the manner in which the operators view potential targets—literally, through a lens—could combine to create a dehumanizing effect. The lives of those being viewed do not carry the same value as those the operator passes on the journey to and from work each day, whom they experience differently and whose humanity is more evident. Significant parts of what we know about the military dimension of the US drone program come via leaks by a whistleblower working in US intelligence to the online investigative publication *The Intercept* in 2015. The source has discussed how the special operations community viewed potential targets: "They have no rights. They have no dignity. They have no humanity to themselves. They're just a 'selector' to an analyst. You eventually get to a point in the target's life cycle that you are following them, you don't even refer to them by their actual name."[48]

David Omand: The wide-ranging policy commission on drones I chaired in 2014 came to the opposite conclusion about the RAF after taking evidence from those involved all the way along the command chain. It is one area where drone operations score over the use of other weapons systems given the persistent observation of the target over many hours or even days, the presence of several pairs of eyes on the target including analysts', the availability of legal advice if required, the ability to manually override attack plans right up to the last moment, and the videotaping of all that goes on, thus leading to a culture of restraint. The practice is quite the opposite to the theorizing of critics that this is a videogame war. The comparison with a fast jet attempting the same mission with only a fleeting glimpse of the target is illuminating in that respect.

Drone pilots are trained aircrew. Although on the ground, not in the air, they share the ethos of a disciplined service, which is an important issue since drone pilots report emotional intimacy that comes from hours spent in close surveillance of targets, sometimes as a prelude to attacking them.[49] In counterinsurgency warfare, where combatants seek to hide among the population, the additional discrimination that drones can provide makes their use when available the ethically sounder choice. As Tony Rogers, author of *Law on the Battlefield*, observes, "There is nothing special in the law of war about the use of drones to deliver missiles. Their use in armed conflict is governed by the normal rules on military objectives, precautions in attack, proportionality, perfidy and persons *hors de combat*."[50] The acquisition and use of drone technology are also subject both to the general principles and rules of weapons law in the law of armed conflict and to the treaty and customary law rules relating to targeting.[51]

Mark Phythian: Even accepting a utilitarian calculation of positive net benefit per sortie, the scale of the US use of armed drones in the war on terror risked being counterproductive for the United States given the level of resentment it generates. One person who showed a clear awareness of this was Gen. Stanley McChrystal, the former head of the US Joint Special Operations Command. He explained, "There's a perception of arrogance, there is a perception of helpless people in an area being shot at like thunderbolts from the sky by an entity that is acting as though they have omniscience and omnipotence. And you can create a tremendous amount of resentment inside populations . . . because of the way it appears and feels. . . . What seems like a panacea to the messiness of war is not that at all. . . . And wars are ultimately determined in the minds of populations."[52]

Similarly, in 2009 David Kilcullen, a former adviser to Gen. David Petraeus in Iraq, coauthored a *New York Times* op-ed piece that criticized the use of armed drones on utilitarian grounds. One of the three reasons why the costs outweighed the benefits, he argued, was that "the drone war has created a siege mentality among Pakistani civilians. . . . While violent extremists may be unpopular, for a frightened population they seem less ominous than a faceless enemy that wages war from afar and often kills more civilians than militants."[53] Within this objection, of course, lies the understanding that despite the assurances of US administrations, targeting errors and collateral damage are killing significant numbers of innocent people.

David Omand: There is much good sense in those observations. Strategic success always depends on a collection of tactical successes, but the logic does not run the other way. Tactical successes themselves do not guarantee strategic success if factors such as the need for a long-term, viable, politically acceptable solution are ignored. But care is needed not to fall into the trap of the instinctive sense of ethical fair play that kicks in when thinking about the asymmetry of a counterterrorism or counterinsurgency conflict in circumstances where, as Hilaire Belloc brutally put it, "whatever happens, we have got the Maxim gun, and they have not."[54] It is not ethically sound to insist on equality of arms between combatants in war. "It is neither intellectually convincing today, nor plausible in historical perspective, to argue that the side with high, even suicidal, commitment is automatically morally superior to opponents with high capital investments, more advanced equipment, and a greater concern for the survival of their troops."[55]

Mark Phythian: Let us now look again at the utility of Just War concepts in aiding our thinking about the ethical acceptability of action-on intelligence by referring to our third example, which involves a different form of targeted killing. In November 2010 Majid Shahriari, a professor of nuclear physics at Shahid Beheshti University in Tehran, was killed when an attacker on a motorcycle attached a bomb to his Peugeot car, sped away, and then detonated the bomb from a distance. Shahriari had been traveling with his wife (like him, a professor of nuclear physics) and a bodyguard, who were both injured in the explosion but survived.[56] A little later that same morning there was a similar attempt to assassinate Fereydoon Abbasi, a nuclear physicist with expertise in nuclear isotope separation. Abbasi noticed the motorcycle approach and make contact with his car. Abbasi quickly got out of the car, pulling his wife out as well. Both were injured in the explosion but survived. Already in January of that year, another professor of physics, Massoud Ali-Mohammadi, had been killed by a remote-controlled bomb.

The suspicion was that these scientists were aiding an Iranian nuclear weapons program. Even assuming such involvement could amount to just cause, surely more than this would be required, such as clear evidence that these individuals were making such a key contribution to the program that their elimination would make them difficult or impossible to replace. In other words, killing them was an act of necessity, not just one of intimidation to deter others from participating in the program. In essence, this judgment seems to have been behind the (unclaimed) assassination of ballistics wunderkind Dr. Gerald Bull in Brussels in 1990, while he was working to develop a supergun for Iraq that could, in theory, have been capable of shelling Israel.

Could these targets be considered to fall into the category of combatants in an intelligence sense? Were they legitimate targets?

David Omand: We cannot know the answer for certain without access to what intelligence was available. Let us assume, for the sake of argument, that the targets were known to be key figures whose absence would significantly delay and disrupt a (covert, denied, and unlawful under international law) nuclear weapons program. The further argument then has to be made that such a delay was necessary to protect the vital interests of the (we are assuming) Israeli state. This nation in 1981 stopped Iraq from acquiring a nuclear capability by bombing and destroying the Osirak reactor near Baghdad when it was under construction. Israel also had made clear over many years that an Iranian nuclear weapons program would be an unacceptable risk to the survival of Israel.

At this point we can refer to the findings of the inquiry by the Israeli Supreme Court (a judicial body of high reputation) on the targeted killing of terrorists. As the president of the court put it, the court addressed the following problem: "The Government of Israel employs a policy of preventative strikes which cause the death of terrorists in Judea, Samaria, or the Gaza Strip. It fatally strikes these terrorists, who plan, launch, or commit terrorist attacks in Israel and in the area of Judea, Samaria, and the Gaza Strip, against both civilians and soldiers. These strikes at times also harm innocent civilians. Does the State thus act illegally? That is the question posed before us."

The judgment of the court included these conclusions:

> Ultimately, when an act of "targeted killing" is carried out in accordance with the said qualifications and in the framework of the customary laws of international armed conflict as interpreted by this Court, it is not an arbitrary taking of life, rather a means intended to save human life. . . .
>
> [T]he State should not be denied that means which, according to the opinion of those responsible for security, constitutes a necessary means for protection of the lives of its inhabitants. However, in light of the extreme character of "targeted killing," it should not be employed beyond the limitations and qualifications which have been outlined in our judgment, according to the circumstances of the merits of each case.
>
> Thus it is decided that it cannot be determined in advance that every targeted killing is prohibited according to customary international law, just as it cannot be determined in advance that every

targeted killing is permissible according to customary international law. The law of targeted killing is determined in the customary international law, and the legality of each individual such act must be determined in light of it.[57]

By extension, we can see that a substantive legal case could be made for lethal action being taken against a key civilian scientist working on a prohibited nuclear weapons program that, if completed, threatened the existence of a state. Although the Supreme Court also concluded that the threshold for assassination would have to be a very high one, a case could be made. There are many problematic steps to the argument, however, including the judgment as to whether the action is *wise* in strategic terms in addition to the need to satisfy legal and ethical concerns.

Mark Phythian: This recalls our earlier discussion about norms being a product of specific intelligence cultures influenced by history and geography. Even assuming the attacks passed such initial legal and ethical scrutiny, did the assassins possess legitimate authority? No one claimed responsibility for these attacks. In terms of the earlier discussion, no one sought to construct a legitimating argument in ethical and/or legal terms. But let us continue to assume they were Israeli covert operations, based on that state's history of engaging in assassination of perceived enemies abroad, including scientists and engineers, and its known concern about the potential threat posed by an Iranian nuclear weapons program. If so, the operatives would have possessed the formal authority of the Israeli state but no international authority; thus, they could not claim they were acting in accordance with UN Security Council resolutions in carrying out these attacks. Would these attacks, then, pass the right authority test?

David Omand: The Iranian leadership, from their public statements, appeared not to accept the existence of the state of Israel. Through the International Atomic Energy Agency, the United Nations had tried to use inspections to ensure Iran complied with its nonproliferation obligations, but it was seen to have failed when Western intelligence revealed in 2009 a covert military uranium enrichment program hidden under a mountain at Fordow in Iran, forcing the Iranians to admit they had this undeclared enrichment facility (itself an excellent example of coercive diplomatic action being taken on secret intelligence). The level of international trust in the Iranians' declared intentions of not pursuing a nuclear weapons ambition at that point was low, and in Israel it was zero. But the prospect that Russia would not veto a resolution based on chapter 7 of the UN Charter to force Iran's compliance with international obligations would also be zero. In such circumstances a right authority defense of unilateral action under Article 51 (self-defense) could be entered. Recall in 1998 NATO took actions in Kosovo to protect the Albanian population despite lacking the authority of the Security Council. The absence of accepting responsibility by any state for the Iranians' killings weakens but does not, I suggest, eliminate the defense.

Mark Phythian: Considering this case in terms of proportionality, were the deaths of the scientists (the aim in all three cases) and of their wives in two of them, plus one bodyguard (which the attackers were clearly prepared to countenance), justified by reference to the scale of the harm the acts were intended to prevent? What is the appropriate scale of measurement if fear of nuclear attack is the basis of the harm that the action is intended to prevent? Given this rationale, presumably many more scientists and their families—indeed, the entire Iranian scientific community—could have been eliminated and a justification in terms of proportionality offered.

A closely related question is whether sufficient discrimination was applied. Would the deaths of Majid Shahriari's wife and bodyguard and of Fereydoon Abbasi's wife have been justified on this basis? Was it possible to target the scientists at a different time when "noncombatant" deaths could have been avoided? If not, should the attacks have gone ahead or been called off? Does the fact that Majid Shahriari's wife was also a nuclear physicist justify killing her? After all, she did not possess the same knowledge as Majid Shahriari, but she may have had some understanding of his scholarship and methods and may have been able to move toward replicating his work.

David Omand: They are the right questions, and we must hope that those authorizing the attacks weighed them in their minds. We can draw an ethical parallel to the wave of bombings and shootings that targeted Algerian Front de Libération Nationale nationalists and their German arms dealers during the Algerian War from November 1954 to March 1962. One of these attacks on the Autobahn targeted the car of a German arms dealer believed to be supplying weapons to the Algerian rebels, but it succeeded in killing only his wife and wounding his young daughter. Another attack scuttled an arms-bearing ship in Hamburg harbor. These attacks on West German territory appear from archival research to have been conducted by the French foreign intelligence service, the Service de Documentation Extérieure et de Contre-Espionnage. The service went to the further step of creating a right-wing cover organization, the Red Hand, to take blame for the attacks, which the highest political authorities in Paris had in fact authorized.[58] As Prime Minister Michel Debré's security and intelligence counselor Constantin Melnik would later note, "There are certain circumstances in which the State, representing . . . the common interest, must, if it does not want to succumb, oppose violence with violence."[59] Melnik echoes the US view given earlier in Ray Cline's comment about not being restricted to fighting by the Queensberry rules.

No doubt the same *raison d'état* (political reason) lay behind the French justification for sinking the Greenpeace ship the *Rainbow Warrior* in Auckland harbor (Opération Satanique) in 1985. Greenpeace had threatened to disrupt French nuclear testing, but tragically the sinking resulted in the death of a photographer who happened to be on board. (The attack took place when the ship was believed unoccupied, but the risk of such accidental deaths should always be factored into consideration.) For France at that time, maintaining the credibility of its nuclear deterrent would have been sufficient reason.

As we have seen, the Just War concepts do provide a framework for examining in detail the ethical components of the decisions to conduct such operations, although they themselves cannot provide answers. The decisions will depend on the facts of each case, as interpreted by the morality of the time (*O tempora, O Mores!*). Perhaps the most pertinent question is whether the threats these attacks were intended to counter really touched the vital interests of the state and were a last resort.

Mark Phythian: We concluded earlier that last resort was of limited relevance in assessing the ethics of intelligence collection. However, here we are talking about action-on arising out of intelligence, where it is reasonable to expect that all alternatives short of high-end interventions, such as attempted assassination, were understood to be exhausted. This issue is closely linked to another, that of the extent to which the problems being faced constituted an imminent threat. Over the years, assessments of the Iranian nuclear program have been numerous and varied, making reliable judgment difficult. Can we assume that because the attacks were (likely to have been) carried out by an intelligence agency, they would have been based on secret intelligence that justified the action? Can international relations—in particular, those of democracies—rest on that assumption in cases such as these? Given the potential stakes here—a hostile neighbor possibly developing a nuclear weapons capability—is an intervention some way short of last resort justified? If so, how far?

David Omand: This is one of those cases where last resort does not mean "at the very last moment," since by then it would be too late and a break-out capability would exist. *Last resort* means absent other reliable ways of achieving the same end.

Around the same period (we do not know for certain when the operation started), the Iranian nuclear program was being subject to cyber attack through the Stuxnet computer worm (which is generally assumed to have been a US and Israeli operation). At the time it would not have been known how effective that tactic would prove to be (it was the first ever recorded major cyber sabotage operation). Even if the worm succeeded in slowing down Iran's enrichment operations, it could not close the program entirely since it had plenty of spare centrifuges and other enrichment sites. Stuxnet itself was also single-site specific, since it had to be engineered to the layout at Natanz. And this site was only one route to Iran's acquiring material for a bomb. Stuxnet is thought, however, to have succeeded in introducing a delay in the Iranian uranium enrichment program.

Mark Phythian: If this is the case, then it begs a more nuanced question: At what stage in the development of the nuclear technology would this situation come to constitute last resort? Certainly, the November 2007 US National Intelligence Estimate "Iran: Nuclear Intentions and Capabilities" provided an assessment that put the Iranian program a long way from acquiring a full nuclear weapons delivery capability, a conclusion confirmed by subsequent US intelligence community analysis.[60] Although the attempted assassinations could be presented as conforming to last resort in temporal terms (adjusted to take into account the possibility that last resort needs to be understood as occurring in advance of its literal meaning), last resort has another dimension, which is clearly of considerable importance when applying Just War insights to intelligence practice: it also refers to the absence or exhaustion of all other options for resolution. As you point out, concurrently, Israel and the United States had been subjecting the Iranian nuclear program to cyber attack through the Stuxnet computer worm, and that constituted an alternative. Moreover, in 2015 the United States and Iran reached a nuclear agreement, demonstrating the potential for diplomacy, although it raised unanswerable questions about the role of the pressure applied by intelligence action-on in bringing Iran to the negotiating table. On this basis, though, last resort criteria had clearly not been met. Assassination was not the only game in town.

David Omand: Another game in town for hawks in the Israeli government was an all-out raid to destroy all the Iranian nuclear infrastructure, and this option was believed feasible following the development of bunker-busting bomb technology. If the Iranians' program had not been slowed down sufficiently to allow negotiations, such an Israeli attack on Iran would have been a real possibility, one that almost certainly would have triggered a wider conflict with a hugely uncertain outcome.

Although it could be argued that the assassination of leading scientists was not temporally a last resort, the stakes for peace and war were as high as they could be. Delay by whatever means to the Iranian program, in the end, proved essential. It took years of very hard negotiations for the United States, the European Union, and Iran to reach a nuclear agreement, yet it is still regarded as inadequate for Israeli security in the eyes of many Israeli security officials and of the advisers to US president Trump. The steps taken to slow down the Iranian program, although they can no doubt be challenged in international law, do have an ethical Just War defense. We cannot of course say definitively that the combination of pressures (and there may have been others of which we are unaware) applied to Iran brought it to negotiate seriously, but there can be little doubt that the resource costs and difficulty of pursuing the Iranians' nuclear ambition were raised. In the end, Iran renounced through negotiation, at least in the short to medium term, the capabilities that would have supported its ambition.

Many Israelis, however, suspect Iran did so knowing that long after sanctions were lifted, it would still be capable of a long-term breakout from the nonproliferation treaty should future circumstances require it. And this exact scenario is what the Israelis fear most.

Mark Phythian: Perhaps, then, this case may illustrate a point we discussed earlier—that is, the way in which intelligence interventions may generate ethical dilemmas that can be acute but nevertheless can spare those concerned the greater ethical dilemma that could well follow if such intelligence intervention was unavailable or deemed impermissible. Our final example of the ethics of intelligence use involves an influence operation mounted by the United Kingdom against a friendly state, the United States, to affect decisively its action—that is, to declare war on Germany in 1917. The operation was made possible by using a deep secret: the British naval cryptographers in Room 40 of the Admiralty led by Director of Naval Intelligence rear admiral Reginald "Blinker" Hall could read enciphered German diplomatic traffic.

In January 1917 Arthur Zimmermann, state secretary for foreign affairs in Berlin, sent a secret telegram to his ambassador in Mexico via the

German embassy in Washington and proposed a military alliance between Germany and Mexico in the event the United States entered the war against Germany.[61] The Germans' main purpose was to make the Mexican government declare war on the United States in hopes of tying down American forces and slowing the export of American arms to the United Kingdom. The British, however, had cut the German transatlantic telegraph cables, so the telegram had to be sent to the United States under an agreement that President Woodrow Wilson had earlier consented to (in the interests of encouraging peaceful diplomacy) that allowed Germany's diplomatic messages to be transmitted via the US transatlantic cable to Washington. The Germans assumed that the US cable was secure and used it extensively, but as that cable passed through Cornwall in western England, Room 40 had already secretly tapped it. As the telegram was sent across the Atlantic and on to Mexico City, it secretly also went to Room 40, where Nigel de Grey, a remarkable cryptographer, started to decipher it.

By the next day, the first few sentences were read and were startling enough: "We intend to begin on the first of February unrestricted submarine warfare. We shall endeavour in spite of this to keep the United States of America neutral. In the event of this not succeeding, we make Mexico a proposal of alliance on the following basis: make war together, make peace together, generous financial support and an understanding on our part that Mexico is to reconquer the lost territory in Texas, New Mexico, and Arizona."[62]

David Omand: At this point the story becomes really interesting. Hall and de Grey had immediately seized the potential anti-German impact that the telegram could make on US public opinion, especially the Germans' offer to Mexico of regaining Texas, New Mexico, and Arizona. The ethical case for using the intelligence to shock President Wilson and Congress into joining the war and thus hasten its end was very strong (and although in the end it was 1918 before Gen. John Pershing's army was sent to Flanders, the presence of a million additional soldiers made Allied victory inevitable). But Hall and de Grey had three challenges to meet if they were going to reveal the cable to President Wilson in the expectation that it would become public: the Germans must not realize that their current high-grade cipher was broken, the United States must not learn that the British were tapping its transatlantic cable, and they must convince the president the cable was genuine.

Hall waited three weeks before informing anyone outside Room 40, during which time the analysts had completed the decryption and prepared their deception plans. To deceive the Germans, they must be persuaded that a human agent in Mexico had stolen the text of the telegram. To deceive the Americans, the British could claim that the telegram had been sent over three routes—by radio and by two transatlantic cables operated by neutral governments for the use of their diplomatic services—thus complicating any eventual search by the Americans (and the Germans) for the source. Hall knew that the German embassy in Washington would have to send it by US commercial telegraph to Mexico and that the Germans would use an older, weaker cipher, so a copy of that enciphered text would be in the Mexico telegraph office. Hall arranged to bribe a Mexican employee, who secured a copy. The British could then show the Americans the decrypted version of that copy. This plan risked revealing their ability to read the old cipher but protected the deep secret of the readability of the current diplomatic cipher. Finally, to convince the US authorities of the cable's authenticity, the British could ask them to compare the enciphered text from the Mexican office with the cipher text that would have been deposited in the records of the US commercial telegraph in Washington, and the British could provide the older cipher so the Americans could retrieve the text themselves. The British could also publicly claim when the news broke that their agents had stolen the telegram's deciphered text in Mexico (a cover story that the Americans agreed to back once they had been convinced of the authenticity of the message).

On February 1, 1917, Germany announced its resumption of unrestricted submarine warfare, an act that led the United States to break off diplomatic relations with Germany on February 3. Hall must have felt the conditions for his operation were ripe, and on February 5 he revealed the cable to the Foreign Office. His contact in the US Embassy in London then arranged for the US ambassador to call on the foreign secretary, who gave him the enciphered text and the plain text in English and German. The ambassador reported the story with due outrage at the Germans to President Wilson, including details to be verified from the telegraph company. Wilson released the text publicly on February 28. The understandable skepticism of pro-German sympathizers in the United States, suspecting a British plot, were stilled by Zimmermann himself at a press conference on March 3, when he told an American journalist, "I cannot deny it. It is true." The German Foreign Office refused to consider its ciphers might be insecure and instead embarked on a witch hunt for a traitor in the embassy in Mexico. On April 6 the US Congress declared war on Germany.

Mark Phythian: That was an elegant set of solutions to a classic ethical problem over taking action on the basis of high-grade intelligence. Perhaps the most famous story about the dilemmas facing those using intelligence, still recounted today but not historically accurate, is that in November 1940 Bletchley Park, having learned from German air force Enigma traffic that Coventry was to be heavily bombed, informed Churchill. According to the conspiracy story, he instructed that in order to preserve the Enigma secret Coventry would have to be sacrificed, and no warning should be issued.[63] The reality is that the warnings were not specific as to the target, but the analysts felt that the most likely target was going to be London on the night of November 14, 1940.[64] However, Coventry was hit that night. Three hundred German bombers dropped five hundred tons of explosives, thirty-three thousand incendiary bombs, and dozens of parachute mines. During the raid, 507 civilians were killed and 420 seriously injured.

Even though the story of sacrificing Coventry is untrue, tales of what are essentially utilitarian trade-offs involving immediate sacrifices in return for ongoing intelligence or other gains recur regularly in intelligence history and folklore. Another example from the same era is the not-widely believed theory that Churchill knew in advance of the Japanese intention to attack Pearl Harbor but chose not to forewarn President Franklin Roosevelt given the prime minister's overriding priority of seeing the United States enter the Second World War.[65] As well as being a staple of intelligence fiction and folklore, such dilemmas as to where the greater good lies—and whether to accept sacrifice in the short term to avoid blowing a source you believe may be critical to longer-term victory, thus accepting the ethical penalty of adverse events unfolding in the interests of the longer-term gains from maintaining the source of high-grade intelligence—are recurrent ones. Knowledge is power and gives rise to options. But access to knowledge can become an end in itself and can risk blinding those responsible for harvesting it to the bigger ethical picture. We saw this issue with human intelligence in chapter 4 regarding the ethical problems of collusion in criminal behavior that accompanied Brian Nelson's reporting from inside a Loyalist terrorist organization in Northern Ireland in the 1980s. A clear lesson from that case is that the ethical issues should not be left to the intelligence community to assess alone within that secret world.

A variant of the dilemma, all too familiar in the contemporary world, concerns how far a terrorist plot should be monitored and allowed to develop in order to maximize the intelligence gain and acquire sufficient evidence to secure convictions in court. Too far and the risk is the plot will reach fruition; intervene too soon and valuable intelligence might be lost and too little evidence collected to convince a jury to convict. In 2006, for example, the United States seems to have felt British monitoring of a plot to explode multiple civilian aircraft flying from Heathrow airport as they crossed the Atlantic had gone beyond the point where the threat needed to be acted on. However, the course of the subsequent trials of the accused, who were eventually convicted and given long sentences, illustrated well the tension between the requirements of conviction in a court of law and the judgments about the point of intervention lest the plot be executed.

David Omand: We might finally pause to reflect on the ethics of maintaining the bulk access the United Kingdom had secured to the US transatlantic cable by 1917. We discussed that ethical issue in chapter 5 regarding the privacy of those who are of no interest to the authorities but whose private communications are also carried on a cable and thus subject to bulk access. In 1917 Hall was right to fear the American public's reaction at the time if the United Kingdom's access to US communications had become known. US-UK intelligence cooperation during the Second World War became very close and would have by then made the access to cable traffic and the techniques used a shared secret between the governments. (When the United States entered the war, Churchill indeed wrote personally to President Roosevelt and warned of the insecurity of US cipher systems; in other words, British cryptographers had been reading US ciphers.) Access to the transatlantic cables, however, was only finally revealed to the public when in 1967 *Daily Express* journalist Chapman Pincher rediscovered the Government Communications Headquarters (the present inheritor of the Room 40 tradition) was tapping the cables and caused a front-page scandal that rocked the Labour government of Harold Wilson.

And, of course, we have had even greater controversy in 2013 following Edward Snowden's leaking NSA documents that revealed the value of transatlantic cable bulk access to the intelligence effort of the Five Eyes partners. The difference today, however, is that the ethical balance is publicly struck on the two sides of the Atlantic by Congress and Parliament in their respective interception legislation while operating under the rule of law.

7

Building Confidence through Oversight and Accountability

David Omand: President Reagan famously declared "trust but verify" was the best approach to arms control with the Soviet Union. These terms are not contradictory if we think of trustworthiness as being earned through verification of consistent rule-observing behavior. In the secret intelligence world, where the general public cannot directly check for themselves what is going on and the nature of the subject is hardly conducive to blind trust, assured verification by reliable parties is needed to establish trustworthiness.

To take a simple example, all advanced societies have public hygiene laws that apply to fast food outlets. You order the burger and trust that the staff person preparing it has clean hands. You rely on trustworthiness— the reputation of the restaurant—that there will be internal rules and that managers will try to ensure compliance with them. But you also know that management cannot be omnipresent; therefore, you have to trust that the rationale behind the rules has been sufficiently internalized by the staff members so that a dropped hamburger will not simply be slid back onto the plate and that knives chopping raw meat will be washed before chopping salads. From time to time, food poisoning scandals appear in the media. Giving the unwashed public open access to the kitchens would defeat the purpose, so additional confidence comes from knowing that an external audit exists—that is, local officials who will from time to time inspect premises, check that the hygiene rules are clearly posted and legal standards are being met, and investigate complaints. With such external oversight, the risk of sanctions if fault is found helps keep managers on task.

So it is with the world of secret intelligence as well. Much must remain inaccessible, out of the public sight, behind closed doors. The public should be able to find out what the law does and does not allow, but greater transparency of everyday operations would be self-defeating. It is all the more important that senior managers can demonstrate through democratic oversight that they take codes of behavior seriously and create environments that encourage staff to uphold ethics, not least by showing that they themselves have a functioning internal moral compass. Managers also need that spur of an external audit by legislators who can be authorized to enter the circle of secrecy around the secret agencies and their activities to check whether the results justify the ethical risks being taken (see chapter 1) and the resources being expended. When things may have gone wrong, oversight can also help establish whether the internal rules were being followed and whether they are adequate. In another incentive for correct behavior, having a judicial component of oversight ensures that activity is being run within the laws governing the conduct of the most intrusive types of operations.

The larger and more internationally based any organization is, the harder it is in practice for the top executives to know how the front line is behaving in relation to the approved codes of conduct. In the world of business, an internal, as well as external, audit has a role in providing assurance to the board that systems of control are adequate (with the emphasis on ensuring the robustness of the system rather than on checking every transaction). The huge size of the US administration, with its very large departments such as the Pentagon and the NSA, led to the appointment of inspectors general who are accountable to the heads of the respective organizations for carrying out an internal oversight role. In 1952, a few years after the CIA was created, an IG was appointed as an independent officer to promote economy, efficiency, effectiveness, and accountability in the management of the agency's activities by performing independent audits, inspections, investigations, and reviews of CIA programs and operations, as well as seeking to detect and deter fraud, waste, abuse, and mismanagement. The IG role came under sustained criticism by the Church Committee (1975–76) and again at the time of the Iran-Contra scandal (1985–87) as being insufficiently independent and critical. To help remedy this, in 1989 the role was made statutory, with the CIA IG being nominated by the president, removable from office by the president only, and with responsibilities to congressional overseers.

The historical record shows that the work of inspectors general is not a substitute for external oversight by legislators, although it provides insights

for top management on the efficiency and morale of their respective organizations, and some of their reports have supplied invaluable material for
external scrutiny. A 2004 CIA IG report to the agency's director, for example, found that the public had been misled by the administration's statements about the harsh treatment of detainees in the terrorist interrogation
program set up after the 9/11 attacks. Critical questions over the legality
of the interrogation methods used were brought to the attention of the
Justice Department. The IG did his job even if the attorney general then
ruled no change was necessary; instead, it took a change of administration
to end the torture program. Praising the work of the IG in exposing unlawful practices, Intelligence Committee member Sen. Ron Wyden (D-OR)
commented publicly that "in the wake of serious breaches of trust by CIA
leadership over the past year, it is more important than ever that the administration appoint a strong, independent CIA Inspector General."[1]

An innovation that the United Kingdom has adopted to provide external perspective to security and intelligence agencies that necessarily operate
in secret is the appointment of independent nonexecutive members to their
management boards, a practice common across civilian government. This
author, when director of the Government Communications Headquarters,
first introduced nonexecutives to the management board in 1995 to help
it deal with the exceptional twin challenges of the coming digital era and
of the post–Cold War restructuring by appointing a senior engineer with
private sector experience in managing large, complex projects and a human
relations director from a major national organization experienced in cultural change. All the UK security and intelligence agencies now have nonexecutive members on their boards, thus offering another way of reducing
the inevitable risk of isolation of highly secretive organizations from cur-
rents of thinking in business and wider society.

LEGISLATIVE OVERSIGHT

Specialist oversight committees are generally thought to be essential to
the effective operation of legislative chambers as they enable members to
develop in-depth knowledge of the matters under their jurisdiction. As
"little legislatures" such committees can monitor current governmental
operations, identify issues suitable for legislative review, gather and evaluate information, and recommend courses of action to their parent body. In

the case of the US Senate, they are almost as old (1789) as the Senate itself, although the interest in secret intelligence is much more recent.

Special investigating committees can be thought of as a form of episodic oversight. It was the evidence gathered in 1973 by the Select Committee on Presidential Campaign Activities (the famous Watergate Committee) that led to the setting up of the US Senate Select Committee to Study Governmental Operations with Respect to Intelligence Activities, chaired by Sen. Frank Church (D-ID), to investigate allegations of illegal intelligence gathering. The findings of the Church Committee uncovered covert action programs to assassinate foreign leaders and efforts by the CIA and other agencies to collect information on the political activities of US citizens and others in the United States, in particular those who opposed the Vietnam War.[2] Church concluded:

> Too many people have been spied upon by too many Government agencies and to [sic] much information has been collected. The Government has often undertaken the secret surveillance of citizens on the basis of their political beliefs, even when those beliefs posed no threat of violence or illegal acts on behalf of a hostile foreign power. . . .
>
> The Constitutional system of checks and balances has not adequately controlled intelligence activities. Until recently the Executive branch has neither delineated the scope of permissible activities nor established procedures for supervising intelligence agencies. Congress has failed to exercise sufficient oversight, seldom questioning the use to which its appropriations were being put. Most domestic intelligence issues have not reached the courts, and in those cases when they have reached the courts, the judiciary has been reluctant to grapple with them.[3]

In a highly significant decision, the Senate then set up the Select Committee on Intelligence to oversee all future US intelligence activity. A parallel move in the House of Representatives led to the establishment of the Select Committee on Intelligence in 1975 and was made permanent in 1977 (known as the House Permanent Select Committee on Intelligence).

In the United Kingdom specialist select parliamentary committees only came into being in 1979 to cover the major government departments such as defense, foreign affairs, and home affairs. Not until 1994 and the avowal of the existence of the Secret Intelligence Service and the GCHQ (see chapter 2) was it possible to set up an Intelligence and Security Committee composed of selected and trusted parliamentarians who were appointed by the prime minister to oversee at least some aspects of their work. The ISC's success in reporting responsibly on intelligence activity, including examining whether the agencies could have prevented terrorist attacks, then led in 2013 to legislation making the ISC a proper parliamentary committee with its members appointed by Parliament and the committee having the right of access to information from the intelligence community.

The role of a democratic oversight body is not an easy one. Intelligence professionals take the need for secrecy about their work seriously. So trust in the reliability of the overseers is important and has to be earned over time, especially confidence that there will not be leaks to the press for political advantage, that grandstanding in open forums will be avoided, and that members will make the effort to understand the nature of intelligence gathering. The US committees have found that hard to do, and experienced intelligence officers have expressed their frustrations. Hank Crumpton, one of the best counterterrorism professionals the United States has ever produced, expressed his dismay with the 9/11 Commission's obsession with intelligence failures: "Why not the policy failures? Perhaps, I figured, because politicians and policy makers had set the rules and they constituted the entire commission. There were no incentives for policy makers to blame themselves. They were protecting their tribe. Not a single intelligence professional held one of the commission's seats. . . .

"Worse, the commission and the public held the CIA to a standard of unattainable tactical perfection in a context of strategic policy failure."[4]

Those people in the world of secret intelligence nevertheless have to recognize that the justification for oversight—and for the occasional excesses in oversight—have their roots in their own behavior. Such was the case for Vietnam War–era spying on radicals (including civil rights activists) in the United States in the 1970s, for the European Court of Human Rights judgments of the 1980s that cast doubt on the lawfulness of much of the domestic surveillance by the United Kingdom's Security Service and Scotland Yard, and most recently for the Snowden revelations about the digital intelligence-gathering programs of the NSA and the GCHQ that, while lawful, were not sufficiently understood by legislators (see chapter 5).

Most European Union nations (the exceptions are Ireland, Malta, Finland, and Portugal) now have legislative oversight of intelligence activity either with specialist committees or, in the case of Greece, Cyprus, and Sweden, through standing committees with broader remits.[5] Most oversee the policies, administrations, budgets, and expenditures of the relevant intelligence services, but modalities vary according to the different national organizational structures for intelligence work. There is no set model, for example, on whether separate external services exist and, if they do, whether they are part of the national defense structure or freestanding; on whether internal services are part of national police structures with police powers or, as in the United Kingdom, a separate civilian service; and, importantly, on how technical and digital intelligence activity is organized. The Venice Commission recommended that nations should set up one parliamentary committee to oversee all the different bodies involved in intelligence work to help with more far-reaching oversight and to cross agency boundaries.[6] Nevertheless, all such oversight mechanisms remain resolutely national, since intelligence activity is ultimately a responsibility of the nation-state.

This principle is incorporated into the Lisbon Treaty of European Union itself: "The Union shall respect the equality of Member States before the Treaties as well as their national identities, inherent in their fundamental structures, political and constitutional, inclusive of regional and local self-government. It shall respect their essential State functions, including ensuring the territorial integrity of the State, maintaining law and order and safeguarding national security. In particular, national security remains the sole responsibility of each Member State."[7]

When intelligence is shared by one nation with another, it is common practice to make it subject to originator control so that an overseas originating agency has to agree (or not) to the oversight body's having access to its material in the course of an investigation. The risk exists therefore that ethical issues posed by international cooperation between intelligence agencies, including sharing of personal information (as we discuss in this chapter), fall between the cracks of national oversight.[8]

One striking difference between the US and European models of government lies in the separation of powers. Congress, as the legislative branch, holds the executive branch to account but is itself part of the government of the United States, sharing in the key policy decisions and responsible for granting the funds to execute them. As Sen. Robert Byrd (D-WV) said to Deputy Secretary of Defense Paul Wolfowitz on seeing the demands for the 2003 Iraq War, "Congress is not an ATM [automated teller machine]."[9] It is therefore constitutionally necessary to give prior notification to the congressional oversight committees of impending expenditures and major operations. Agencies within the intelligence community are expected to keep the committees "fully and currently informed" of their activities, including any "significant anticipated activities" for which consent can be given or withheld. US law provides that where prior notice is not given, the president will inform the committees "in a timely fashion" and provide a statement explaining why prior notice had not be given.

In the European tradition the executive is drawn from the legislature. A European oversight committee would not want to be asked in advance to approve of government decisions that might thereby constrain its ability to examine them objectively after the fact and therefore its freedom to criticize. This undoubtedly makes the role of European oversight committees such as the British ISC simpler than that of a US Senate oversight committee.

Notwithstanding national differences, the broad conditions for effective oversight are easily stated. A panel of legislators must be in a position to devote the not inconsiderable time needed to master the arcana of intelligence work. They have to be sufficiently senior and experienced to command wider confidence in the legislative body, since we are dealing here with trust by proxy; that is, on behalf of the body politic, a few have access to the ring of secrecy. What they conclude about what is going on needs to matter. Thus, the legislators involved need sufficient staff support, including these days competent technical support, to help them understand the often complex issues and to do much of the digging. Leadership is required that can overcome bipartisan and party politics to take a national view. The committee also must be able to work behind closed doors in a physical environment that allows the most sensitive material to be received and read (what the Five Eyes community calls a secure compartmented intelligence facility). As the CIA's own account relates, "Despite the evident goodwill in both branches, however, profound misgivings lay beneath the surface. Could committees of Congress, inherently political institutions, do hands-on oversight of intelligence activities without revealing them? At this point, no other country in the world had seen fit to entrust their legislatures with such an intrusive role."[10] We can conclude, therefore, that in any polity, the overseers who will have access to information that may potentially make or break an administration, and thereby get themselves on the front pages, need to exercise self-restraint and agree to act collectively and responsibly.

JUDICIAL OVERSIGHT

The part judges or judicial commissioners play in many jurisdictions in approving intrusive surveillance or comparable operations (such as the FISA Court in the United States) has been covered in chapter 2. Where the public has high regard for judicial independence, then arguably such processes add to the public's feelings that the secret agencies are trustworthy at least in their domestic investigations since the public can be confident that agencies are staying within the domestic law. Both the European Court of Human Rights and the European Court itself, reflecting much liberal legal opinion, have tended to emphasize the need for independent judicial scrutiny of any intrusive activity that engages privacy rights. The risk of going too far down such a track is that judges will be drawn into decisions that are essentially for the executive to take and to be accountable for. An independent judge is accountable to the law, not to a democratic parliament, and should not be required to justify his or her decisions beyond the judgment of lawfulness itself. Otherwise, the risk is the politicization of the judiciary. The Snowden revelations in the United Kingdom, for instance, led to the interception commissioner, a very senior retired judge, having to appear as a witness before a parliamentary committee to answer accusations that he had failed to be sufficiently critical in a televised session where the questioning was overtly political in tone. The conflict between judicial rationality and raw politics did not help public understanding of either.

ETHICS SAFETY VALVES

Finally, we should consider the position of the individual members who staff an intelligence agency when they feel they are facing an ethical dilemma. Perhaps an individual either has become aware of activity in the agency that seems to lie outside known guidance or has been asked to carry out a task that seems improper or even unlawful.

In a well-run modern intelligence agency, everyone will have had ethical issues addressed in their training, along with explanations of the legal framework within which they must operate, the authorities required for different activities, and so on. An ethical code of behavior is published with instructions on what to do when issues appear to arise. The first call should be to management, since an individual may not be aware of all the facts.

That in turn requires trust on the part of the employee that raising issues will not result in sanctions or be career limiting. For that reason many organizations (including the British services) employ staff counselors to whom employees can go in confidence and explore issues. The inspectors general, where they exist, fulfill a similar function. Many jurisdictions have whistleblower protection in law, although some exclude intelligence agencies from the scope. Some intelligence analytic organizations (such as the US Defense Intelligence Agency) have analytic dissent mechanisms so that if analysts feel that their opinion has been overridden or ignored for political or other reasons, they can enter a formal reservation, triggering an examination of the issue by the head of profession or a similarly senior, independent individual.

That staff members feel they have secure channels in which they can raise issues and have them seriously addressed without fear is important. Edward Snowden has claimed that because of the NSA's harsh treatment of a previous whistleblower (Thomas Drake), he did not feel he could pursue the internal channels, including the NSA IG, in practice.[11] It can be argued, however, that even if internal processes are not trusted, then the legislative oversight bodies also exist as channels to be tried before a decision is made to make highly classified material public through the media.

Mark Phythian: Throughout the book we have treated the practice of secret intelligence as posing particular dilemmas for liberal democratic states, given that so much behavior seems to run counter to liberalism's core principles. It is not surprising that post-9/11 developments and revelations should have contributed to a certain liberal pessimism regarding intelligence. For some, George Orwell's *Nineteen Eighty-Four* no longer carries the power of dystopian warning; they feel the recent past has been much worse than Orwell imagined. Orwell's emphasis on the various forms of state surveillance can be seen to be prescient, with helicopters in the novel conducting the agile aerial snooping that drones will increasingly perform in the future. ("In the far distance a helicopter skimmed down between the roofs, hovered for an instant like a bluebottle, and darted away again with a curving flight. It was the police patrol, snooping into people's windows."[12]) However, if *Nineteen Eighty-Four* were written today, Winston Smith's lover Julia could well be an undercover Special Demonstration Squad officer, and if she wasn't, the novel could end somewhat earlier, with the two of them being killed by a drone strike as they secretly meet in the country to avoid the concealed microphones and overt patrols that are part and parcel of life in London. In the contemporary world, then, the sense of pervasive surveillance that is a key part of the experience of reading *Nineteen Eighty-Four* has lost much of its former power to shock.

However, nil desperandum. The road to reassurance that intelligence can comply with liberal values while doing what is deemed necessary to protect the liberal state and its populace lies in external oversight. In a liberal democratic context, legislative oversight has been considered a cornerstone of any oversight regime. This understanding proceeds from the principle that although intelligence agencies are creatures of the executive, liberal theory holds that they serve the public and as such should be answerable to the public in some form. Legislative oversight, on this reading, has a role in that overseers must satisfy themselves that intelligence practice is conducted effectively, efficiently, and in line with national values. That this road to reassurance simply exists will itself satisfy some. However, those who study the route maps closely will see that there are areas where the road surface is less clearly marked and less well maintained than others and where, consequently, the going gets tougher. They will note that the road is required to pass through some areas where it meets with local resistance from people who object to it and where travelers do not enjoy full local cooperation. They will further observe that some promising side roads that seem important are simply closed off to oversight traffic. To travel such a road successfully requires a team of experienced drivers, considerable preparation, adequate time, and an on-call roadside support infrastructure.

The historical record shows that oversight can meet with resistance (and, to be clear, I include obstruction or noncooperation as forms of resistance) even in the most advanced liberal democratic oversight contexts, because the degree of active cooperation experienced, or resistance encountered, will vary by issue rather than be a constant across issues. On a related point, because intelligence organizations are bureaucracies, they seek, as all bureaucracies do, to protect and advance their institutional interests. This likely involves attempting to resist or minimize any criticism of the organization that could adversely affect these interests.[13] We would perhaps expect such bureaucratic resistance to be most evident in the context of democratic transitions, where states have undertaken a process of democratization of intelligence as part of a wider process of transitioning from authoritarian military governments and intelligence structures—as, for example, in the cases of Argentina and Brazil—or from one-party communist systems and intelligence structures such as that in Romania. In the latter case, for example, resistance was particularly related to the question of the former Securitate personnel working in the new intelligence structure. One form it took was energetic file destruction.[14]

However, forms of resistance are by no means confined to transitional contexts. In the United States, for example, the Senate Select Committee on Intelligence (SSCI) investigation into the CIA's detention and interrogation program during the war on terror met with acute resistance from both the CIA and the wider executive branch. One form this resistance took was not so much file destruction as the destruction of videotapes of the enhanced interrogation techniques being applied to two detainees, something the SSCI became aware of only after the fact was leaked to the *New York Times*.[15] CIA director Michael Hayden explained that they were destroyed to protect the identity of undercover officers and because they had ceased to have any intelligence value; however, other quarters suggested alternative explanations.[16] Another form was testimony by senior CIA figures such as Hayden to the SSCI; the committee believed it was inaccurate and designed to mislead about the effectiveness of these interrogation techniques.[17] In a similar vein, in chapter 5 we noted James Clapper's March 2013 testimony to the SSCI on whether bulk collection of US citizens' data occurred. Even in the most advanced oversight systems, then, overseers need to be aware that they are potentially involved in a contest. As Peter Gill and I have written, "There is no neat solution to the oversight problem—there will always be tensions within democratic states between security professionals and their overseers. If there are no tensions the oversight system is simply not working."[18]

In the case of the United Kingdom, intelligence oversight did not follow automatically from the US example of establishing legislative oversight. The 1980s nevertheless saw growing pressure for intelligence to be placed on a firm statutory footing in the United Kingdom and for greater light to be shone on the activities of intelligence agencies. The Thatcher governments of that decade stoutly resisted this pressure, but among officials there was a recognition of the problems that the absence of legislative cover was creating.[19] For example, the news in the summer of 1980 that BBC television's *Panorama* program was making a documentary on the intelligence services induced mild panic in Downing Street. Pressure was applied to the BBC's director general to drop the program, and formally banning the program was considered. Cabinet Secretary Robert Armstrong floated the idea of exercising some control over the program by steering the BBC to focus on the question of accountability. As he explained to Mrs. Thatcher:

The Government would be wholly justified in seeking to prevent a programme about the functions and working of the Services, but it is less clear that we should be justified in seeking to prevent a programme genuinely confined to the question of [their] accountability. This is a matter of which there is bound to be some discussion in Parliament, because of Mr. [Robin] Cook's Bill on the Security Services; and though the issue of accountability may have come to public notice because of the activities and articles of Duncan Campbell, it is arguably a matter of legitimate public interest. If we were minded not to object to a programme on accountability, however, the difficulty would be to make sure that it was confined to that: on its own it would be a pretty boring and unvisual subject. And its conclusion can be taken as foregone: how can it fail to conclude that the intelligence services ought to be more publicly accountable?[20]

In chapter 2 we discussed the emergence of legislative oversight in the United Kingdom via the 1994 Intelligence Services Act, which created the ISC.[21] Hence, by the time of the Edward Snowden leaks, the ISC had existed for almost twenty years. In its early work, it had successfully established itself and gained the trust of those within the intelligence community that it would be a secure body and not degenerate into partisan politics. The committee was able therefore to develop its remit without controversy beyond the administration of the agencies and into operational activity. In its second decade, however, its performance in investigating a series of issues related to the war on terror attracted criticism for a tendency not to probe too deeply and thus to exonerate the agencies of any responsibility for any apparent failures. For example, the need to have a freestanding inquiry by Lord Butler into the evident WMD intelligence failures in the run-up to the 2003 Iraq War, an inquiry that included the chair of the ISC as a member, drew attention to the limitations of the ISC itself. The conclusions of other ISC reports had to be corrected because the agencies failed to provide key information at the time, raising questions (as did the ISC itself) about the extent to which the committee enjoyed their full cooperation. Subsequent revelations also exposed the committee's structural inability to investigate adequately allegations of UK involvement in extraordinary rendition and torture in the war on terror. Essentially, the committee seemed to lack the political will that is widely considered an essential element of effective intelligence oversight, and, not unconnected, it had only qualified independence from government and a limited investigatory capacity and support staff at best.[22] To an extent, it was hobbled by design.

By 2012 it was becoming apparent to the government, the agencies, and the ISC itself that intelligence oversight in the United Kingdom was failing. It was not delivering the public trust, and hence the democratic legitimacy, that the agencies themselves wanted and ultimately require. Consequently, the ISC itself put forward proposals for reform that fed into the Justice and Security Act of 2013, which sought both to make the committee more independent of the government and, importantly, to demonstrate that it was independent. Previously criticized as the creature of the prime minister, the committee would now be accountable directly to Parliament, which would appoint its members, albeit on the recommendation of the prime minister after consultation with the parties. This meant, on the one hand, that Parliament still could not appoint to the ISC anyone the prime minister (and the agencies) did not want there; and, on the other hand, in theory, Parliament could challenge (and ultimately veto) the composition of a committee that it felt was not appropriately balanced. The ISC would choose its chair from among its members, but this would not guarantee one commonly recommended reform—the chair should be drawn from an opposition party rather than the government party—thus missing an opportunity to enhance the appearance of independence.

Like select committees, the ISC would now have right to access the information it needed for its inquiries (where previously it could only request the information from the agencies), unless the secretary of state vetoed the right on clearly defined grounds. Its reports would be laid before Parliament but only after being seen by the prime minister (and the agencies), and the ISC would still need to exclude from the reports any information the prime minister considered prejudicial to the continued work of the agencies. Finally, the ISC's role in investigating operational matters—a role not included in the 1994 act but which had developed in practice in the years since—was recognized through the new act, though it was subject to prime ministerial approval. On balance, then, it was possible to discern a shift, albeit a limited one, in the balance of power from the executive to the legislature.

Still, the reforms had the effect of giving the ISC a clean slate, as all criticisms had related to an anterior oversight regime. However, within weeks the new ISC faced the fallout generated by the publication of the Snowden leaks and the criticism of the preceding ISC that it had either not known or failed to act when the GCHQ bypassed UK law in accessing information from the NSA's PRISM program, but in either case the ISC would have failed to provide effective oversight.

David Omand: The allegation against the GCHQ of operating outside the then understood law was in fact not true.[23] The ISC issued a statement in July saying so, although without disclosing evidence for its assurance that the GCHQ had complied with UK law. At the same time the ISC announced that it would examine the "complex interaction" between the relevant pieces of legislation—the Regulation of Investigatory Powers Act, the Intelligence Services Act, and the Human Rights Act—"and the policies and procedures that underpin them."[24] This statement masked that, as we noted in chapter 5, the ISC was placed in an awkward situation over the exposure of the NSA-GCHQ relationship and the PRISM allegations. The committee was fully aware of the nature and extent of the NSA-GCHQ (and other Five Eyes) relationship prior to the Snowden revelations, but it was not free to make public the detailed mechanisms of cooperation and that requests to the NSA were covered by the requisite authority under UK law (and vice versa[25]). It took the case brought by Liberty and other NGOs against the UK government to force an agreement to disclose to the court (the Investigatory Powers Tribunal) what the safeguards were. Without that disclosure the government might well have lost the case. The court then reached the important conclusion (see chapter 5) that, as correctly applied as the authorization procedures might be, the rule of law required sufficient transparency so members of the public can find out how the law might apply to them. That, in the end, had to be achieved by brand-new legislation, the Investigatory Powers Act 2016, as finally recommended by the ISC.

Mark Phythian: This example does raise key issues of the nature and form of briefings to overseers, of the need to be able to involve those with appropriate specialist expertise who advise the overseers (that is, to be able to bring them into the "ring of secrecy"), and of the resources necessary to conduct effective legislative oversight of intelligence in the contemporary environment (that is, to have access to sufficient specialist expertise in the first place). Not surprising, ISC members conceded nothing in public about whether parts of the Snowden material came as a surprise to them, but, as we argued in chapter 5, the wider significance of what they would have learned seemed to elude them.

This general point is further illustrated by returning to the United States and the example of the SSCI's oversight of intelligence practices in

the war on terror. One core assertion of those CIA managers who over-
saw the enhanced interrogation program was that congressional oversight
committees were briefed on and supported the program.[26] However, the
conditions under which such briefings take place can impact how full an
understanding the overseers come away with. It is quite possible, in theory, for a briefing of overseers to have taken place but for overseers to be
less than fully aware of its full significance and, by extension, what they
appear to be supporting. Sen. Jay Rockefeller (D-WV), a former chair of
the SSCI, recalled his briefings on the CIA's use of enhanced interrogation
techniques:

> I first learned about some aspects of the CIA's detention and inter-
> rogation program in 2003 when I became vice chair of the com-
> mittee. At that point and for years after, the CIA refused to provide
> me or anybody else with any additional information about the pro-
> gram. They further refused to notify the full committee about the
> program's existence. My colleagues will remember there was always
> the Gang of 4, the Gang of 6, or the Gang of 8. They would take
> the chairman and vice chairman, take them to the White House,
> give them a flip chart, 45 minutes for the Vice President, and off he
> would go. Senator [Pat] Roberts [R-KS] and I went down by car and
> were instructed we couldn't talk to each other on the way back from
> one of those meetings. It was absurd. They refused to do anything to
> be of assistance.
>
> The briefings I received provided little or no insight into the
> CIA's program. Questions or followup requests were rejected, and
> at times I was not allowed to consult with my counsel. I am not a
> lawyer. There are legal matters involved here. They said we couldn't
> talk to any of our staff, legal counsel or not, or other members of the
> committee who knew nothing about this because they had not been
> informed at all.
>
> It was clear these briefings were not meant to answer any ques-
> tions but were intended only to provide cover for the administration
> and the CIA.
>
> It was infuriating to me to realize I was part of a box checking
> exercise that the administration planned to use, and later did use, so
> they could disingenuously claim they had—in a phrase I will never
> be able to forget—"fully briefed Congress."[27]

Oversight of intelligence, then, involves a contest over power, where there is a close relationship between secrecy and power. For some, this makes oversight of intelligence, even in entrenched liberal democratic contexts, an inherently uneven contest. As John le Carré wrote in apparent exasperation:

> Parliamentary oversight? Have you ever spotted those weird recruit-ment ads that MI6 puts out in our newspapers at our expense? Boiled down, they're all about: how good are you at talking people into betraying their country? I'm not sure how high that particular skill rates on the credibility and legitimacy charts, but one thing that won't have changed in the 50-odd years since I left the secret world, and never will, is the gullibility of the uninitiated when faced with real-life spies. In a flash, all rational standards of human judgement fall away.[28]

To return to the challenges confronting the ISC in the United King-dom, in his 2015 *A Question of Trust* report (discussed in chapter 5), David Anderson was only too aware of the limitations of the ISC. His report noted that the ISC "as an institution did not receive significant support from those making submissions to us," with some advocating its abolition.[29] Moreover, Anderson was not supportive of the continuation of the ISC in its current form. His report suggested that Parliament should consider whether to maintain the ISC but strengthen it by appointing a chair from outside the governing political party, or whether to transfer its investigative resource to a proposed judicial commission, or whether to recast it as a select com-mittee, possibly merging it with the Defence Select Committee.[30] This set of options underlined the overall failure of the ISC as an oversight body.

Important questions flow from this discussion. Does the nature of con-temporary surveillance technology and the need for legislation to keep pace with technological development require overseers who are as much technicians as they are politicians? In light of the Snowden revelations—and what they reveal about oversight capacities as much as state prac-tices—is the idea of legislative oversight, at least as the primary expression of intelligence accountability, now a "busted flush"? Is this area just too complex to be entrusted to politicians? As Anderson's recommendations might indicate (he described the work of the statutory commissioners as a model of its kind), should the judiciary gradually supplant the politicians as the primary guardians of the public interest in overseeing intelligence? What would be the implications of conceding this in a liberal democratic context? For example, would this shift in effect reduce the role of overseers in terms of providing a normative as well as a legal check (bearing in mind Senator Rockefeller's sense that he had been used as part of a "box checking exercise")?

In posing such questions we confront the reality that the executive branch, including intelligence agencies, on the one hand, and the legislature, on the other hand, have somewhat different understandings of the purpose of oversight and of the role of overseers. From the perspective of the executive branch and intelligence agencies, oversight is a means of delivering public confidence and, with it, trust in the intelligence agencies. As then UK home secretary Jacqui Smith helpfully explained in 2008 in opening a debate on the ISC's latest annual report, from the executive's perspective, "it is essential that Parliament and, through Parliament, the wider public can be assured that the security and intelligence agencies are fulfilling their lawful duties efficiently and effectively. That is the role of the Intelligence and Security Committee—the ISC."[31] This is all well and good, but what happens when the overseers find evidence—for example, cases of ethical misbehavior by intelligence officers or possible intelligence failure— that is likely to adversely affect trust in the agencies? Does the role outlined by Smith generate a conflict or create a pressure on overseers?

Parliamentarians are clearly aware of the potential pressures. Speaking in the same debate, then shadow home secretary Dominic Grieve (and a future chair of the ISC) worried:

> To an extent, we are guided by what members of the [ISC] say, although I am always conscious that there is a danger of them going native and ceasing to be the upholders of the interests of the House. When that happens, it is because they are lured magnetically into a world where the fact that rooms and secret information are made available to them gently and subtly affects their judgment. They are grateful for being made privy to matters that are not available to other people. . . . That is one of the inherent tensions in the different roles that one plays in Government and in the House.[32]

This is, in effect, a restatement of le Carré's point. This idea that the member of the legislative oversight body owes a primary duty to Parliament rather than to the intelligence services can, it seems, result in a form of cognitive dissonance.

As then ISC member Richard Ottaway conceded in the same debate:

> I feel most uncomfortable with the question about the precise role of the ISC. Is it with the agencies or against them? Does it provide oversight or a check or balance? The Committee's job is defined, as is the job of a Select Committee, as the provision of oversight of policy, finance and administration. That definition is wide and vague, and can be broadly or narrowly interpreted. During my time on the ISC, I have seen a narrow interpretation. A Select Committee has more freedom to range and is wide-ranging in its scope.[33]

At the same time, it would be wrong to suggest that the ISC, together with an emerging greater role for judges in supervising the legality of the exercise of surveillance powers, constitutes the entire legitimate universe of intelligence oversight. In the United States and the United Kingdom, and elsewhere, the media has often been the primary source of revelations about intelligence practice that then spurs further inquiries by legislative overseers, subverting what might be considered the normal relationship whereby the media reports the findings of intelligence overseers. The most significant controversies concerning intelligence in the United States and the United Kingdom in recent years, in terms of the scale of the democratic deficit they exposed and the normative values the two societies subscribe to, have come to the public's attention through newspapers, not overseers. Nor should we overlook the significant role that commissions of inquiry continue to play in pulling together vast amounts of material and offering postmortem judgments on past intelligence activities and performance.

We should also be aware of gaps that domestic legislation alone cannot fill—the inability of domestic overseers to access details arising out of international intelligence cooperation (the promising side roads closed off to oversight traffic), for example—and consider the implications of, and national-level responses to, this situation. In an increasingly networked intelligence world, this accountability gap arising from international intelligence cooperation is set to grow in significance in the future and render national oversight arrangements partial and without access to the full picture.[34]

David Omand: As in so many aspects of secret intelligence, the trustworthiness of those involved turns out to be a central question. As you have set out, a skeptical public must be convinced that overseers drawn from the legislature are independent of those they are examining and that they neither have fallen under the spell of the professional intelligence officer, with a lifetime's experience in deceiving the adversary, nor stand in thrall to the inherent secrecy of intelligence activity and the apparent glamour of secret service and its tradecraft. Some of what the overseers will learn will indeed be extraordinary as are the feats of some of those they will meet, whether through their sheer mathematical or scientific wizardry or through their courage under fire in war zones. But the overseers must remain vigilant and persistent in their questioning. Yet, I would submit, they should not be inherently adversarial toward those they are overseeing, for that way lies constant confrontation and suspicion, where the advantages will always go to those with the secret and whose work lies outside the direct observation of outsiders.

The overseen also need to feel that those overseeing them are trustworthy in their unique role, through evident objectivity and fairness, as well as firmness, and in their receipt of secrets on which lives may depend. The overseers must avoid the temptation to make party political capital out of what they learn in confidence about the attitudes of previous administrations. Any activity of secret agencies can almost guarantee media interest, so overseers must also be trusted not to turn their inquiries into political theater. It may well be that what you criticized as the CIA's destruction of material relating to the coercive interrogation program had its real roots in a lack of trust that overseers would play fair with the lives, reputations, and livelihoods of those involved. It may also be hard for the busy elected politician who is appointed to an oversight committee to accept that the large amount of time they need to devote to intelligence oversight meetings and visits will be spent in activities that their constituents or the wider public will never properly recognize, unlike others who serve on select committees where the opportunities for political profile are greater. (This is one of the reasons why oversight work is less attractive to the young politician who has yet to make his or her mark.)

The current concerns over the privacy risks associated with domestic surveillance should not lead us to undervalue the need for oversight of all the other work (the greater part) of intelligence agencies, including the support for foreign policy and military operations. In the concluding chapter we look ahead at some of the ethical issues that are likely to arise in the future for intelligence communities, including in relation to open source intelligence, how to balance civilian efforts with that best contributed from military sources, how to use cyber intelligence to help achieve the increasingly important mission of cyber security, and how far to use contractors from the private sector. Recruiting staff with the relevant technical skills for the digital world will remain a challenge, as will ensuring adequate security vetting and cover in a world of ubiquitous social media. Whether it is sensible to maintain or to change intelligence structures, to merge or demerge functions including links to law enforcement, and to determine how best to invest the funds available for future capability are the sorts of issues on which overseers should be challenging governments. It matters how well governments seize opportunities and avoid simply papering over cracks.

We should be realistic therefore about what oversight by busy legislators can achieve and what is best sought by other means. Checking the ethical compass of those in the secret world is a task that is best shared with judicial oversight. Judges are well placed by their experience to test cases put forward for the use of the most intrusive powers in terms of lawfulness, necessity, and proportionality. But experienced legislators can also test the moral fiber of the leaders of the intelligence community from whom they take evidence and the extent to which they are setting an example with ethical awareness and training for their staffs.

When, as is inevitable, allegations of scandal or ineffectiveness occasionally hit the headlines, oversight committees can provide a means of relatively rapid investigation (at least in comparison to the painful experience of the inordinate length of any judicial inquiry in which legal representation is needed). Like other parts of the government, the secret world now will have to absorb the age-old lesson that mistakes are best admitted swiftly and faults clearly seen to be tackled quickly. In some cases it will be evident that claims are not well founded, and oversight can impartially defend the reputations of those who cannot defend themselves publicly. But here care is needed not to undermine confidence in oversight by asking overseers to take on inquiries beyond their reach, such as into potential criminality that ought to be conducted by the police or that on rare occasions do require the apparatus of a formal inquiry including legal representation and evidence given under oath. Nor should they hold frequent public evidence sessions at which official witnesses are obliged to stonewall questions that take them to the edge of what is disclosable in open session, thus creating an unhelpful and false image of a lack of cooperation.

Legislative overseers must resist any rush to judgment in response to the clamor of the media to assign blame for any alleged intelligence failure and to name names. They must also not succumb to bland assurances from the secret world that there is nothing to the claims without first establishing in depth and to the committee's own satisfaction what they need to know to answer the questions they are addressing. For that effort, there is no alternative to having experienced staff support to dig on their behalf.

By what criteria should overseers opine that there has been an intelligence failure? A rational consideration of the question of failure was the ISC report into the killing of a young soldier, Trooper Lee Rigby, by jihadist extremists on a London street.[35] The identities of the killers were known previously to the Security Service and the police, and they had featured in no less than seven previous inquiries. So could the attack have been prevented? The committee answered this question with a detailed examination (many of the details were included for the first time in its report) of the prioritization processes in the Security Service and the triage methods by which cases were assessed and scare surveillance resources allocated. The committee members showed that they recognized a very important truth: an in-depth investigation into any complex, high-pressure human activity (from transport accidents to lost football matches) will uncover mistaken judgments and errors in procedure that are important in themselves but are not germane to the proximate cause of the outcome being investigated. As the ISC concluded:

> We have discovered a number of errors, and this Report therefore contains criticisms where processes have not been followed or decisions have not been recorded. That, in itself, may not be surprising: any in-depth inquiry, with the benefit of time and hindsight, is always likely to reveal opportunities for improvement, particularly in an organisation such as MI5 where staff operate under significant pressure. However, what we have been seeking to determine is whether they would have made a difference, and what might have prevented the murder of Fusilier Lee Rigby. Based on the evidence we have seen, we do not consider that any of the Agencies' errors, when taken individually, were significant enough to have affected the outcome.[36]

What was also helpfully and publicly made clear was the high threshold that the Security Service felt had to be reached in terms of evidence of a violent threat before a warrant would be sought from the secretary of state for the most intrusive investigative methods. That ISC conclusion was a useful corrective to the assumptions of the media and nongovernmental organizations about the authorities' presumed readiness to engage in mass surveillance.

In some cases, such as investigating intelligence surprises, internal and external reviewers of performance also need to develop a sense of what in the circumstances would be a reasonable expectation of success. In counter-terrorism, as the ISC recognized, a perfect record of stopping attacks is not a sensible expectation on the part of the public. We would not expect the goal-keeper of a premier soccer team to keep out every shot at goal, nor would it be sensible to sack the goalkeeper or his teammates after a single defeat. We can rightly expect the players to have been doing their best on each occasion to win and to be penalized for breaking the rules. After a loss, managers cannot shirk the duty of examining the team's morale and will to win and of taking steps when they are found to have flagged. Too many errors and a rest or a replacement may be called for, and the position of the manager himself may be called into question if there is no evidence of a willingness to be open to constructive criticism and to show attention to the need for improvement.

Judging failure in preventing unwelcome foreign policy surprises through intelligence assessment is harder and involves examining the past priorities as set by government, as well as the receptiveness and the use made of intelligence assessments. As many as eight stages have to be navigated successfully for intelligence to contribute to effective counter-surprise actions:

1. There must be relevant data points that would be collectible in the first place, but if deception is being practiced by an adversary, this may be problematic.
2. To access them, the agencies need well-placed sources, which may depend on the priorities set previously through intelligence requirements and may call into question the past size and distribution of resources across the intelligence community.
3. The agencies have to interpret and report impartially and responsibly (with the appropriate caveats) what they have found.
4. Reports and warnings (including oral briefings), and including tip-offs to police and border officials, must reach the right parts of the government securely and in time.
5. The all-source analysts have to assess correctly the significance of all the reporting and open source information to explain what is going on and

where it might lead, including identifying lower-probability but high-impact scenarios of likely concern to the government.
6. Analysts have to explain the assessments, including probabilistic estimates of likelihood, sufficiently clearly, and customers have to understand what they are saying (and what they are *not* saying).
7. Customers have to accept the implications of the assessments and judge how they might impact present and future policy and operations.
8. Customers then have to make sensible decisions on what to do.

With the benefit of hindsight, the route from the past to the present will usually appear as a linear series of linked steps, each of which ought to have been apparent at the relevant time to the intelligence analysts. What the backward examination by an oversight inquiry will not observe, unless it takes great care, are the alternative branching paths from the past to the present that were not taken but at the time would have been perfectly reasonable possibilities to consider and possibly to act on. As the investigation into the run-up to the 2005 London bombings subsequently showed, when a group of suspects being covertly observed split up, the watchers had to decide which of them to follow, making a tactical spur-of-the-moment judgment with huge strategic consequences. What overseers should be looking for most of all are systemic sources of error. When problems do occur, the fiercest critics are likely to be found within the intelligence and security community, since these people best know what might have been possible had matters been disposed differently.

All that said, external oversight has inherent limitations. All parents of teenagers know that you need some house rules and that the youngsters need them explained and monitored such as the time when they return from parties (and the state they are in). But when they are out of your sight and you cannot know what they are really up to (including these days on the Internet), your main reassurance is the trustworthiness they have demonstrated by consistent past behavior that shows they have internalized your values and ethics and that they are likely to try to stay safe and self-regulate to avoid at least the worst excesses. In the case of secret intelligence agencies, visits by members of the oversight committee and by judicial commissioners and inspectors or their equivalent can confirm from contacts with staff at all levels that self-regulation appears to be effective, that an appropriate ethical code is in place, and that the staff takes it seriously.

Mark Phythian: The recent past has been a time of significant evolution in both intelligence and its oversight. Twenty-five years ago I doubt it would have been possible to meaningfully discuss the idea of the ethics of intelligence over such a space as we have here. Allocating a full chapter to the subject of intelligence oversight would have proved challenging to say the least. Oversight has come a long way in a range of countries in this period. Nevertheless, I think we need to take care not to be seduced by the surface charms of what we might term a Whig interpretation of intelligence history in this respect, one that would see ethical concerns and failures or underperformance in the practice of intelligence or its oversight as features of a bygone era.

To go back to a point made earlier, if we accept that the need for intelligence arises out of (1) the nature of the international system and the impact of the international on the national and (2) domestically, from forms of resistance to aspects of state power, then we must also accept that the contexts in which intelligence is both vital and challenged may ebb and flow but will certainly arise. The record of the past fifteen years shows that when intelligence practice is placed under strain and is required to respond to fresh or evolving challenges, so too intelligence oversight will need to respond and face challenges of its own in doing so. What might have been considered the forward march of intelligence oversight was halted, or even in some ways reversed, by the advent of the war on terror and the role of intelligence in it. However, Loch Johnson's careful periodization of the historical relationship between the US Congress and the intelligence community since 1947 shows that the reality is often more complex than broad narratives of progress might lead us to believe.[37]

I agree that overseers should not approach their task in an adversarial fashion. At the same time, as you say, it is important that the legitimacy and necessity of oversight is fully embraced by intelligence communities in liberal democracies. At the very least, the suspicion of limited cooperation and forms of obstruction have clearly persisted into the twenty-first century on occasion, even in those liberal democratic states where intelligence oversight is most deeply embedded. For legislative overseers, though, it is also important that they are not too credulous. Skepticism is a healthy liberal attribute in this respect.

Intelligence history is, of course, partly responsible for this state of affairs. I cited John le Carré earlier, but an even more stark warning in a similar vein focuses on the perils of inquiring into intelligence controversies.

It can be found in Desmond de Silva's report into the murder of Patrick Finucane, which we discussed in chapter 4, that was published less than five years prior to writing this chapter:

> I have borne in mind throughout that intelligence agents and their handlers have of necessity to deal in deceit, duplicity and subterfuge. In pursuit of the truth reviewers such as myself have to enter a murky world of uncertainty, cover stories and cover-ups, of misinformation and accounts re-formatted. I am acutely aware that things said, representations made and records kept may well not reflect the truth, and that records not made when one expects them to have been may speak volumes and undermine an "official" version of the truth. There are those who may fear the exposure of the truth and who may, for a variety of reasons, engage in dissembling, distorting or embellishing the account of activities in which they were involved.[38]

But I also think a certain skepticism on the part of overseers is important for a slightly different reason, and that this makes it important that there is a robust form of *legislative* oversight that commands widespread respect (and, in the United Kingdom context, a more robust and effective Intelligence Security Committee emerges and thrives). As any student of intelligence would, I hope, recognize, there is no such thing as total security.[39] It follows that the extent to which security is pursued and which dimensions are prioritized and at what price (both in terms of financial costs and the normative opportunity costs) rest on political choices. Informed and engaged overseers are necessary to reflect on and apply tests to such judgments and to provide a check that, in terms of necessity and efficacy, the investment is worthwhile. Overseers should also be the motors that facilitate informed public discussion. David Anderson highlighted this role in his *A Question of Trust* report, but it seems to have been beyond the ISC up to that point. Moreover, in providing this form of check, overseers need to recognize that intelligence communities themselves constitute a bureaucratic interest that both logic and history suggest they will look to defend and advance.

Conclusion

Toward Principled Spying

We hope that our dialogue in this book between a political science academic and a former practitioner in the worlds of defense, security, and intelligence has demonstrated that sound ethical thinking and good intelligence practice are not contradictory concepts, even though there will inevitably at times be a tension between them. To be safe *and* sound is within our grasp. Managing that tension should be a core aim of intelligence practice in liberal democratic contexts so that the public can benefit from both security and liberty while enjoying freedoms and rights that are integral to the society that the security and intelligence agencies exist to defend.

For the reasons we have discussed in this book, there always will be potential threats to the state and society that the government must counter; not least they come from the activities of other states in a competitive international system and from a kaleidoscope of non-state groups that include terrorists, organized criminal gangs, cyber criminals, child abuse networks, people and narcotics traffickers, and illegal weapons proliferation networks. Collectively, if the risks are not well managed, the very health of society is undermined. In a variety of ways, those within the realm, citizens and visitors alike, look to the authorities of the state for at least a minimum assurance of safety and security.

In this context Philip Bobbitt has suggested that "the most difficult intelligence challenge of all [is] . . . how to develop rules that will effectively empower the secret state that protects us without compromising our commitment to the rule of law."[1] We agree but would want to take a broader view by adding "and without compromising the ethical principles that underpin the operation of liberal democracies, notably the exercise of restraint in the use of the coercive powers of the state." When individual cases are considered it becomes clear that not everything that may be legal should be considered ethical. An initial reluctance to exercise the coercive powers of the state is a healthy instinct to foster in those authorizing intelligence operations and in the intelligence officers carrying them out. Stansfield Turner's dictum discussed in chapter 1 has an evident relevance: "There is one overall test of the ethics of human intelligence activities. That is whether those approving them feel they could defend their decisions before the public if their actions became public."[2] Any convincing ethical justification genuinely has to include the sentiment, it was the *right* thing to do.

In terms of principles that should be generally applicable, we debated (in chapter 3) how helpful it is to draw on the Just War tradition of jus ad bellum and jus in bello, with their provisions that seek to place constraints on the use of force to minimize the inevitable suffering and risk to the innocent that war brings. We repeat here the Just War tradition concepts that we identified are relevant to the ethics of intelligence:

- *just cause*—being in accordance with the constraints of statute law, transparent to the public, and with the intended meaning of terms such as "national security" explained in published government documents
- *right intention*—acting with integrity and having no hidden political or other agenda behind the authorization of intelligence activity or the analysis, assessment, and presentation of intelligence judgments to decision-makers
- *proportionality*—keeping the ethical risks of operations in line with the harm that the operations are intended to prevent
- *right authority*—establishing the level appropriate to the ethical risks that may be run and that will then allow for accountability for decisions and oversight of the process
- *reasonable prospect of success*—having adequate justification for individual operations based on sound probabilistic reasoning that also prevents general fishing expeditions or mass surveillance
- *discrimination*—determining the human and technical ability to assess and manage the risk of collateral harm, including privacy intrusion into the lives of those who are not the intended targets of intelligence gathering
- *necessity*—finding no other reasonable way to achieve the authorized mission at lesser ethical risk but still applying any intrusive investigation with restraint

Our discussion of the utility of these Just War concepts has, we hope, brought out clearly a number of problems that can arise in translating from the ethics of warfare to those of intelligence. What is most important to recognize here, though, is that it is the habit of thought—borne out of centuries of philosophical struggle over how to reconcile conflicting moral considerations—that really matters. Such thinking should be universal.

We also explored in chapter 2 the development of what began as an assumed, but these days is an increasingly explicit, bargain between the citizen and state. Its terms are made clear through democratic debate and the resulting clearly drafted legislation under which the citizen, in return for safety and security, empowers the state with coercive powers, including intrusive means of investigation, and the right to levy taxes to pay for them. We might see this as constituting a shift from the "secret states" of European nations in the nineteenth and twentieth centuries to the "protecting states" of the early twenty-first century in which secret intelligence is avowed and its use encouraged to support law enforcement in its detection and prevention of serious crime.[3] Counterterrorism is a national security matter and features heavily in national security strategies, but terrorism itself is a crime. Thus, in most jurisdictions the objective of the intelligence authorities is to help law enforcement bring terrorist suspects before a court.

The ethical issues are not confined to the work of the intelligence officers who design and operate intelligence collection. The intelligence analysts have a responsibility to behave ethically in the way they infer rational conclusions from intelligence material and in the confidence they ascribe to those judgments, for their conclusions may well have serious, even fatal, consequences for those individuals against whom action is subsequently taken. Excessive reluctance to collect or to analyze intelligence also has consequences for society at large if it were to result in terrorist attacks or other threats not being detected. As John Stuart Mill warned, "A person may cause evil to others not only by his actions but by his inaction, and in either case he is justly accountable to them for the injury."[4] Actions will always have consequences, sometimes unintended, but so does the failure to act. This point also reminds us that intelligence managers have ethical obligations to tell truth to power and not withhold or adapt intelligence that might be considered unwelcome because it does not support a preferred policy direction.

We have explored the way that ethical issues permeate every aspect of intelligence work. For human intelligence, the methods of recruitment, the management of risks to agents and their families, and the dangers that can arise from collusive relationships with agents who operate inside criminal organizations—all can pose acute ethical challenges. The use of digital means to gain access to personal communications and to gather information about individuals and their use of the Internet also involve managing tricky ethical issues around intrusions into privacy.

Some of these core issues over the morality of spying are as ancient as history itself. However, it is important to recognize that the digital revolution has had a transformative impact and greatly expanded the scale of what intelligence activity is affordable even for relatively poor nations and for non-state actors, thereby giving a new twist to some of these old problems. We have to be aware, for example, of the consequences for society of applying cheap computing and artificial intelligence to the widespread collection of personal data by the private sector that is justified for commercial purposes but generates results that can be of great value to intelligence and law enforcement.

It is becoming increasingly easy to harness virtually unlimited cloud computing power and the latest algorithms using artificial intelligence and deep learning methods to create personal profiles of individuals from their online purchases, their Web-browsing activity, their location, and their travel. From those profiles it is possible to infer educational levels and social activity, personal preferences, likes and dislikes, ambitions in life, and much more. Already such profiles can be bought and used for marketing purposes and targeted advertising. The Trump administration has signaled that it is prepared to lift the Federal Communications Commission's restrictions that the Obama administration imposed on Internet providers that gather and sell the Web use profiles of their customers.[5]

Intelligence agencies undoubtedly will find ways of exploiting such techniques to help meet their requirements for information about individuals deemed potential threats. One example might be identifying for investigation those who are deemed likely to be susceptible to violent jihadist influence and so are considered to be at risk of being drawn into threatening behavior. The ethical issue will then be whether that is a step too far toward unacceptable profiling, especially if the same techniques are then used to try to nudge the individuals into more socially acceptable ways of looking at events by directing carefully chosen counterpropaganda into their online world.

In this book we argue that governments would be well advised to get ahead of such developments and promote an informed, open, democratic debate with the public not only about how far it is necessary to allow the use of personalized profiles by the intelligence and law enforcement agencies but also about how best to apply ethical principles and embed them in legal regulations governing the authorities' use of such techniques. The larger question for society is how far liberal democracies should seek to regulate the profit-seeking activities of the global Internet companies whose economic viability depends on monetizing the underlying information (the global annual online advertising market is estimated at $83 billion[6]), but that question goes way beyond intelligence and security considerations.

It can no longer be considered science fiction to envisage in the near future machines that are capable of knowing us better than we know ourselves (in the sense of their being able instantly to recall and make inferences from all the digital data we have ever provided in the course of our lives during the twenty-first century). It is no longer fanciful to imagine computer-assisted purchases of vacations or computer-assisted decisions over such lifestyle choices as where to live, what car to drive, or what partner to seek. We should no doubt expect to feel very comfortable with the results since such decisions will rest on soundly based inferences about our preferences and tastes—some of which we may be only dimly aware of or indeed they may lie in our subconscious hopes, desires, and fears.

We may come to see that use of personalized data as the next empowering step in human evolution, one that will allow us to harness the ability of intelligent machines to overcome our human limitations. Alternatively, we may come to fear such developments as the beginning of the end of human autonomy, or the free will that makes us truly human. Based on the historical experience of the last century or more, we can be confident that the inventive minds of national security intelligence communities will seek ways of harnessing such technological advances to achieve their missions, as they have done with every innovation from the discovery of radio waves to that of quantum electrodynamics. Waiting until after the technology is covertly deployed and used (as we can reasonably expect to be the case in a number of authoritarian states) before having our own public debate about how such activity can best be regulated in the public interest risks a rerun of the 2013 crisis of confidence over state surveillance after the Snowden material was published.

A different example that illustrates the need to think ahead about ethical issues can be seen in the coming of small, cheap automated drones carrying high-resolution cameras connected to software in the cloud that is capable of advanced facial recognition, thus identifying suspects even from fleeting glimpses. The security application to spotting known terrorists or criminal suspects in the vicinity of crowded national, sporting, or social events is obvious. But, again, the approach to ethics we have set out in this book would point to the importance of securing prior public confidence, based on democratic debate and legislation, that these systems cannot be abused for state snooping on the general population (or on political opponents) and that any deployment will be regulated with adequate oversight arrangements in place to satisfy the ethical criteria we outlined of right authority, necessity, and proportionality.

A different set of ethical issues for the future surrounds the increasing ability to use cyberspace to mount intelligence-gathering operations, to plant destructive malware, or to corrupt data. As we argued in chapter 5, and as demonstrated by the British experience, it should be possible for liberal democracies to regulate their own use of such techniques in accordance with sound ethical and legal principles (recognizing that the debate is likely to be a vigorous one). But against adversaries who show no such transparency or restraint, as demonstrated in their use of more traditional forms of sabotage or terrorism, active defensive measures will likely have to be deployed against aggressive cyber attacks. In such cases sound intelligence attribution of responsibility will be essential to the ethical and legal justification for armed responses (or their cyber equivalents) in self-defense.

Cyberspace is also becoming a vehicle for both intense open propaganda and covert information operations by states, notably Russia. Based on today's trends, we can expect intensified covert attempts to manipulate social media to propagate *fake news* (which we define as information known to be false when sent and designed to divert and distract attention, or as a form of intelligence deception) or to sow confusion and dissent to the advantage of the originator. The US intelligence community, for example, has accused Moscow of an influence campaign using a messaging strategy that blends covert intelligence operations—such as cyber activity—with overt efforts by government agencies, state-funded media, third-party intermediaries, and social media "trolls." The United States sees Russia, like the former Soviet Union, as having a history of conducting covert influence campaigns focused on US presidential elections and of using intelligence officers, agents, and press placements to disparage candidates seen as hostile to the Kremlin. The assessment of the US national intelligence community is unequivocal:

We assesses with high confidence that Russian President Vladimir Putin ordered an influence campaign in 2016 aimed at the US presidential election, the consistent goals of which were to undermine public faith in the US democratic process, denigrate Secretary [Hillary] Clinton, and harm her electability and potential presidency. We further assess Putin and the Russian Government developed a clear preference for President-elect Donald Trump. When it appeared to Moscow that Secretary Clinton was likely to win the election, the Russian influence campaign then focused on undermining her expected presidency.[7]

That will undoubtedly not be the last such active information operation from Russia or other states. An obvious new intelligence priority for Western nations thus must be to identify overseas actors that are covertly exploiting cyberspace to mount hostile information operations. Analysts must be trained to be aware of the likelihood of deception operations, including those aimed at encouraging misattribution of hostile cyber activity. In addition, democratic governments will need to organize their own information effort to rebut untrue material. More work may be needed with the Internet companies to get their technical help in identifying illegal material and taking it down quickly while still consistently respecting freedom of speech.

These ethically charged digital information issues are only some of what governments will have to face in the years to come. In tackling them governments will have to decide how far to allow (and encourage in future) the differing worlds of national security and law enforcement to join forces in confronting threats such as cyber crime and terrorism. When the postwar West German constitution was being drawn up, the fear of any future re-creation of a secret police led to legal barriers being placed between the domains of overseas intelligence, security, and policing, both national and regional. The US Congress set legal boundaries around the FBI as a law enforcement agency and stipulated that the CIA should not operate inside the United States. The UK Parliament, when it first legislated in 1989 to provide a statutory basis for the operation of the Security Service, did not give it powers of arrest, as the members no doubt were similarly wary of the taint of a secret police. But Parliament did state that one of the three statutory purposes of secret intelligence activity should be the detection and prevention of serious crime (along with national security and the economic well-being of the nation from threats overseas). There has therefore been no legal bar in the United Kingdom to the development of close relationships and full information exchanges on investigations between the worlds of law enforcement and intelligence, not least to gather and prepare admissible evidence for trial. Joint counterterrorism and cyber crime investigations have become the UK norm in the twenty-first century.

Such a close intelligence-police relationship has great advantages in managing ethical issues that arise when dealing with cyber crime, where tension is likely between the action to disrupt attacks and protect the public (including children from child abuse) and the due process of bringing suspects before the courts, especially when the suspects concerned are hiding in jurisdictions that do not care to, or cannot, enforce the law. Disruptive actions in the interests of the public's safety may well carry ethical risks but would normally be expected to take priority over the important but abstract value of upholding the law through prosecution. As we discussed in chapter 6, in the same way, decisions will have to be made as to whether to allow an investigation into a terrorist group to continue in the hope of identifying all its members and of gathering leads to instigators overseas, or to act quickly in the interests of public safety even at the expense of not having the evidence on which a prosecution can be mounted.

Most countries have traditionally organized separate services to gather intelligence externally from those managing internal security. That domestic-external distinction can be traced to the inevitable political sensitivity governments feel toward electors at home, as against populations abroad, and thus the need for additional controls over domestic surveillance than for foreign intelligence collection. A few nations, including the United States and the United Kingdom but not France or Germany, have placed national responsibilities for cyber security alongside national digital intelligence gathering on the well-understood application of the adage that "former poachers make the best gamekeepers."

At first sight, however, domestic security activity involves violating Kant's categorical imperative: "Act only according to that maxim whereby you can, at the same time, will that it should become a universal law."[8] We might advance one practical justification for having stricter rules domestically than might apply to those overseas: within the jurisdiction it is reasonable to expect the police or intelligence agency to be able to specify the names of the suspects, or the premises where they may be found, and thus to apply some system of warranting with a high degree of discrimination that would not be reasonable to expect for targets overseas (for example, to discover the capabilities of the Russian air force in Syria or to know the names or exact locations of terrorists operating there). This practical line of argument, long recognized by the courts, is that states can reasonably be expected to exercise a duty of care, such as the important task of protecting privacy rights, only for those within their own jurisdictions or areas of control.

Nevertheless, as we have argued, in accordance with the circumstances of each case the ethical principles of necessity and proportionality should still apply to intelligence activity overseas, including the search for human sources. In garnering digital intelligence overseas, even if accessed in bulk, discrimination must still be applied to what is retained and accessed by analysts. Certainly when the mission is to keep the public safe, there is unlikely in many cases to be any clear boundary between investigating suspect domestic and suspect overseas activity. This reflects the rise of the intermestic as a key location of potential security risks that intelligence must navigate. One consequence of this dynamic environment is that intelligence and security agencies with traditionally separate spheres of activity must learn to work together as an intelligence community on joint investigations and to share information if potential threats such as cyber attacks and terrorism are to be managed.

Organizational issues for national intelligence communities also arise from the expansion of traditional secret sources into the digital world and the plethora of open sources available through the Internet. The ethical risks of intelligence gathering will be lessened if more organized use can be made of sources of information that can be accessed lawfully and straightforwardly with the appropriate legal authorization or that are openly available, especially nowadays using the power of advanced Internet search engines. Those sources that involve the theft of secrets, or equivalently deceitful measures such as planting malware on suspects' devices, are bound to be ethically more problematic. Chapter 4 explored the ethics involved in using human intelligence methods to obtain a secret against the wishes of its holder, including by persuading someone close to the secret to betray the holder's trust and act as an agent. Such sources bring valuable insights into the thinking of targets and will not be rendered redundant by digital technology. We must also expect technical operations will increasingly be facilitated by agents tasked with planting bugging devices or providing access to networks, and in such cases the ethical issues will relate to the management of human sources as well as the privacy issues associated with technical access.

In addition to human and technical sources of secret intelligence, there is already a large body of personal digitized information legitimately held by governments and private companies. These data sets are rapidly growing in number. Although statutory privacy rights apply, these databases can be lawfully accessed in many circumstances for a variety of purposes, ranging from checking that taxes have been paid to verifying that an airline passenger has not previously been identified as a potential terrorist and placed on a watch list. Among the mass of such data (either as directly observed data points or as capable of being inferred from them) will be specific personal information that an individual wishes to keep private. An individual may also not want personal information to be retained in digital form. In most cases those preferences should be respected, and data protection legislation is there in the commercial world to enable their enforcement. But there may well be circumstances where after public debate, society deems it right through clearly drafted legislation to override privacy in the wider interest—for example, by having Internet service providers retain Internet connection records for a reasonable time.

We have identified the need to manage the ethical risk to third parties in the course of legitimate intelligence operations. Some collateral intrusion is inevitable even in targeted interception intelligence operations; therefore, the right to respect for one's family and private life in ECHR Article 8 is, in the words of the former British lord chief justice Lord Bingham, "being qualified by what may be called a community exception—a recognition that the rights of the individual may properly be restricted in the interests of the community at large, if certain fairly demanding conditions are met."[9] From the start, the authorities must then accept that since some collateral intrusion is inevitable, the privacy rights of all those innocent parties potentially within reach of the intelligence operation are engaged *from the outset* and must be respected even in the planning and authorization of the operation.

A substantive ethical issue that then arises is to what extent it is acceptable to retain Internet-accessed data in bulk to enable a subsequent search for information of legitimate intelligence interest given that inevitably suspect communications are mixed with those of the public at large. If the methods of selection are insufficiently discriminating and if there is no reasonable likelihood of a proportionate gain from such searches, then the result would be open to the accusation of having conducted mass surveillance, which is a characteristic practice of totalitarian regimes. That risk perception itself may in turn chill normal behavior for fear of privacy intrusion and represent an attack on the fundamental liberal value of freedom of speech if sentiments cannot be expressed for fear of being overheard.[10] Of course, recognizing that such a danger exists in principle is one thing; identifying the point at which ethical limits are anywhere near to being approached in practice is another and constitutes an ongoing ethical and legal dilemma.

A balance also has to be reached that is appropriate to the circumstances of each nation between its military and civilian intelligence activity. Intelligence is an accepted military staff function, and most armed forces have specialist units dedicated to collecting and interpreting tactical intelligence. There are peacetime constraints: international law recognizes territorial waters (of at least three miles) into which intelligence-gathering ships and aircraft should not penetrate; international humanitarian law lays down conditions, such as the wearing of uniforms and the treatment of spies found in civilian clothes; and other international law governs innocent passage for warships on the high seas and not using hospital ships for intelligence gathering (and consequent restrictions on the use of encrypted communications from vessels flying the red cross or red crescent).

Intelligence gathering for force protection has become an integral part of operations, including today's use of satellites and reconnaissance drones. Well-trained and well-led military forces will exhibit an institutional concern for responsibility, legality, proportionality, and distinction in their use of their weapons systems. They will also exercise other important military virtues such as prudence, circumspection, and judgment, not least with regard to minimizing civilian casualties. It is obviously important that this ethos should be conscientiously and self-critically maintained when acting on intelligence tip-offs in war zones such as using the geo-location of an insurgent leader and striking by drone or a Special Forces or other military raid (as we discussed in chapter 6). Military intelligence capabilities can be enhanced by those of national civilian agencies (as was done to support NATO operations in Afghanistan).

There is an inevitable tension in intelligence activity between secrecy and transparency. As we saw in chapter 3, with privacy given a greater weight than in past eras, the use of the cloak of traditional secrecy associated with intelligence work was bound to conflict with the rise of the ideology of universal human rights and the modern requirements of the rule of law under which the citizen should be able to discover under what circumstances the law would allow intelligence agencies and law enforcement to conduct investigations that intrude on personal privacy. A tension must be navigated between maintaining the effectiveness of intelligence activity through secrecy and obtaining informed public consent to intelligence capability through transparency in regulating the different methods of intrusive surveillance. Nevertheless, most will recognize the type of source or method being used to provide intelligence on a specific target must remain secret. If the possessor of the secret knows the sources and methods of the signals, human, imagery, or other intelligence techniques being used to try and obtain the secret, then resistance becomes easier. But that simple observation remains, of course, the justification for having such organizations as secret intelligence agencies in the first place. Not only do the secrets that have been acquired, if possible, have to be kept secret but also, if they are to be most effective, so do the human and technical methods by which they were obtained.

In the first instance, the responsibility to manage these ethical tensions is national since, as we have seen, matters of national security are at the heart of the responsibilities of the contemporary nation-state. We conclude by considering how far an international perspective can be taken.

We have debated in this book what can distinguish the legitimate use of an intelligence method in the hands of some governments from the illegitimate use of exactly the same method in the hands of others. Kant's categorical imperative can be interpreted here as meaning that we should not be quick to condemn activity on the part of others and view their motives as ignoble while condoning the same activities on the part of our own governments for what we consider noble motives. But that observation should not lead us to a state of moral relativism and hopelessness about international anarchy over intelligence activity. We believe that the norms suggested in this book can be promoted internationally to encourage responsible conduct in the realm of secret intelligence and its use.

We have recognized a historical process that has led from the unconstrained use of sovereign power, *pour raison d'état*, to the gradual development of control by elected governments over the secret activities of the state. We have identified in particular the model, still prevalent in many nations, of the hidden guardians licensed by the government to operate in secret regardless of legal niceties to protect the state from external threats and internal subversion, and we have suggested that the model is no longer compatible with contemporary liberal democratic practice.[11]

The social compact model of security and intelligence activity has thus emerged from a long historical journey from the exercise of prerogative powers to a democratic statutory license being given to the secret servants of the state. The journey has been one of gradual acceptance of the need for democratic control of secret activity, recognizing the full implications of the rule of law and the importance of human rights being respected even in the secret world. The journey has also involved years of persistent investigative journalism, consequent reaction to scandal, and loss of public deference to authority, as well as growing acknowledgment of the salience of intelligence work in protecting the public from potential threats such as terrorism and crime.

We identified in particular in chapter 5 how the very rapid growth in the use of digital techniques such as accessing communications data in bulk, interfering with electronic devices and servers, and mining bulk personal databases in search of intelligence about suspects, although legitimized by (sometimes obscure) statutory provisions, had overtaken the public's understanding of what was happening. As a result, such practices rested on a dubious legitimacy that led to the creation of a significant trust gap. It follows that, as we discussed in chapter 2, the law must be arrived at by legislatures after open debate that exposes and explores not only the purposes of the powers being given statutory authority but also how they will operate in practice, the outcomes that may result, and the safeguards that will apply to protect the public from unintended consequences. In the case of the United States, the Obama administration brought the relevant NSA collection programs more clearly under the purview of the FISA Court and published his directive that governs how digital intelligence is collected by the NSA. For the United Kingdom, the controversy has resulted in a completely new act of Parliament, extensively examined and debated, that regulates all forms of intrusive digital intelligence gathering and added the safeguards of judicial review and oversight.

Such an outcome would not have happened for many years without the spur of public debate following media disclosures. The most significant ethical lesson to be learned from recent experience is that the unparalleled transparency we have seen concerning the lawful use of intrusive powers will have to be maintained as both threats and intelligence methods continue to evolve so that a new trust gap does not open up. This democratic license to operate represents a milestone in the development of liberal intelligence and, in keeping with this, should be renewed regularly.

Nations also must be encouraged to conduct their gathering and use of intelligence ethically in the context of a global struggle over the governance of the Internet itself.[12] Measures are needed that reinforce the nature of the Internet as a secure, open, and safe medium; that are technically sound; and that make business sense, as well as encouraging the "permissionless innovation" that is the hallmark of the Internet.[13] Multi-stakeholder Internet governance must continue to engage governments, the Internet companies, the tech community, and civil society in that objective. A promising approach is to encourage the development from the ethical principles we have identified of norms of responsible conduct in cyberspace for liberal democratic states (accepting that although not all states will initially comply, the reputational cost of bad behavior will increase over time):

- Insist on the application of international humanitarian law to reduce harm from offensive intelligence and military activity in cyberspace just as it should do in the everyday physical world.
- Uphold the rule of law so that where accessing data is legally warranted, companies cooperate to provide data when it is practicable or technically feasible to do so and when doing so does not unreasonably risk harms to others by endangering the security of their data.[14]
- Press governments to promote the integrity of the Internet itself, for example, by not weakening or compromising encryption or other standards on which the Internet depends so that its core infrastructure remains stable and secure and so that we do not see mandatory data localization and the fragmentation of the Internet into national blocks.
- Maintain the open nature of the Internet, where data flows are based on efficient routing principles and protocols and on clear, publicly arrived-at standards; where the development of the Internet of Things includes security and thus does not introduce new sources of harm to the citizen; and where—unlike in closed, proprietary systems—the integrity of the system can be demonstrated.
- Build cyber security partnerships between the government agencies, the private sector operators of critical national infrastructure, and the tech community; and encourage their development of new trust architectures, such as may come from blockchain innovation, and common standards of data protection across borders to build confidence in data hosting and processing where most efficient.
- Insist that freedom of speech be upheld in the digital world as in the real world and that any restrictions on Internet content are only for the purposes of public safety and security and as provided by law.

Applying such ideas to the development of ethical solutions not just nationally but internationally will build effective international information and evidence arrangements to tackle current issues of terrorism, organized global criminality, and cyber security.

Ultimately, the distinguishing characteristics of liberal intelligence will be the adherence to a legal framework that is regularly reviewed, giving rise to high levels of confidence that ethical considerations are being applied, and that is underpinned by robust oversight arrangements, and the role of an inquiring free press to provide reassurance and ensure any slippage is identified and addressed rather than swept under the carpet. We welcome the recent development in an increasing number of democratic nations to an open commitment to conducting secret intelligence activity under the rule of law and supported by an increasingly global culture of intelligence oversight. If followed through, it has the potential to lead to a new era in the democratic control of secret intelligence activity. We strongly encourage those countries whose intelligence activities still are regarded as part of the deep state, and not for open discussion, to follow suit.

NOTES

Preface

1. Omand and Phythian, "Ethics and Intelligence."
2. Loch K. Johnson, ed., "An *INS* Special Forum: Implications of the Snowden Leaks," *Intelligence and National Security* 29, no. 6 (2014): 793–810.
3. Data taken from each journal's website, May 9, 2017.
4. Bingham, *Rule of Law*, viii.
5. See website for the Centre for International Governance Innovation, https://www.cigionline.org/activity/global-commission-internet-governance; and Independent Surveillance Review, *Democratic Licence to Operate*.

Introduction

1. See, for example, Perry, *Partly Cloudy*.
2. A definition from the *Collins English Dictionary*, http://www.collinsdictionary.com/dictionary/english/ethics, accessed July 26, 2016.
3. Editorial, "The Guardian View on Trump and Russia: Playing Putin's Game—Again," *The Guardian*, January 8, 2017.
4. Hennessy, *New Protective State*.
5. As explained in chapter 1, these schools of thought involve respectively judging the rightness of an action by its consequences, by whether it matches up to religious or other ethical codes, or by whether it represents conduct worthy of a well-lived human life.
6. BBC News, "Spy Law 'Used in Dog Fouling War,'" April 27, 2008, http://news.bbc.co.uk/1/hi/uk/7369543.stm.
7. Well-known examples include Philip Zimbardo's Stanford prison experiment and Stanley Milgram's obedience to authority experiment (supposedly) using the application of electric shocks. For an outline explanation of each, see Saul McLeod, "Stanford Prison Experiment," Simply Psychology, 2008, http://www.simplypsychology.org/zimbardo.html; and Saul McLeod, "The Milgram Experiment," 2007, http://www.simplypsychology.org/milgram.html.

1. Thinking about the Ethical Conduct of Secret Intelligence

1. Quoted in Lathrop, *Literary Spy*, 207.
2. Herman, "Ethics and Intelligence," 342.
3. Gill and Phythian, *Intelligence in an Insecure World*, 19. See also the definitional discussion at 17–20.
4. Realist thinkers explain international relations in terms of power politics, with the nation-state as the principal international actor. Neorealists (also termed structural realists) see the imperative to acquire power as arising out of the structure of the international system, which is understood to be competitive and a "self-help" system. See, for example, the explanation in Mearsheimer, *Tragedy of Great Power Politics*, chaps. 1 and 2. A classic account of revisionist states in the international system is E. H. Carr's *The Twenty Years' Crisis, 1919–1939: An Introduction to the Study of International Relations* (London: Macmillan, 1939).
5. Mearsheimer, *Tragedy of Great Power Politics*, 33.
6. Lathrop, *Literary Spy*, 245.
7. See, for example, Robert M. Gates, *From the Shadows: The Ultimate Insider's Story of Five Presidents and How They Won the Cold War* (New York: Simon & Schuster, 1997); Tenet, *At the Center*; Rodriguez, *Hard Measures*; and Panetta, *Worthy Fights*.
8. John Lewis Gaddis, *Surprise, Security, and the American Experience* (Cambridge, MA: Harvard University Press, 2004), chap. 4; and Cogan, "Hunters Not Gatherers," 304–21.
9. Turner, *Secrecy and Democracy*, 178.
10. See United States Senate, *Final Report*; Loch K. Johnson, *A Season of Inquiry: The Senate Intelligence Investigation* (Lexington: University Press of Kentucky, 1985); and Turner, *Secrecy and Democracy*, 178.
11. Turner, *Secrecy and Democracy*, 178.
12. Ibid.
13. This forms part of Leffler's definition of national security. See Melvyn P. Leffler, "National Security," in *Explaining the History of American Foreign Relations*, 2nd ed., ed. Michael J. Hogan and Thomas G. Paterson (New York: Cambridge University Press, 2004), 123. Andrew Preston traces the rise of the ideology of national security back to the 1930s and the administration of Franklin Delano Roosevelt in "Monsters Everywhere: A Genealogy of National Security," *Diplomatic History* 38, no. 3 (2014): 477–500.
14. David E. Hoffman, *The Billion Dollar Spy: A True Story of Cold War Espionage and Betrayal* (New York: Doubleday, 2015), 6.
15. United States Senate, *Final Report*, 9.
16. Moyn, *Last Utopia*, 13. He locates the origins of this shift to the mid-1970s.
17. See Rosenau, *Along the Domestic-Foreign Frontier*, 4. Victor D. Cha, in "Globalization and the Study of International Security," *Journal of Peace Research* 37, no. 3 (2000): 391–403, provides a useful discussion of the impact of globalization on thinking about security.

18. On Elizabethan-era state security measures, see Stephen Alford, *The Watchers: A Secret History of the Reign of Elizabeth I* (London: Allen Lane, 2012). In reviewing this book, Keith Thomas pointed to the parallels between the threat faced by the Elizabethan state and the nature of its responses to it and those of the post-9/11 terrorist threat: "It is tempting to regard William Allen as a 16th-century Osama Bin Laden, and the English College at Rome as the equivalent of a terrorist training-camp in Pakistan. Young Catholic priests, blessed by the Pope, and knowingly heading for a terrible death, were the suicide bombers of their time, even though their only weapons were spiritual ones. Walsingham's counter-terrorists resemble their modern counterparts in their eagerness to bypass normal legal process by using torture. Unlike some of their successors, they seem to have drawn the line at targeted assassination, but if the Elizabethans had had telephones they would undoubtedly have tapped them." Keith Thomas, "Uneasy Lies the Head," *The Guardian*, August 18, 2012, https://www.theguardian.com/books/2012/aug/17/watchers-elizabeth-stephen-alford-review.

19. Max Weber, "The Profession and Vocation of Politics," in *Weber: Political Writings*, ed. Peter Lassman and Ronald Speirs (Cambridge: Cambridge University Press, 1994), 309–69.

20. John Hoffman, *Beyond the State: An Introductory Critique* (Cambridge: Polity Press, 1995), 5. Emphasis in original.

21. John Hoffman suggests that we "imagine a state which successfully monopolizes all legitimacy within a given territory. Under these circumstances none of its subjects have cause to dissent from the moral justifications the state invokes in passing laws. No dissent, no subversion, no law-breaking, no criminals. As a result there would be no need for force. Government . . . would exist but the state disappears." Ibid., 65.

22. Rodney Barker, *Political Legitimacy and the State* (Oxford: Clarendon Press, 1990), 114.

23. Ibid.

24. Hoffman, *Beyond the State*, 100. In this, he is following David Easton, "Walter Bagehot and Liberal Realism," *American Political Science Review* 43, no. 1 (1949): 17–37.

25. Andrew Levine, *The End of the State* (London: Verso, 1987), 36.

26. Alford, *Watchers*; and Robert Hutchinson, *Elizabeth's Spy Master: Francis Walsingham and the Secret War that Saved England* (London: Weidenfeld & Nicolson, 2006).

27. Hare, *Moral Thinking*, provides a useful framework for thinking about these issues.

28. Here an *overseas-related communication* is defined as one sent or received by an individual outside the British Islands.

29. See the discussion in Bingham, *Rule of Law*, 110–29.

30. Philip Cunliffe, ed., *Critical Perspectives on the Responsibility to Protect: Interrogating Theory and Practice* (Abingdon: Routledge, 2012).

31. The European General Data Protection Regulation of 2016 guidance can be found at European Commission, "Reform of EU Data Protection Rules," http://ec.europa.eu/justice/data-protection/reform/index_en.htm.

32. Regarding controversy, see the 2016 judgment of the European Court of Justice on the retention of bulk data under the constraints of the European charter of rights, in Court of Justice of the European Union, Press Release no. 145/16, Luxembourg, December 21, 2016, http://curia.europa.eu/jcms/upload/docs/application/pdf/2016-12/cp160145en.pdf. See the approach taken by the US National Academy of Sciences in the report from its National Research Council, *Bulk Collection of Signals Intelligence: Technical Options* (Washington, DC: National Academies Press, 2015); and Anderson, *Bulk Powers Review*, 3.

33. Omand, *Securing the State*.

34. The quoted phrase is used in the Notes on Clauses of the Investigatory Powers Bill published in Theresa May, *Draft Investigatory Powers Bill: Guide to Powers and Safeguards* (London: Williams Lea Group for Her Majesty's Stationery Office, November 2015), 27, https://www.gov.uk/government/uploads/system/uploads/attachment_data/file/473770/Draft_Investigatory_Powers_Bill.pdf.

35. See Omand, Bartlett, and Miller, "Introducing Social Media Intelligence," 801–23.

36. See Jeffreys-Jones, *We Know All about You*.

37. Liberty, "Article 8 Right to a Private and Family Life," https://www.liberty-human-rights.org.uk/human-rights/what-are-human-rights/human-rights-act/article-8-right-private-and-family-life, accessed November 10, 2015.

38. Bellaby, *Ethics of Intelligence*, esp. chap. 2.

39. Set at the level of a police superintendent in the United Kingdom by order under the Regulation of Investigatory Powers Act 2000.

40. The order is known as a terrorism prevention and investigation measure (TPIM).

41. Security Service MI5, "What We Do," https://www.mi5.gov.uk/what-we-do, accessed August 10, 2017.

42. The French operations are powerfully depicted in Gillo Pontecorvo's fictional film *The Battle of Algiers* (1966), and the British operations are described in General Sir Frank Kitson, *Bunch of Five* (London: Faber and Faber, 1977).

43. John Finnis, "Judicial Power: Past, Present and Future," Policy Exchange lecture, London, October 21, 2015, http://judicialpowerproject.org.uk/john-finnis-judicial-power-past-present-and-future/.

44. Henry Porter, "Don't Be Fooled by Spook Propaganda: The State Still Wants More Licence to Pry," *The Guardian*, October 31, 2015, https://www.theguardian.com/commentisfree/2015/oct/31/investigatory-powers-bill-henry-porter.

45. Max Weber, *Politik als Beruf* (Berlin: Duncker & Humblot, 1964).

46. As identified by Michael Freeden in *Liberalism*, 15.

47. Ibid., 12–13, 37–54.

48. As described by Anderson, *Question of Trust*, app. 9, case study 6. Available at https://terrorismlegislationreviewer.independent.gov.uk/wp-content/uploads/2015/06/IPR-Report-Print-Version.pdf.

49. See Duncan Bell, "What Is Liberalism?," *Political Theory* 42, no. 6 (2014): 682–715.

50. Pekel, "Integrity, Ethics and the CIA," 85–94.

51. Ibid., 87.

52. Ibid., 88.

53. Ibid.

54. Ibid.

55. Indeed, watch out for those who don't! From an organizational perspective, this is often an early indication of trouble to come.

56. For a discussion of "thin" and "thick" ethical approaches, see, for example, Mervyn Frost, *Global Ethics: Anarchy, Freedom and International Relations* (Abingdon: Routledge, 2009), chap. 1; and Michael Walzer, *Thick and Thin: Moral Argument at Home and Abroad* (Notre Dame, IN: University of Notre Dame Press, 1994).

57. Saunders, *Who Paid the Piper?*, 5.

58. Dujmovic, "Hearts and Minds," 180.

59. Peter Finn and Petra Couvée, *The Zhivago Affair: The Kremlin, the CIA, and the Battle over a Forbidden Book* (London: Harvill Secker, 2014), 264.

60. Sidney Webb and Beatrice Webb, *Soviet Communism: A New Civilization?* (New York: Scribner's, 1935). The second and third editions of 1938 and 1941, respectively, dropped the question mark from the title.

61. It is worth bearing in mind that even the assassins of former Russian intelligence officer and dissident Alexander Litvinenko believed their own legitimating narrative. One of them told an acquaintance in Germany that he was traveling to London to kill Litvinenko, explaining that "Litvinenko is a traitor! There is blood on his hands! He does deals with Chechnya!" Cited in Luke Harding, *A Very Expensive Poison: The Definitive Story of the Murder of Litvinenko and Russia's War with the West* (London: Guardian Books / Faber and Faber, 2016), 114.

62. Writing in 1999 the historian Bernard Porter made a similar point, commenting on how "until recently, MI5 and MI6 had no official existence. Questions about them in Parliament were ignored; writing to them was like sending messages to Father Christmas; they operated from invisible headquarters; shoddy office blocks in London, blanks on the Ordnance Survey map. The contrast here with Russia is obvious. Everyone there was aware of the KGB, its headquarters were a landmark in Moscow, people shuddered as they hurried by. Millions must have passed MI5's old registry in Curzon Street without a tremor. We just did not know it was there." Bernard Porter, "Boarder or Day Boy?," review of *The Culture of Secrecy in Britain, 1832–1998*, by David Vincent, *London Review of Books* 21, no. 14 (July 15, 1999): 13–15, https://www.lrb.co.uk/v21/n14/bernard-porter/boarder-or-day-boy.

63. Sir Anthony May, *Annual Report of the Interception of Communications Commissioner*, HC 1184 (London: House of Commons, April 8, 2014), para. 6.6.20.

64. Garton Ash, *File*, 205. Emphasis in original.

65. Ibid., 207, 149.

66. Ibid., 208.

67. As summarized in Sisman, *John le Carré*, 543. In an interview for BBC television at around this time, Cornwell said that spying "felt like betrayal, but it had a voluptuous quality: this was a necessary sacrifice of morality and that is a very important component of what makes people spy, what attracts them." Ibid.

68. See Tony Diver, "Historian Investigates Cold War Oxford Spy Ring," Cherwell, September 27, 2016, http://www.cherwell.org/2016/09/27/oxford-spy-ring/.

69. Garton Ash, *File*, 209.

70. Ibid., 220.

71. Ibid.

2. Ethics, Intelligence, and the Law

1. When the king first saw her in the flesh, he claimed he had been duped by the pretended likeness painted at Cromwell's request (by the court painter Hans Holbein).

2. George Washington's innovative use of espionage is duly celebrated at the museum at his home, Mount Vernon. See Mount Vernon Ladies' Association, "Spying and Espionage: George Washington, Spymaster," http://www.mountvernon.org/george -washington/the-revolutionary-war/spying-and-espionage/george-washington -spymaster/, August 10, 2017.

3. Walter Bagehot, *The English Constitution* (1867; Oxford: Oxford University Press, 2009), chap. 1.

4. "If you knew what I know" was a favorite saying of the now discredited MI5 officer Peter Wright, who was obsessed with his theory that the then director general of MI5 was himself a Soviet spy. Cited in Andrew, *Defence of the Realm*, 520. For the postwar threat, see Andrew and Mitrokhin, *Mitrokhin Archive*.

5. The Maxwell Fyfe Directive of 1952 also required that the (undefined) powers of MI5 were to be "strictly limited to what is necessary for the purpose of their task."

6. In the Commander Crabb scandal, an unauthorized attempt was made to examine covertly the hull of the latest Soviet cruiser, which had brought the Soviet leaders Nikita Khrushchev and Nikolai Bulganin on their first visit to the United Kingdom in 1956, and resulted in the death of the diver, Cdr. Lionel Crabb. It cast a long shadow over the summit meeting.

7. John Helgerson, *Getting to Know the President: Intelligence Briefings of Presidential Candidates, 1952–2004*, 2nd ed. (Washington, DC: US Government Printing Office, 2012), https://www.cia.gov/library/center-for-the-study-of-intelligence /csi-publications/books-and-monographs/getting-to-know-the-president/index .html.

8. From a report by Sir Findlater Stewart, chairman of the Security Executive, dated November 27, 1945, and cited in Andrew, *Defence of the Realm*, 322.

9. Consultation Paper, "Interception of Communications in the United Kingdom," Cm4368 (London: Her Majesty's Stationery Office, June 1999), 11.

10. Chapman Pincher, "Cable Vetting Sensation," *Daily Express*, February 21, 1967, 1.

11. Council of Europe, "European Convention on Human Rights," Strasbourg, Article 8(2), http://www.echr.coe.int/Documents/Convention_ENG.pdf. Italics added.

12. Notably against the Metropolitan Police in the Malone case, Application no. 8691/79, Judgment of August 2, 1984.

13. See Harding, *Snowden Files*, chap. 4.

14. See the discussion in Bok, *Secrets*, esp. chaps. 12, 13.

15. National Archives (NA), Kew, KV2/3941/73A: Source report, August 1, 1950.

16. NA, Kew, KV2/3941/84: Minute by J. L. Vernon, B.1.A., December 10, 1951.

17. Simon Blackburn, *Ethics: A Very Short Introduction* (Oxford: Oxford University Press, 2001), 53.

18. Independent Surveillance Review, *Democratic Licence to Operate*, which the government (deputy prime minister) commissioned as part of the preparations for the Investigatory Powers Act 2016.

19. Finnis, "Judicial Power."

20. Roubiczek, *Ethical Values*.

21. NA, "Education: Victorian Britain, Activity 1," http://www.nationalarchives .gov.uk/education/victorianbritain/lawless/activity1_2.htm, accessed January 6, 2016.

22. Hansard, June 10, 2013, col. 32.

23. Hague is referring to the Data Retention and Investigatory Powers Act of 2014. In July 2015 the High Court issued an order that sections 1 and 2 of the act were unlawful and not to be applied. They were suspended until March 31, 2016, thereby giving the government a deadline to come up with alternative legislation (now in the Investigatory Powers Act 2016).

24. Jan Goldman, "Ethics Phobia and the US Intelligence Community: Just Say 'No,'" in *Intelligence Ethics: The Definitive Work of 2007*, ed. Michael Andregg (St. Paul, MN: Center for the Study of Intelligence and Wisdom, 2007), 16.

25. On this, see Bob Brecher, *Torture and the Ticking Bomb* (Malden, MA: Blackwell Publishing, 2007), chap. 3.

26. Gordon Rayner and Richard Alleyne, "Council Spy Cases Hit 1,000 a Month," *Daily Telegraph*, April 12, 2008; Steven Morris, "Council Used Terror Law to Spy on Fishermen," *The Guardian*, May 14, 2008; Nicholas Watt, "Councils Told to Stop Using Spy Laws for 'Trivial' Issues," *The Guardian*, June 23, 2008; and Press Association, "Council Spied on Family over School Place, Hearing Told," *The Guardian*, November 6, 2009.

27. Investigatory Powers Tribunal, Case Liberty/Privacy No. 2, Reported in [2015] 3 AER 212.

28. Anderson, *Question of Trust*, para. 35.

29. See Savage, *Power Wars*, on how utilizing "legally available" arguments helped make the legal case for actions in the war on terror and, in so doing, helped expand the scope of what was deemed permissible in international law.

30. We return to this point in chapter 7.

31. Such as the United Kingdom's release in 1964 of the Soviet spy Gordon Lonsdale in return for the Soviets' release of the British businessman Greville Wynne, who had helped MI6 communicate with its agent Oleg Penkovsky.

32. "Intelligence Services Act, 1994: Section 7," National Archives, http://www.legislation.gov.uk/ukpga/1994/13/section/7, August 17, 2017.

33. Graham Greene, *The Human Factor* (Harmondsworth: Penguin, 1978), 34.

34. Tenet, *At the Center*, 241.

35. David Margolis, "Memorandum for the Attorney General," US Department of Justice, Washington, DC, January 5, 2010, 67, http://graphics8.nytimes.com/packages/pdf/politics/20100220JUSTICE/20100220JUSTICE-DAGMargolisMemo.pdf; and Eric Lichtblau and Scott Shane, "Report Faults 2 Who Wrote Terror Memos," *New York Times*, February 19, 2010, http://query.nytimes.com/gst/fullpage.html?res=9E02E0DA1239F933A15751C0A9669D8B63&pagewanted=all.

36. Carol J. Williams, "Poland Feels Sting of Betrayal over CIA 'Black Site,'" *Los Angeles Times*, May 10, 2015, http://www.latimes.com/world/europe/la-fg-poland-cia-blacksite-20150510-story.html.

37. Intelligence and Security Committee, *Report on Rendition*, July 2007, available at http://isc.independent.gov.uk/committee-reports/special-reports.

38. Walzer, *Just and Unjust Wars*, chap. 16; and Michael Walzer, "Emergency Ethics: The Joseph A. Reich, Sr., Distinguished Lecture on War, Morality, and the Military Profession," US Air Force Academy, Colorado, November 21, 1988, https://archive.org/stream/walzer_emer_ethics/walzer_emer_ethics_djvu.txt.

39. Walzer, *Just and Unjust Wars*, 251. For a critique of Walzer's "supreme emergency" as a concept, see Michael Neu, "The Supreme Emergency of War: A Critique of Walzer," *Journal of International Political Theory* 10, no. 1 (2014): 3–19.

40. Bruce Hoffman, "Intelligence and Terrorism: Emerging Threats and New Security Challenges in the Post–Cold War Era," *Intelligence and National Security* 11, no. 2 (1996): 212.

41. Ibid.

42. Walzer, "Emergency Ethics," 11.

43. Richard Norman, *Ethics, Killing and War* (Cambridge: Cambridge University Press, 1995), 11.

44. A question discussed by Bernard Williams in "A Critique of Utilitarianism," in *Utilitarianism: For and Against*, ed. J. J. C. Smart and Bernard Williams (Cambridge: Cambridge University Press, 1973).

45. From Harvard Classics edition of John Stuart Mill, "Introductory," in *On Liberty* (New York: P. F. Collier & Son, 1909; Kindle ed., Adelaide: University of Adelaide, ebooks@Adelaide, 2014), chap. 1, https://ebooks.adelaide.edu.au/m/mill/john_stuart/m645o/chapter1.html.

46. Hayden, *Playing to the Edge*.

47. United States Senate Select Committee on Intelligence, *Committee Study*, Executive Summary.

48. Hayden, *Playing to the Edge*, 217.

49. Vice Chairman Dianne Feinstein, "Factual Errors and Other Problems in 'Playing to the Edge: American Intelligence in the Age of Terror,' by Michael V. Hayden," Staff Summary, March 2016, 4–5, http://fas.org/irp/congress/2016_cr/feinstein-hayden.pdf. Emphasis in original.
50. CIA Inspector General, "Special Review: Counterterrorism Detention and Interrogation Activities (September 2001–October 2003) (2003-7123-IG)," May 7, 2004, paras. 231–32, http://media.luxmedia.com/aclu/IG_Report.pdf.
51. Amy Davidson, "I Really Resent You Using the Word 'Torture'": Q & A with Jose Rodriguez," *New Yorker*, July 18, 2012, http://www.newyorker.com/news/amy-davidson/i-really-resent-you-using-the-word-torture-q-a-with-jose-rodriguez. See also Rodriguez, *Hard Measures*.
52. Ibid.
53. Hayden, *Playing to the Edge*, 217.
54. Ibid., xiv.
55. For example, Brecher, *Torture and the Ticking Bomb*.
56. See, for example, Tyler Hamilton and Daniel Coyle, *The Secret Race: Inside the Hidden World of the Tour de France: Doping, Cover-Ups, and Winning at All Costs* (London: Bantam Press, 2012); and Tom Cary, "Cycling Doping Report: Drug Taking Remains Widespread," *Daily Telegraph*, March 9, 2015, http://www.telegraph.co.uk/sport/othersports/cycling/11458133/Cycling-doping-report-Drug-taking-remains-widespread.html.

3. From Just War to Just Intelligence?

1. See, for example, Robin W. Lovin, *Reinhold Niebuhr and Christian Realism* (Cambridge: Cambridge University Press, 1995).
2. Walzer, "Triumph of Just War Theory."
3. Suárez, *De Legibus*, 2.19 (1610), cited in Corey and Charles, *Just War Tradition*, 137.
4. See the explanatory documentation of article 52 (2) of the International Committee of the Red Cross, "Protocol Additional to the Geneva Conventions of 12 August 1949, and Relating to the Protection of Victims of International Armed Conflicts (Protocol 1), 8 June 1977," https://ihl-databases.icrc.org/ihl/INTRO/470.
5. Reed and Ryall, in *Price of Peace*, provide a series of essays that reexamine Just War thinking in the context of the twenty-first century.
6. William H. Rehnquist, *All the Laws but One: Civil Liberties in Wartime* (New York: Vintage Books, 2000).
7. Michael Quinlan, "The Just War Tradition and the Use of Armed Force in the Twenty-First Century," annual lecture of the War Studies Department, King's College London, January 25, 2006.
8. As argued in Corey and Charles, *Just War Tradition*, chap. 7.
9. President Obama complained of Chinese commercial cyber espionage; see Tal Kopan, "White House Readies Cyber Sanctions against China ahead of State

Visit," CNN, September 24, 2015, http://edition.cnn.com/2015/08/31/politics /china-sanctions-cybersecurity-president-obama/. See also Buchanan, *Cybersecurity Dilemma*.

10. Available at Global Commission on Internet Governance, 30–37, https://www .cigionline.org/activity/global-commission-internet-governance, accessed January 2016. See also Group of Governmental Experts, "Developments in the Field of Information and Telecommunications in the Context of International Security," UN General Assembly, July 22, 2015, http://www.un.org/ga/search/view _doc.asp?symbol=A/70/174.

11. Council of Europe, "European Convention on Human Rights," Strasbourg, Article 8(2), http://www.echr.coe.int/Documents/Convention_ENG.pdf.

12. See, for the United States, Ellen Nakashima and Steven Mufson, "U.S., China Vow Not to Engage in Economic Cyberespionage," *Washington Post*, September 25, 2014, https://www.washingtonpost.com/national/us-china-vow-not-to -engage-in-economic-cyberespionage/2015/09/25/90e74b6a-63b9-11e5-8e9e -dce8a2a2a679_story.html; and for the United Kingdom, Rowena Mason, "Xi Jinping State Visit: UK and China Sign Cybersecurity Pact," *The Guardian*, October 21, 2015, http://www.theguardian.com/politics/2015/oct/21/uk-china -cybersecurity-pact-xi-jinping-david-cameron.

13. UK Government, "National Security Strategy and Defence and Security Review, 2015: A Secure and Prosperous United Kingdom" (London: Williams Lea Group for Her Majesty's Stationery Office, November 23, 2015), https://www.gov.uk /government/publications/national-security-strategy-and-strategic-defence -and-security-review-2015.

14. Georges Fenech, "Rapport fait au nom de la Commission d'Enquête relative aux moyens mis en oeuvre par l'Etat pour lutter contre le terrorism depuis le 7 janvier 2015," French National Assembly Report 3922, July 5, 2016. See "avant-propos par le Président."

15. "The National Security Act of 1947—July 26, 1947," P.L. 253, 80th Cong., chap. 343, sec. 102, https://global.oup.com/us/companion.websites/9780195385168 /resources/chapter10/nsa/nsa.pdf.

16. House Permanent Select Committee on Intelligence, "Report of the Joint Inquiry into Intelligence Community Activities before and after the Terrorist Attacks of 11 September 2001," H.Rept. 107-792 (Washington, DC: US Government Printing Office, December 2001), https://www.gpo.gov/fdsys/granule/CRPT -107hrpt792/CRPT-107hrpt792.

17. White House, Office of the Press Secretary, "Presidential Policy Directive—Signals Intelligence Activities, PPD-28," January 17, 2014, section 1(c), https:// obamawhitehouse.archives.gov/the-press-office/2014/01/17/presidential-policy -directive-signals-intelligence-activities.

18. Andrea Peterson, "LOVEINT: When NSA Officers Use Their Spying Power on Love Interests," *Washington Post*, August 24, 2013, https://www.washingtonpost .com/news/the-swtch/wp/2013/08/24/loveint-when-nsa-officers-use-their -spying-power-on-love-interests/?utm_term=.e56cc1308054.

19. As reported in Richard Norton-Taylor, "Britain's Spy Agencies: The Only Watchdog Is the Workforce," *The Guardian*, March 12, 2015, https://www.theguardian.com/news/defence-and-security-blog/2015/mar/12/britains-spy-agencies-the-only-watchdog-is-the-workforce.

20. Immanuel Kant, *Groundwork of the Metaphysics of Morals* (1785; Cambridge: University Press, 2012), discussed in Corey and Charles, *Just War Tradition*, 165.

21. Anderson, *Question of Trust*, 76.

22. See, for example, the inquiries by the Canadian judge Peter Cory into allegations of collusion between the British Army and loyalist paramilitary groups at the Committee on the Administration of Justice, "Legal & Inquiries," http://www.caj.org.uk/legal-inquiries, accessed January 2016.

23. *Klass v. Germany* (application no. 5029/71), judgment of September 6, 1978, para. 56.

24. A point made by Anderson in *Question of Trust*, para. 5.42–5.43, p. 81.

25. The most detailed description of how this operates can be found in National Research Council, *Bulk Collection of Signals Intelligence*.

26. Anderson, *Question of Trust*, 76, para. 5.21. In this he was probably relying on the vernacular use of "absolutely necessary" to be the equivalent of "indispensable."

27. Retter et al., *Moral Component*.

28. Strawser, "Moral Predators."

29. Walzer, *Just and Unjust Wars*, 3. Note that Walzer's book was first published in the United States in 1977.

30. See Preston, "Monsters Everywhere."

31. For example, Quinlan, "Just Intelligence," 7–8.

32. Mark Phythian and Peter Gill, "From Intelligence Cycle to Web of Intelligence: Complexity and the Conceptualisation of Intelligence," in *Understanding the Intelligence Cycle*, ed. Mark Phythian (Abingdon: Routledge, 2013), 21–42.

33. Cited in Lathrop, *Literary Spy*, 41.

34. Jo Becker and Scott Shane, "Secret 'Kill List' Proves a Test of Obama's Principles and Will," *New York Times*, May 29, 2012.

35. See Walzer, *Just and Unjust Wars*, chap. 16.

36. Ibid., 144.

37. For a discussion of the intelligence "action" role, see Gill and Phythian, *Intelligence in an Insecure World*, chap. 6.

38. Walzer, "Emergency Ethics."

39. See the discussion in ibid.

40. A. J. Coates, *The Ethics of War* (Manchester: Manchester University Press, 1997), 189.

41. Guthrie and Quinlan, *Just War*, 33–34.

42. "Article 51," Charter of the United Nations, last updated August 23, 2016, http://legal.un.org/repertory/art51.shtml.

43. See Brecher, *Torture and the Ticking Bomb*.

44. For example, Quinlan, "Just Intelligence."

45. Cited in Lathrop, *Literary Spy*, 205.

46. Thomas Hobbes, *Leviathan* (1651; London: Penguin, 1985), chap. 13, pp. 186–87.

47. See Meredith Reid Sarkees, "The COW Typology of War: Defining and Categorizing Wars," Correlates of War Project, version 4, http://correlatesofwar.org/data-sets/COW-war/the-cow-typology-of-war-defining-and-categorizing-wars/view?searchterm=def, accessed August 17, 2017.

48. For an account of the historical evolution of hybrid warfare, see Williamson Murray and Peter R. Mansoor, eds., *Hybrid Warfare: Fighting Complex Opponents from the Ancient World to the Present* (New York: Cambridge University Press, 2012). On Russia, see the essays in Janne Haaland Matlary and Tormod Heier, eds., *Ukraine and Beyond: Russia's Strategic Security Challenge to Europe* (London: Palgrave Macmillan, 2016).

49. See, for example, the essays in Guillaume Lasconjarias and Jeffrey A. Larsen, eds., *NATO's Response to Hybrid Threats* (Rome: NATO Defense College, 2015).

50. Cogan, "Hunters Not Gatherers," 317.

51. For example, Daniel Brunstetter and Megan Braun, "From *Jus ad Bellum* to *Jus ad Vim*: Recalibrating Our Understanding of the Moral Use of Force," *Ethics and International Affairs* 27, no. 1 (2013): 87–106.

52. Richard J. Aldrich and Rory Cormac, *The Black Door: Spies, Secret Intelligence and British Prime Ministers* (London: William Collins, 2016), 65.

53. Documents from the Snowden leak revealed the existence of a network known as the SIGINT Seniors Europe (SSEUR) group (the Fourteen Eyes), which comprises the Five Eyes states plus France, Germany, Spain, Italy, Belgium, the Netherlands, Denmark, Norway, and Sweden. See "14-Eyes Are 3rd Party Partners Forming the SIGINT Seniors Europe," Elecrospaces.net, April 16, 2014, http://electrospaces.blogspot.co.uk/2013/12/14-eyes-are-3rd-party-partners-forming.html.

54. Alison Smale, "Anger Growing among Allies on US Spying," *New York Times*, October 23, 2013, http://www.nytimes.com/2013/10/24/world/europe/united-states-disputes-reports-of-wiretapping-in-Europe.html.

55. Philip Sherwell and Louise Barnett, "Barack Obama 'Approved Tapping Angela Merkel's Phone 3 Years Ago,'" *Daily Telegraph*, October 27, 2013, http://www.telegraph.co.uk/news/worldnews/europe/germany/10407282/Barack-Obama-approved-tapping-Angela-Merkels-phone-3-years-ago.html.

56. "German Intelligence under Fire for NSA Cooperation," *Spiegel Online*, April 24, 2015, http://www.spiegel.de/international/germany/german-intelligence-agency-bnd-under-fire-for-nsa-cooperation-a-1030593.html.

57. Alison Smale, "Germany, too, Is Accused of Spying on Friends," *New York Times*, May 5, 2015, https://www.nytimes.com/2015/05/06/world/europe/scandal-over-spying-shakes-german-government.html.

58. Sherwell and Barnett, "Barack Obama."

59. Cited in Lathrop, *Literary Spy*, 247. In a similar vein, former French foreign minister Bernard Kouchner responded to the Merkel mobile phone controversy by telling a French radio station, "Let's be honest, we eavesdrop, too. Everyone is listening to everyone else. But we don't have the same means as the United States, which makes us jealous." Cited in Max Fisher, "Why America Spies on Its

Allies (and Probably Should)," *Washington Post*, October 29, 2013, https://www
.washingtonpost.com/news/worldviews/wp/2013/10/29/why-america-spies-on
-its-allies-and-probably-should/?utm_term=.57f275c4c069. More generally, see
Leif-Eric Easley, "Spying on Allies," *Survival* 56, no. 4 (2014): 141–56.

60. A January 2016 version of the UK Code of Practice provides in section 4 special
rules for intercepting such categories of person. See Home Office, "Interception of
Communications: Code of Practice—Pursuant to Section 71 of the Regulation of
Investigatory Powers Act, 2000" (London: The Stationery Office, January 2016),
https://www.gov.uk/government/uploads/system/uploads/attachment_data
/file/496064/53659_CoP_Communications_Accessible.pdf.

61. Israeli Supreme Court, HCJ 769/02, December 11, 2005, para. 45.

62. Amnesty International, "Document: Israel/Occupied Palestinian Territo-
ries: The Conflict in Gaza: A Briefing on Applicable Law, Investigations and
Accountability," January 19, 2009, para. 1.3.1, https://web.archive.org/web
/20090512141943/http://www.amnesty.org/en/library/asset/MDE15/007/2009
/en/4c407b40-e64c-11dd-9917-ed717fa5078d/mde150072009en.html#6.5.
%20Accountability|outline.

63. Andrew, *Defence of the Realm*, 591.

64. Ibid.

65. French Code Penal, Art. 421-2-1.

66. Omand, "Ethical Guidelines," 613–28.

67. Independent Surveillance Review, *Democratic Licence to Operate*.

68. Omand, *Securing the State*, 286.

69. Herman, "11 September," 227–41.

70. Ibid., 237.

4. Secret Agents and Covert Human Sources

1. See the discussion in Warner, *Rise and Fall of Intelligence*, chap. 1.

2. Herodotus, *Histories*, bk. 3, pp. 154, 231.

3. Ibid., bk. 3, pp. 157, 233.

4. Ibid., bk. 3, p. 158.

5. Griffith, *Sun Tzu*, 145. See also Warner, "Divine Skein," 483–92.

6. Griffith, *Sun Tzu*, 146.

7. Ibid.

8. Ibid., 146–47.

9. Quoted in Kant, *Kant's Political Writings*, 18.

10. Ibid., 133. Emphasis in original.

11. Ibid.

12. Ibid. Emphasis in original.

13. Ibid.

14. Ibid., 134.

15. Ibid., 96.

16. Ibid., 97.

17. George Orwell, *Nineteen Eighty-Four* (1949; London: Penguin, 2013), pt. 2, chap. 8, p. 107.

18. Ibid., pt. 2, chap. 10, p. 256.

19. De Silva, *Patrick Finucane Review*, vol. 1, *Executive Summary and Principal Conclusions*, 18, para. 84, https://www.gov.uk/government/uploads/system/uploads/attachment_data/file/246867/0802.pdf.

20. The definition of *collusion* is, as de Silva noted, "a complex and contested issue." Ibid., 1:30, para. 1.28. De Silva adopted the definition found in para. 1.30; see also the definitional discussion at paras. 1.15–1.30.

21. Ibid., 1:18, para. 87. De Silva's overall assessment was that "a series of positive actions by employees of the State actively furthered and facilitated his murder." Ibid., 1:23, para. 115.

22. Sir John Stevens, "Stevens Enquiry 3: Overview and Recommendations" (London: The Stationery Office, April 2003), para. 4.3, http://cain.ulst.ac.uk/issues/collusion/stevens3/stevens3summary.htm. Nelson was put on trial in 1992 and pleaded guilty to five charges of conspiracy to murder (two charges of first degree murder were dropped as part of a plea bargain), and he was sentenced to ten years' imprisonment. He was released after six years and died in 2003 while living under the witness protection program somewhere in England.

23. Ibid., para. 4.7. See also John Stevens, *Not for the Faint-Hearted: My Life Fighting Crime* (London: Weidenfeld & Nicolson, 2005), 171–76.

24. Cory Collusion Inquiry, *Report*, 107, para. 1.293. It should be noted that Cory's definition of collusion was much broader than that used by de Silva. Cory adopted a broad definition given his belief that "because of the necessity for public confidence in the army and police, the definition of collusion must be reasonably broad when . . . applied to" such government agencies. To this end, Cory's definition of collusion includes state agencies (the army and police force in this case) that are "ignoring or turning a blind eye to the wrongful acts of their servants or agents or supplying information to assist them in their wrongful acts or encouraging them to commit wrongful acts." Ibid., 21–22, para. 1.39. It should be noted that working to a narrower definition, de Silva concluded that "the threshold for a finding of collusion is met" in the Finucane murder case. De Silva, *Patrick Finucane Review*, 1:23, para. 114.

25. See Ed Moloney, *A Secret History of the IRA* (London: Allen Lane / Penguin, 2002), 4–33.

26. Ingram and Harkin, *Stakeknife*, 64.

27. Ibid.

28. Ibid., 215–16.

29. Ibid., 39.

30. Ibid., 36.

31. Joseph Fitsanakis, "Analysis: How Does Israel Recruit Palestinian Informants in Gaza?," *Intelnews*, September 19, 2014, https://intelnews.org/2014/09/19/01-1558/.

32. See, for example, Phoebe Greenwood and Hazem Balousha, "Hamas Promises Amnesty to Palestinian Collaborators Spying for Israel," *The Guardian*, March 13, 2013, http://www.theguardian.com/world/2013/mar/13/hamas-amnesty-palestinian-spying-israel.

33. Godfrey, "Ethics and Intelligence," 629.

34. Ibid., 630.

35. Funder, *Stasiland*, 198. In line with Martin Ingram's explanation in the context of Northern Ireland, Bock thought that some acted as informers because they "got the feeling that, doing it, they were somebody. You know—someone was listening to them for a couple of hours a week, taking notes. They felt they had it over other people." Ibid., 201. Mike Dennis lists five motivations for such collaboration: political and ideological conviction, coercion and fear, personal advantage, emotional needs, and a desire to influence official policy. Mike Dennis, *The Stasi: Myth and Reality* (Harlow: Pearson, 2003), 97.

36. Wolf, *Man without a Face*, 123.

37. John O. Koehler, *Stasi: The Untold Story of the East German Secret Police* (Boulder: Westview, 1999), 174–87.

38. Frederick Forsyth, *The Day of the Jackal* (London: Hutchinson, 1971), chap. 3.

39. See, for example, the accounts in the BBC Two television program *True Spies: Subversive My Arse*, broadcast on October 27, 2002. See "Watching 'Subversives,'" BBC News, October 17, 2002, https://assets.documentcloud.org/documents/2642522/Transcript-True-Spies-E1-Proofed-Transcript.pdf.

40. Ibid.

41. Rob Evans and Paul Lewis, "Police Spies Had Children with Activists," *The Guardian*, January 21, 2012. See also Lewis and Evans, *Undercover*, chap. 4.

42. Rob Evans, "I Thought I Knew Him Better Than Anyone," *The Guardian*, November 21, 2015.

43. Rob Evans, "Met Apologises to Women Deceived by Police Spies," *The Guardian*, November 21, 2015.

44. Paul Lewis and Rob Evans, "Police Spies Case Shocking and Violated Rights, Says UN Official," *The Guardian*, January 24, 2013.

45. Mick Creedon, *Operation Herne: Operation Trinity, Report 2—Allegations of Peter Francis* (Ashbourne: Derbyshire Constabulary, 2014), 45–46, para. 16.2, http://www.derbyshire.police.uk/Documents/About-Us/Herne/Operation-Herne---Report-2---Allegations-of-Peter-Francis.pdf.

46. Mick Creedon, *Operation Herne: Report 1—Use of Covert Identities* (Ashbourne: Derbyshire Constabulary, 2013), 10, para. 4.2; 11, 5.1, http://www.derbyshire.police.uk/Documents/About-Us/Herne/Operation-Herne---Report-1---Covert-Identities.pdf.

47. Ibid., 21, para. 11.9.

48. Creedon, *Operation Herne: Report 2*, 46, para. 17.2.

49. Paul Lewis and Rob Evans, "Kennedy Unlawfully Spied on Climate Activists, Say Judges," *The Guardian*, July 21, 2011.

50. In a UK context, the role of the Security Service in the 1984–85 miners' strike is a good example of an intervention in or close to the political realm that divided public opinion in terms of its legitimacy. The Security Service monitored the miners' leaders, particularly National Union of Miners leader Arthur Scargill on the basis that he was an "unaffiliated subversive," but it also resisted pressure to undertake greater surveillance—for example, to extend surveillance to the association of miners' wives or to monitor picket lines. See Andrew, *Defence of the Realm*, 677, 679. On claims that the Security Service had at least one covert human intelligence source inside the union, see Seumas Milne, *The Enemy Within: The Secret War against the Miners*, 3rd ed. (London: Verso, 2004).

51. De Silva, *Patrick Finucane Review*, 1:23, para. 112–13.

52. Essentially the conclusion reached by the army's own history of the conflict. See *Operation Banner: An Analysis of Military Operations in Northern Ireland*, Army Code 71842 (London: Ministry of Defence, July 2006), http://www.vilaweb.cat /media/attach/vwedts/docs/op_banner_analysis_released.pdf.

53. Jonathan Powell, *Great Hatred, Little Room: Making Peace in Northern Ireland* (London: The Bodley Head, 2008).

54. M. L. R. Smith, *Fighting for Ireland: The Military Strategy of the Irish Republican Movement* (London: Routledge, 2002), 20.

55. Howard, *British Intelligence*, 5, chap. 8. Further detail is in Andrew, *Defence of the Realm*, 241–62.

56. Part 2 of the Regulation of Investigatory Powers Act, 2000; and Home Office, "Covert Human Intelligence Sources: Code of Practice" (London: The Stationery Office, December 2014), https://www.gov.uk/government/uploads /system/uploads/attachment_data/file/384976/Covert_Human_Intelligence _web.pdf.

57. College of Policing, "Code of Ethics: A Code of Practice for the Principles and Standards of Professional Behaviour for the Policing Profession of England and Wales" (Coventry: College of Policing, July 2014), http://www.college.police.uk /What-we-do/Ethics/Documents/Code_of_Ethics.pdf.

58. Mark Ellison, "The Stephen Lawrence Independent Review: Possible Corruption and the Role of Undercover Policing in the Stephen Lawrence Case—Summary of Findings," HC 1094 (London: Home Office, March 2014), 20, https://www.gov .uk/government/uploads/system/uploads/attachment_data/file/287030/stephen _lawrence_review_summary.pdf.

59. Ibid., 20–21.

60. Presented to Parliament under the Regulation of Investigatory Powers Act 2000, Home Office, "Cover Human Intelligence Sources."

61. Dominic Casciani, "Met Police Apology for Women Tricked into Relationships," BBC News, November 20, 2015, http://www.bbc.co.uk/news/uk-34875197.

62. College of Policing, "Code of Ethics," 17.

63. Herbert Scoville Jr., "Is Espionage Necessary for Our Security?," *Foreign Affairs* 54, no. 3 (1976): 483.

64. Rob Evans, "Undercover Police Unit Broke Rules, Met Finds," *The Guardian*, July 27, 2015.

65. Ibid.

66. Ellison, "Stephen Lawrence Independent Review," 30.

67. See de Silva, *Patrick Finucane Review*, vol. 2.

68. Ibid., 2:221.

69. Ibid.

70. Memo from Attorney General Sir Patrick Mayhew to Secretary of State for Defence Tom King, March 11, 1991, in ibid., 2:240.

71. Ibid. Emphasis in original.

72. As the attorney general wrote, "It has to be said, however, that, at least in the cases I have seen, the action taken seems to have been far from adequate to meet the objective of frustrating crime by the use of Nelson." See ibid.

73. See the cases of the murders of Terence McDaid and Gerald Slane and of the conspiracy to murder Alex Maskey and Brian Gillen that are included as an appendix to the attorney general's March 11, 1991, memo, in ibid., 2:242–44.

74. Letter from John Stevens to Hugh Annesley, Chief Constable RUC, April 12, 1991, in ibid., 2:276.

75. De Silva, *Patrick Finucane Review*, 1:493–94, para. 24.226.

76. Memorandum, March 19, 1991, in de Silva, *Patrick Finucane Review*, 2:255.

77. Memorandum from Secretary of State for Defence (Tom King) to Attorney General (Sir Patrick Mayhew), March 19, 1991, in ibid., 2:265.

78. Ibid., 2:278. Indeed, given his activities, the number could reasonably have been expected to fall.

79. Ibid., 2:255.

80. Ibid.

81. Ibid., 2:255–56.

82. De Silva, *Patrick Finucane Review*, 1:5–6, paras. 18 and 19.

83. Article 2, point 1 of the European Convention on Human Rights states: "Everyone's right to life shall be protected by law" (6).

84. De Silva, *Patrick Finucane Review*, 1:7, para. 25.

85. Ibid., 1:7, para. 24.

86. Part of the definition of *covert intelligence source*, under UK legislation, is a relationship that is established or maintained for a covert purpose if and only if it is conducted in a manner calculated to ensure that one of the parties to the relationship is unaware of the purpose.

87. Thatcher's communications with Reagan are now available on the National Security Archive website, along with the relevant US assessments.

88. Butler, *Review of Intelligence*, para. 414.

89. Andrew and Mitrokhin, *Mitrokhin Archive*, xix.

90. See Andrew, *Defence of the Realm*, section D.

91. For example, see David Brown, "Notorious Spies: The Other NSA Spy, Ronald Pelton," Clearance Jobs, August 31, 2014, https://news.clearancejobs.com/2014/08/31/notorious-spies-nsa-spy-ronald-pelton/.

5. Digital Intelligence and Cyberspace

1. The Internet of Things refers to everyday objects, from household items such as Internet-enabled TVs and refrigerators to sensors embedded in vehicles and devices such as electricity meters, that can send and receive data from the Internet.

2. A good explanation of these issues can be found in Her Majesty's Government, "National Cyber Security Strategy, 2016–2021," November 1, 2016, https://www.gov.uk/government/publications/national-cyber-security-strategy-2016-to-2021; and the US Department of Defense, "The DoD Cyber Strategy," April 2015, https://www.defense.gov/Portals/1/features/2015/0415_cyber-strategy/Final_2015_DoD_CYBER_STRATEGY_for_web.pdf.

3. David Omand, *Understanding Digital Intelligence and the Norms That Should Govern It* (Ottawa: Center for International Governance Innovation, 2015).

4. Clarke et al., *NSA Report*.

5. A remarkable account of Dark Net underworld activity can be found in Bartlett, *Dark Net*.

6. Herbert Simon, "Rational Choice and the Structure of the Environment," Psychological Review 63, no. 2 (1956): 129–38.

7. The first major recorded cyber espionage campaign, code-named Moonlight Maze, was conducted by Russia against US defense targets in the late 1990s. See Rid, *Rise of the Machines*, 316–39.

8. A good introduction is given by the US National Academy of Sciences, *At the Nexus of Cybersecurity and Policy* (Washington, DC: National Academies Press, 2014).

9. See Corera, *Intercept*.

10. William Safire, "You Are a Suspect," *New York Times*, November 14, 2002.

11. See Hampson and Jardine, *Look Who's Watching*, 84–85.

12. Council of Europe, "European Convention on Human Rights," Strasbourg, Article 8(2), http://www.echr.coe.int/Documents/Convention_Eng.pdf.

13. For example, as described in the Vodafone Group, "Law Enforcement Disclosure Report, 2015," http://www.vodafone.com/content/index/about/sustainability/law_enforcement.html, accessed April 1, 2016.

14. For a critical analysis, see Donohue, "Bulk Metadata Collection."

15. "Administration White Paper: Bulk Collection of Telephony Metadata under Section 215 of the USA Patriot Act," August 9, 2013, 2, https://www.documentcloud.org/documents/750211-administration-white-paper-section-215.html.

16. Samuel D. Warren and Louis D. Brandeis, "The Right to Privacy," *Harvard Law Review* 4, no. 5 (December 1890): 205.

17. Anderson, *Bulk Powers Review*.

18. Order of February 6, 2015, relating to Case Nos: IPT/13/77/H, IPT/13/92/CH, IPT/13/168-173/H, IPT/13/194/CH, IPT/13/204/CH, available at http://www.ipt-uk.com/judgments.asp?id=25.

19. Intelligence and Security Committee of Parliament, *Privacy and Security*; Anderson, *Question of Trust*; and Independent Surveillance Review, *Democratic Licence to Operate*.

20. Anderson, *Bulk Powers Review*.

21. Lowenthal, "Towards a Reasonable Standard," 306.

22. Cited in Lathrop, *Literary Spy*, 41.

23. Ellen Nakashima and Joby Warrick, "For NSA Chief, Terrorist Threat Drives Passion to 'Collect It All,'" *Washington Post*, July 14, 2013, https://www.washingtonpost.com/world/national-security/for-nsa-chief-terrorist-threat-drives-passion-to-collect-it-all/2013/07/14/3d26ef80-ea49-11e2-a301-ea5a8116d211_story.html; and Greenwald, *No Place to Hide*, 95–96.

24. See Budiansky, *Code Warriors*. As Budiansky puts it, "*Every* country was a legitimate target, friend and foe alike; intelligence on everything from its industry to agriculture, from its politics to internal social forces, might provide the one crucial detail that would make the difference between triumph and catastrophe for American policy" (20). Emphasis in original.

25. Cited in ibid., 22.

26. James Clapper, interview by Andrea Mitchell, NBC News, Liberty Crossing, Tysons Corner, VA, June 8, 2013, https://www.dni.gov/index.php/newsroom/speeches-interviews/speeches-interviews-2013/item/874-director-james-r-clapper-interview-with-andrea-mitchell. The more accurate analogy here, perhaps, lies in the fact that libraries do not usually order a book every time someone requests one. They collect as many of the books most likely to be requested as they can afford and have the capacity to store. This makes accessing a specific element of the collection much more efficient when a user wants to look at it.

27. Ibid.

28. Tempora is the name given to the GCHQ program of intercepting Internet communications carried underwater via fiber-optic cables, storing the acquired data to facilitate sifting and analysis, and sharing this information with the NSA. See, for example, Greenwald, *No Place to Hide*, 118–24; and Ewen MacAskill et al., "GCHQ Taps Fibre-Optic Cables for Secret Access to World's Communications," *The Guardian*, June 21, 2013, https://www.theguardian.com/uk/2013/jun/21/gchq-cables-secret-world-communications-nsa.

29. Chris Huhne, "Cabinet Was Told Nothing about Prism and Tempora," *The Guardian*, October 7, 2014.

30. Patrick Wintour, "Only 'Tiny Handful' of Ministers Knew of Mass Surveillance, Clegg Reveals," *The Guardian*, November 5, 2015; and Nick Clegg, "The Surveillance Bill Is Flawed but at Last We Have Oversight," *The Guardian*, November 5, 2015.

31. For discussions of the relationship between uncertainty, risk, and threat, and the role of intelligence, see the following articles published in *Intelligence and National Security* 27, no. 2 (2012): Mark Phythian, "*Policing Uncertainty: Intelligence, Security and Risk*," 187–205; Peter Gill, "Intelligence, Threat, Risk and the Challenge of Oversight," 206–22; and David Strachan-Morris, "Threat and Risk: What Is the Difference and Why Does It Matter?," 172–86.

32. Intelligence and Security Committee, *Privacy and Security*, 33, para. 90.

33. Clarke et al., *NSA Report*, 57.

34. Anderson, *Question of Trust*, appendix 9, para. 3.

35. Ibid., appendix 9, para. 5.

36. Intelligence and Security Committee, *Privacy and Security*, 5. See also paras. 78–90.

37. Anderson, *Bulk Powers Review*, executive summary, 1.

38. Intelligence and Security Committee, *Privacy and Security*, 5.

39. Ibid., 6.

40. For a discussion of the link between political and intelligence cultures, see Mark Phythian, "Cultures of National Intelligence," in *Routledge Companion to Intelligence Studies*, ed. Robert Dover, Michael S. Goodman, and Claudia Hillebrand (Abingdon: Routledge, 2014), 33–41.

41. Kantar TNS, "Public Opinion Monitor: Britons Give Safeguarding Security a Higher Priority Than Protecting Privacy," TNS-BMRB Poll, February 3, 2014, http://www.tnsglobal.com/uk/press-release/public-opinion-monitor-britons -give-safeguarding-security-higher-priority-protecting-p. See also the discussion in Anderson, *Question of Trust*, paras. 2.32–2.34.

42. Cited in Independent Surveillance Review, *Democratic Licence to Operate*, para. 2.34.

43. To use the summary of panel member Heather Brooke, "Our Victory over Omnipotent Surveillance," *The Guardian*, July 14, 2015.

44. Anderson, *Bulk Powers Review*, para. 4.22. My emphasis.

45. In this respect, it is notable that all three reports discussed previously comment on the lack of clarity in the existing legislation. The Anderson report called for the law that would replace RIPA to be "written so far as possible in non-technical language" and to be "structured and expressed so as to enable its essentials to be understood by intelligent readers across the world." Anderson, *Question of Trust*, paras. 15.3–15.4.

46. That privacy is no longer a social norm is a claim associated with Facebook founder Mark Zuckerberg. See Emma Barnett, "Facebook's Mark Zuckerberg Says Privacy Is No Longer a 'Social Norm,'" *Daily Telegraph*, January 11, 2010. Regarding issues of control and consent, see Independent Surveillance Review, *Democratic Licence to Operate*, para. 2.12.

47. Ibid., para. 5.26.

48. This is implicit in ibid., para. 5.29.

49. See, for example, David E. Sanger, "New NSA Chief Calls Damage from Snowden Leaks Manageable," *New York Times*, June 29, 2014.

50. Ewen MacAskill, "Snowden: My Leak Aided US and I Should Be Pardoned," *The Guardian*, September 14, 2016.

51. Aid, *Secret Sentry*; James Bamford, *The Shadow Factory: The Ultra-Secret NSA from 9/11 to the Eavesdropping on America* (New York: Doubleday, 2008); and a leading example is the comprehensive technical guide by Bruce Schneier to all things cryptographic, *Applied Cryptography*, which explains how digital intelligence can be gathered.

52. Ewen MacAskill and Paul Johnson, "MI5 Chief Warns of Growing Russian Threat to UK," *The Guardian*, November 1, 2016.

53. See, for example, Spencer Ackerman and Ewen MacAskill, "Privacy: Campaigners Fear Unfettered Surveillance," *The Guardian*, November 12, 2016.

54. Ed Pilkington, "Obama Puts Hurdle in Way of Trump Plan to Introduce Muslim Registry," *The Guardian*, December 23, 2016.

55. Mearsheimer, *Tragedy of Great Power Politics*, 33.

56. Joshua Rozenberg, "The Power to Intrude," *Prospect*, February 2016, 40.

57. Curry, *Security Service*, 158, 170.

58. The Berne Group consists of the heads of the internal services of the twenty-eight EU members, Switzerland, and Norway.

59. Richard Wright, Matthew Addis, and Ant Miller, "The Significance of Storage in the 'Cost of Risk' of Digital Preservation," presentation at iPRES 2008, London, September 2008, https://www.bl.uk/ipres2008/presentations_day1/21_Wright.pdf; and David Rosenthal et al., "The Economics of Long-Term Digital Storage," 2012, http://www.unesco.org/fileadmin/MULTIMEDIA/HQ/CI/CI/pdf/mow/VC_Rosenthal_et_al_27_B_1330.pdf.

60. Crabtree appears to have been an elaborate prewar academic joke involving spoof orations at British universities. See R. V. Jones, *Reflections on Intelligence* (London: Mandarin, 1989), 88.

61. Sir Francis Richards, address to Royal Society seminar on the social implications of cyber technology, London, June 9, 2014, http://www.cs.bham.ac.uk/research/groupings/security-and-privacy/royalsoc2014/programme/Richards_text.pdf.

62. David Kaye, "Promotion and Protection of the Right to Freedom of Opinion and Expression," A/71/373, United Nations General Assembly, September 6, 2016, http://www.un.org/ga/search/view_doc.asp?symbol=A/71/373.

63. The conclusion of the NATO Group of Experts. See Michael N. Schmitt, ed., *Tallinn Manual 2.0 on the International Law Applicable to Cyber Operations*, 2nd ed. (Cambridge: Cambridge University Press, 2017).

6. The Ethics of Using Intelligence

1. Cited in Peritz and Rosenbach, *Find, Fix, Finish*, 5.

2. Examples taken from Richard J. Aldrich, *The Hidden Hand* (New York: The Overlook Press, 2002).

3. Quoted in Treverton, *Covert Action*, 6.

4. See Christopher Mayhew, *Time to Explain: An Autobiography* (London: Hutchinson, 1987); and Andrew Lownie, *Stalin's Englishman: The Lives of Guy Burgess* (London: Hodder & Stoughton, 2015), chap. 24.

5. In his memoirs, Owen wrote that although the IRD "did essential service" in combating Soviet propaganda and "there is no need for anyone associated with it to feel shame," nevertheless, "its style of operation got out of step with our more open democracy." Owen felt its operation represented a "grey area, which for too

long escaped proper scrutiny, falling neither in the open area of diplomacy nor in the closed area of spying." David Owen, *Time to Declare* (London: Penguin, 1992), 348.

6. Timothy Garton Ash, "Orwell's List," *New York Review of Books*, September 25, 2003, http://www.nybooks.com/articles/2003/09/25/orwells-list/.

7. Aldrich, *Hidden Hand*, 343.

8. On the idea of forming an ethical "ladder of escalation," see Johnson, *Secret Agencies*, 62–63; and Johnson, *National Security Intelligence*, 99–104. Ross Bellaby uses the ladder of escalation as an ordering device in his *Ethics of Intelligence*. Bellaby's focus is on the methods used in intelligence collection, while Johnson is concerned with covert action as a form of "action-on," which is our focus in this chapter.

9. Falk, "CIA Covert Action," 40.

10. Savage, *Power Wars*, 236.

11. An example is in its treatment of offensive cyber. See Her Majesty's Government, "National Cyber Security Strategy," 25.

12. Greg Miller, "White House Approves Broader Yemen Drone Campaign," *Washington Post*, April 26, 2012.

13. David S. Cloud, "CIA Drones Have Broader List of Targets," *Los Angeles Times*, May 5, 2010.

14. Declaration of Mary Ellen Cole, information review officer, National Clandestine Service, Central Intelligence Agency, in *American Civil Liberties Union et al. v. Department of Justice et al.* (Case No. 1:10-CV-00436-RMC), September 2010.

15. Ibid.

16. Scott Shane, "US Approves Targeted Killing of American Cleric," *New York Times*, April 6, 2010; Peter Finn, "Secret US Memo Sanctioned Killing of Aulaqi," *Washington Post*, September 30, 2011; and Shane, *Objective Troy*.

17. Hansard, September 7, 2015, col. 23.

18. Owen Bowcott, "Attorney General Calls for New Legal Basis for Pre-emptive Military Strikes," *The Guardian*, January 10, 2017, https://www.theguardian.com/uk-news/2017/jan/11/attorney-general-calls-for-new-legal-basis-for-pre-emptive-military-strikes.

19. Bethlehem, "Self-Defense against an Imminent," 770–77.

20. Andrew Robotham, House of Commons Debates (2013), written answer col. 37W, February 25, 2013, http://www.publications.parliament.uk/pa/cm201213/cmhansrd/cm130225/text/130225w0002.htm#130225w0002.htm_wqn32.

21. Harold Hongju Koh, "The Obama Administration and International Law," speech to the annual meeting of the American Society of International Law, Washington, DC, March 25, 2010, https://www.state.gov/documents/organization/179305.pdf.

22. Ibid.

23. Ibid. My emphasis.

24. For example, Mary Ellen O'Connell, "When Is a War Not a War? The Myth of the Global War on Terror," *ILSA Journal of International & Comparative Law* 12

(2005–6): 535–39. Regarding Article 51, see Mary Ellen O'Connell, "Enhancing the Status of Non-state Actors through a Global War on Terror?," *Columbia Journal of Transnational Law* 43, no. 2 (2003–5): 435–58; and for preemptive action, see the views collected in Elizabeth Wilmhurst, "Principles of International Law on the Use of Force by States in Self-Defence," Working Paper (London: Chatham House, October 1, 2005), http://www.chathamhouse.org/publications /papers/view/108106.

25. UN Office of the High Commissioner for Human Rights, "UN Expert Criticizes 'Illegal' Targeted Killing Policies and Calls on the US to Halt CIA Drone Killings," June 2, 2010. See summary at http://reliefweb.int/report/afghanistan/un -expert-criticizes-illegal-targeted-killing-policies-and-calls-us-halt-cia.

26. Washington Post/ABC News Poll, conducted February 1–4, 2012, www .washingtonpost.com/wp-srv/politics/polls/postabcpoll_020412.html. Hence, the armed drone policy passes the Stansfield Turner test mentioned earlier.

27. Perina, "Black Holes," 566.

28. Walzer, "On Fighting Terrorism Justly," 480. Elsewhere, he has written similarly that "covert action is also necessary, and I confess that I don't know what moral rules apply to it." Walzer, *Arguing about War*, 139.

29. Glennon, "How International Rules Die," 956.

30. Ibid.

31. Falk, "CIA Covert Action."

32. William H. Boothby, *Conflict Law: The Influence of New Weapons Technology, Human Rights and Emerging Actors* (The Hague: Asser Press, 2014), chap. 5; and citing approvingly Yoram Dinstein, *The Conduct of Hostilities under the Law of International Armed Conflict*, 2nd ed. (Cambridge: Cambridge University Press, 2010), 103–4.

33. Solis, *Law of Armed Conflict*, 452–53n27.

34. See, for example, the objections UN special rapporteur Philip Alston raised regarding assertions of the existence of a state of non-international armed conflict with al-Qaeda in Philip Alston, "Report of the Special Rapporteur on Extrajudicial, Summary or Arbitrary Executions: Addendum—Study on Targeted Killings" (Geneva: UN General Assembly, Human Rights Council, May 28, 2010), http://www2.ohchr.org/english/bodies/hrcouncil/docs/14session/A.HRC .14.24.Add6.pdf, 17–19, paras. 52–56.

35. Perina, "Black Holes," 575.

36. Richard Boucher, "Excerpts from Press Briefing Relating to Isracl/Palestinians," Washington, DC, August 27, 2001, https://2001-2009.state.gov/p/nea/rt/4697 .htm.

37. Jeh Johnson explained, "On occasion, I read or hear a commentator loosely refer to lethal force against a valid military objective with the pejorative term 'assassination.' Like any American shaped by national events in 1963 and 1968, the term is to me one of the most repugnant in our vocabulary, and it should be rejected in this context. Under well-settled legal principles, lethal force against a valid *military* objective in an armed conflict is consistent with the law of war and does

not, by definition, constitute an 'assassination.'" Jeh Charles Johnson, "National Security Law, Lawyers, and Lawyering in the Obama Administration," Dean's Lecture at Yale Law School, New Haven, CT, February 22, 2012, 147–48, http:// digitalcommons.law.yale.edu/ylpr/vol31/iss1/5/. Emphasis in original.

38. According to recently declassified accounts available at the National Security Archive. See Peter Kornbluh, ed., "Secret CIA Report: Pinochet 'Personally Ordered' Washington Car-Bombing," National Security Archive Electronic Briefing Book no. 532, October 8, 2015, http://nsarchive.gwu.edu/NSAEBB /NSAEBB532-The-Letelier-Moffitt-Assassination-Papers/.

39. Kean and Hamilton, *9/11 Commission Report*, 132.

40. Charlie Savage, "How 4 Federal Lawyers Paved the Way to Kill Osama bin Laden," *New York Times*, October 28, 2015, http://www.nytimes.com/2015/10/29 /us/politics/obama-legal-authorization-osama-bin-laden-raid.html?_r=0; and Department of Justice White Paper, "Lawfulness of a Lethal Operation Directed against a US Citizen Who Is a Senior Operational Leader of al-Qa'ida or an Associated Force," n.d., http://msnbcmedia.msn.com/i/msnbc/sections/news/020413 _DOJ_White_Paper.pdf, accessed August 17, 2017.

41. David Cole, "We Kill People Based on Metadata," *New York Review Daily*, May 10, 2014, http://www.nybooks.com/daily/2014/05/10/we-kill-people-based -metadata/.

42. Cited in Jeremy Scahill and Glenn Greenwald, "Death by Metadata," in *The Assassination Complex: Inside the US Government's Secret Drone Warfare Programme*, ed. Jeremy Scahill and the Staff of the *Intercept* (London: Serpent's Tail, 2016), 98.

43. See, for example, Scott Shane, "Drone Strikes Reveal Uncomfortable Truth: US Is Often Unsure about Who Will Die," *New York Times*, April 23, 2015, http://www .nytimes.com/2015/04/24/world/asia/drone-strikes-reveal-uncomfortable-truth -us-is-often-unsure-about-who-will-die.html; and Office of the Press Secretary, "Fact Sheet: U.S. Policy Standards and Procedures for the Use of Force in Counterterrorism Operations outside the United States and Areas of Active Hostilities," White House, Washington, DC, May 23, 2013, https://www.whitehouse.gov /the-press-office/2013/05/23/fact-sheet-us-policy-standards-and-procedures -use-force-counterterrorism.

44. Birmingham Policy Commission, "The Security Impact of Drones: Challenges and Opportunities for the UK" (Birmingham: University of Birmingham, October 2014), chap. 4, http://www.birmingham.ac.uk/Documents/research /policycommission/remote-warfare/final-report-october-2014.pdf.

45. Jim Acosta, "Obama to Make New Push to Shift Control of Drones from CIA to Pentagon," CNN, April 27, 2015, http://edition.cnn.com/2015/04/27/politics /drones-cia-pentagon-white-house/.

46. Shane, *Objective Troy*, 16–17.

47. Supreme Court, judgment, Smith, Ellis, Allbutt and Others v. the Ministry of Defence, [2013] UKSC 41, 19 June 2013, p. 21 para. 57, https://www .supremecourt.gov.uk/decided-cases/docs/UKSC_2012_0249_Judgment.pdf.

48. Cited in Jeremy Scahill, "The Drone Legacy," in Scahill et al., *Assassination Complex*, 9.

49. McDonald, *Enemies Known and Unknown*, 158–59.

50. A. P. V. Rogers, *Law on the Battlefield*, 3rd ed. (Manchester: Manchester University Press, 2012), 52–3, citing Melzer, *Targeted Killing*, 419.

51. See, for example, ICRC Customary Law Study, rules 1–45, in Jean-Marie Henckaerts and Louise Doswald-Beck, *Customary International Humanitarian Law*, vol. 1, *Rules*, with Carolin Alvermann, Knut Dörmann, and Baptiste Rolle (Cambridge: Cambridge University Press, 2005), https://www.icrc.org/eng/assets/files/other/customary-international-humanitarian-law-i-icrc-eng.pdf.

52. Cited in David Cole, "The New America: Little Privacy, Big Terror," *New York Review of Books*, August 13, 2015, 20.

53. David Kilcullen and Andrew McDonald Exum, "Death from Above, Outrage from Below," *New York Times*, May 16, 2009, http://www.nytimes.com/2009/05/17/opinion/17exum.html.

54. Hilaire Belloc, *The Modern Traveller* (London: Edward Arnold, 1898).

55. Birmingham Policy Commission, "Security Impact of Drones," 57.

56. William Yong and Robert F. Worth, "Bombings Hit Atomic Experts in Iran Streets," *New York Times*, November 29, 2010; and Kim Zetter, *Countdown to Zero Day: Stuxnet and the Launch of the World's First Digital Weapon* (New York: Broadway Books, 2014), 239–42.

57. Israeli Supreme Court, HCJ 769/02, December 13, 2006, https://www.law.upenn.edu/institutes/cerl/conferences/targetedkilling/papers/IsraeliTargetedKillingCase.pdf.

58. Mathilde Von Bülow, "Myth or Reality: The Red Hand and French Covert Action in Federal Germany during the Algerian War, 1956–61," *Intelligence and National Security* 22, no. 6 (2007): 787–820.

59. Constantin Melnik, *1000 Jours à Matignon* (Paris: Grasset, 1988), 80.

60. See James Risen and Mark Mazzetti, "US Agencies See No Move by Iran to Build a Bomb," *New York Times*, February 24, 2012.

61. The classic account is Barbara Tuchman's *Zimmermann Telegram*.

62. Ibid., 5–7.

63. Such as in the 2008 play by Alan Pollock, *One Night in November*.

64. Hinsley et al., *British Intelligence*, 1:316–18.

65. James Rusbridger and Eric Nave, *Betrayal at Pearl Harbor: How Churchill Lured Roosevelt into War* (London: O'Mara, 1991).

7. Building Confidence through Oversight and Accountability

1. Ali Watkins, "Central Figure in CIA-Senate Spying Scandal to Leave Post," Huffington Post, January 5, 2015, http://www.huffingtonpost.com/2015/01/05/cia-senate-spying_n_6418862.html.

2. First revealed in detail by Seymour Hersh in "Huge C.I.A. Operation Reported in U.S. against Antiwar Forces, Other Dissidents in Nixon Years," *New York Times*,

December 22, 1974, http://www.nytimes.com/1974/12/22/archives/huge-cia -operation-reported-in-u-s-against-antiwar-forces-other.html.

3. United States Senate (Church Committee), *Intelligence Activities and the Rights of Americans*, Book 2, *Final Report of the Select Committee to Study Governmental Operations with Respect to Intelligence Activities together with Additional, Supplemental, and Separate Views*, Report 94-755 (Washington, DC: US Government Printing Office, April 1976), 5, 6, https://www.intelligence.senate.gov/sites /default/files/94755_II.pdf.

4. Crumpton, *Art of Intelligence*, 310.

5. A useful survey of EU practice can be found in the report of the EU Agency for Fundamental Rights, *Surveillance by Intelligence Services: Fundamental Rights Safeguards and Remedies in the EU* (Vienna: Fundamental Rights Agency, 2015).

6. European Commission for Democracy through Law, *Democratic Oversight*.

7. European Union, "The Lisbon Treaty," Article 4(2), http://www.lisbon-treaty .org/wcm/the-lisbon-treaty/treaty-on-european-union-and-comments/title-1 -common-provisions/5-article-4.html, accessed July 26, 2016.

8. Born, Leigh, and Wills, in *Making International Intelligence Cooperation Accountable*, emphasize the risk in their Norwegian Parliamentary Oversight Committee–funded study.

9. Quoted in *US Army War College Guide to National Security Policy and Strategy*, 5th ed. (Carlisle Barracks, PA: US Army War College, 2012), 74, http://ssi .armywarcollege.edu/pdffiles/pub1110.pdf.

10. Snider, *Agency and the Hill*, chap. 2.

11. See Lucinda Shen, "Edward Snowden Had No Choice but to Leak to the Media," *Fortune*, May 23, 2016, http://fortune.com/2016/05/23/edward-snowden-might -have-had-no-choice-but-to-leak-to-the-media/.

12. Orwell, *Nineteen Eighty-Four*, 4.

13. A good example of bureaucratic aversion to criticism in an intelligence context is flagged in the report of the UK (Chilcot) inquiry into the Iraq War that was published in 2016. Regarding SIS's postwar withdrawal of key prewar intelligence on Iraq's WMD program, the report noted, "The lack of evidence to support pre-conflict claims about Iraq's WMD challenged the credibility of the Government and the intelligence community, and the legitimacy of the war," and that the "Government and the intelligence community were both concerned about the consequences of the presentational aspects of their pre-war assessments being discredited." Section 4.4, "The Search for WMD," in Sir John Chilcot, *The Report of the Iraq Inquiry*, HC 264 (London: Her Majesty's Stationery Office, July 6, 2016), paras. 910–11.

14. On the issue of intelligence and democratization, see Peter Gill, *Intelligence Governance and Democratisation: A Comparative Analysis of the Limits of Reform* (Abingdon: Routledge, 2016).

15. Mark Mazzetti, "CIA Destroyed 2 Tapes Showing Interrogations," *New York Times*, December 7, 2007, http://www.nytimes.com/2007/12/07/washington /07intel.html.

16. For example, Tom Malinowski, the director of Washington, DC–based Human Rights Watch, said, "Millions of documents in C.I.A. archives, if leaked, would identify C.I.A. officers. The only difference here is that these tapes portray potentially criminal activity. They must have understood that if people saw these tapes, they would consider them to show acts of torture, which is a felony offense." Ibid.

17. United States Senate Select Committee, *Committee Study*. See appendix 3, "Example of Inaccurate CIA Testimony to the Committee—April 12, 2007."

18. Gill and Phythian, *Intelligence in an Insecure World*, 172.

19. Ian Beesley, *The Official History of the Cabinet Secretaries* (Abingdon: Routledge, 2017), 464.

20. Memorandum, Robert Armstrong to Margaret Thatcher, "BBC Panorama: Proposed Programme on Intelligence Services," July 21, 1980, Margaret Thatcher Foundation Archive, 4, http://www.margaretthatcher.org/document/127095. "Should we be prepared to see go forward a programme dealing strictly with the accountability of the Services and not extending to their functions and working?" asked Armstrong. "No," replied Mrs. Thatcher. Ibid.

21. I discuss the background to this in Mark Phythian, "The British Experience with Intelligence Accountability," *Intelligence and National Security* 22, no. 1 (February 2007): 75–98.

22. For a discussion of the elements necessary for effective oversight, see Born and Johnson, "Balancing Operational Efficiency," in Born, Johnson, and Leigh, *Who's Watching the Spies?*, 225–39.

23. As noted in the multiplicity of complex statutes we considered in chapter 5.

24. Sir Malcolm Rifkind, "Statement on GCHQ's Alleged Interception of Communications under the US PRISM Programme," Intelligence and Security Committee of Parliament, July 17, 2013, http://isc.independent.gov.uk/news-archive /17july2013.

25. The GCHQ issued a vigorous denial of the 2017 allegation on Fox News, and repeated by President Trump's spokesman in the White House, that the Obama administration had sidestepped US law by getting the GCHQ to spy on Trump Tower. See Lauren Gambino and Kevin Rawlinson, "GCHQ Dismisses 'Utterly Ridiculous' Claim It Helped Wiretap Trump," *The Guardian*, March 17, 2017, https://www.theguardian.com/us-news/2017/mar/16/gchq-denies-wiretap -claim-trump-obama.

26. For example, see Rodriguez, *Hard Measures*.

27. Jay Rockefeller, floor speech, US Senate, Select Committee on Intelligence Study of the CIA's Detention and Interrogation Program, December 9, 2014, http://votesmart.org/public-statement/942456/senate-select-committee -on-intelligence-study-of-the-cias-detention-and-interrogation-program# .VdAn5Bfugqt.

28. John le Carré, "I Have Contributed to Spies' Mythological Status—but Their Influence Has Become Too Much; It's Time Politicians Said No to These Bush-Style Tactics," *The Guardian*, June 15, 2013.

29. Anderson, *Question of Trust*, para. 12.93.

30. Ibid., paras. 118–20.

31. Hansard, July 17, 2008, col. 455.

32. Ibid., col. 465.

33. Ibid., col. 483.

34. For a discussion, see the contributions in Born, Leigh, and Wills, *International Intelligence Cooperation*.

35. See Sir Malcolm Rifkind, "Report on the Intelligence Relating to the Murder of Fusilier Lee Rigby," HC 795 (London: Her Majesty's Stationery Office, November 2014), http://isc.independent.gov.uk/committee-reports/special-reports.

36. Ibid., 4, para 10.

37. Loch K. Johnson, "Accountability and America's Secret Foreign Policy: Keeping a Legislative Eye on the Central Intelligence Agency," *Foreign Policy Analysis* 1, no. 1 (2005): 99–120.

38. De Silva, *Patrick Finucane Review*, 1:32, para. 1.39.

39. See, for example, the excellent discussion by Eliza Manningham-Buller, *Securing Freedom* (London: Profile Books, 2012), in chap. 2, "Security," based on her 2011 Reith Lectures.

Conclusion: Toward Principled Spying

1. Philip Bobbitt, *Terror and Consent: The Wars for the Twenty-First Century* (New York: Alfred A. Knopf, 2008), 289.

2. Turner, *Secrecy and Democracy*, 178.

3. See Omand, *Securing the State*.

4. John Stuart Mill, *On Liberty* (1859; Oxford: Oxford University Press, 1998), chap. 1.

5. Brian Fung, "The House Just Voted to Wipe away Landmark Internet Privacy Protections," *Washington Post*, March 28, 2017, https://www.washingtonpost.com/news/the-switch/wp/2017/03/28/the-house-just-voted-to-wipe-out-the-fccs-landmark-internet-privacy-protections/?utm_term=.b77439687430&wpisrc=nl_headlines&wpmm=1.

6. "Google, Facebook Increase Their Grip on Digital Ad Market," eMarketer, March 14, 2017, https://www.emarketer.com/Article/Google-Facebook-Increase-Their-Grip-on-Digital-Ad-Market/1015417.

7. Director of National Intelligence, "Assessing Russian Activities and Intentions in Recent US Elections," ICA 2017-01D (Washington, DC: DNI, January 6, 2017).

8. See the discussion in chapter 4. Immanuel Kant, *Grounding for the Metaphysics of Morals*, 3rd ed., trans. James W. Ellington (Cambridge MA: Hackett Classics, 1993), 30.

9. Bingham, *Rule of Law*, 74.

10. An argument advanced by UK Supreme Court judge Lord Neuberger, Hong Kong Foreign Correspondents' Club, "The Third and Fourth Estates: Judges, Journalists and Open Justice," Hong Kong, August 26, 2014, https://www.supremecourt.uk/docs/speech-140826.pdf.

11. Or we might term the guardians "hidden gatekeepers" after the title of the 2012 Academy Award–nominated documentary film by Dror Moreh, *The Gatekeepers*, about the Israeli internal security agency, Shin Bet. In the film six former heads of Shin Bet discuss the successes and failures of Israeli internal security operations since the 1967 Six Day War.

12. See the 2016 report of the Global Commission on Internet Governance, "One Internet," available at https://www.ourinternet.org/report.

13. Adam Thierer, "Does 'Permissionless Innovation' Even Mean Anything?," remarks prepared for the Fifth Annual Conference on Governance of Emerging Technologies: Law, Policy, and Ethics, Arizona State University, Phoenix, May 18, 2017, and reprinted in The Technology Liberation Front, https://techliberation .com/2017/05/18/does-permissionless-innovation-even-mean-anything/.

14. Of note is that the UK intelligence agencies and law enforcement did not seek a backdoor provision on encryption in the major Investigatory Powers Act 2016.

SELECT BIBLIOGRAPHY

SELECTED BIBLIOGRAPHY

Aid, Matthew M. *The Secret Sentry: The Untold History of the National Security Agency*. New York: Bloomsbury, 2009.

Anderson, David. *A Question of Trust: Report of the Investigatory Powers Review*. London: Her Majesty's Stationery Office, June 2015.

———. *Report of the Bulk Powers Review*. CM 9326. London: Her Majesty's Stationery Office, August 2016.

Andrew, Christopher. *The Defence of the Realm: The Authorized History of MI5*. London: Allen Lane, 2009.

Andrew, Christopher, and Vasili Mitrokhin. *The Mitrokhin Archive: The KGB in Europe and the West*. London: Allen Lane, 1999.

Bartlett, Jamie. *The Dark Net: Inside the Digital Underworld*. London: Heinemann, 2014.

Bellaby, Ross W. *The Ethics of Intelligence: A New Framework*. Abingdon: Routledge, 2014.

Bethlehem, Daniel. "Self-Defense against an Imminent or Actual Armed Attack by Nonstate Actors." *American Journal of International Law* 106 (2012): 770–77.

Bingham, Tom. *The Rule of Law*. London: Allen Lane, 2010.

Bok, Sissela. *Secrets: On the Ethics of Concealment and Revelation*. New York: Vintage Books, 1989.

Born, Hans, and Loch K. Johnson. "Balancing Operational Efficiency and Democratic Legitimacy." In *Who's Watching the Spies? Establishing Intelligence Service Accountability*, edited by Hans Born, Loch K. Johnson, and Ian Leigh, 225–39. Washington, DC: Potomac Books, 2005.

Born, Hans, Ian Leigh, and Aidan Wills, eds. *International Intelligence Cooperation and Accountability*. Abingdon: Routledge, 2011.

———. *Making International Intelligence Cooperation Accountable*. Geneva: Centre for the Democratic Control of Armed Forces, 2015.

Buchanan, Ben. *The Cybersecurity Dilemma: Hacking, Trust, and Fear between Nations*. London: Hurst, 2017.

Budiansky, Stephen. *Code Warriors: NSA's Codebreakers and the Secret Intelligence War against the Soviet Union*. New York: Knopf, 2016.

Butler, Robin. *Review of Intelligence on Weapons of Mass Destruction: Report of a Committee of Privy Counsellors*. HC 898. London: Her Majesty's Stationery Office, July 2004.

Clarke, Richard A., Michael J. Morell, Geoffrey R. Stone, Cass R. Sunstein, and Peter Swire. *The NSA Report: Liberty and Security in a Changing World*. Princeton, NJ: Princeton University Press, 2014.

Cogan, Charles. "Hunters Not Gatherers: Intelligence in the Twenty-First Century." *Intelligence and National Security* 19, no. 2 (2004): 304–21.

Corera, Gordon. *Intercept: The Secret History of Computers and Spies*. London: Weidenfeld and Nicholson, 2015.

Corey, David D., and J. Daryl Charles. *The Just War Tradition: An Introduction*. Wilmington, DE: ISI Books, 2016.

Cory Collusion Inquiry. *Report: Patrick Finucane*. London: The Stationery Office, 2004. http://cain.ulst.ac.uk/issues/collusion/cory/cory03finucane.pdf.

Crumpton, Henry A. *The Art of Intelligence: Lessons from a Life in the CIA's Clandestine Service*. New York: Penguin Books, 2012.

Curry, John Court. *The Security Service, 1908–1945: The Official History*. Kew: Public Record Office, 1999.

de Silva, Sir Desmond. *The Report of the Patrick Finucane Review*. Vols. 1 and 2. HC 802-I/II. London: The Stationery Office, December 2012.

Donohue, Laura K. "Bulk Metadata Collection: Statutory and Constitutional Considerations." *Harvard Journal of Law and Public Policy* 37, no. 3 (2014): 757–900.

Dujmovic, Nicholas. "Hearts and Minds: The CIA as White Hats in the Cold War." *International Journal of Intelligence and Counterintelligence* 29, no. 1 (2016): 179–86.

European Commission for Democracy through Law. *Democratic Oversight of Security Services*. Strasbourg: Council of Europe, December 2015. http://www.venice.coe .int/webforms/documents/?pdf=CDL-AD(2015)010-e.

European Union Agency for Fundamental Rights. *Surveillance by Intelligence Services: Fundamental Rights Safeguards and Remedies in the European Union*. Vienna: Publications Office, 2015.

Falk, Richard A. "CIA Covert Action and International Law." *Society* 12, no. 3 (March/April 1975): 39–44.

Freeden, Michael. *Liberalism: A Very Short Introduction*. Oxford: Oxford University Press, 2015.

Funder, Anna. *Stasiland: Stories from behind the Berlin Wall*. London: Granta Books, 2003.

Garton Ash, Timothy. *The File: A Personal History*. London: HarperCollins, 1997.

Gill, Peter, and Mark Phythian. *Intelligence in an Insecure World*. 2nd ed. Cambridge: Polity Press, 2012.

Glennon, Michael J. "How International Rules Die." *Georgetown Law Journal* 93 (2005): 939–91.

Godfrey, E. Drexel, Jr. "Ethics and Intelligence." *Foreign Affairs* 56, no. 3 (1978): 624–42.

Greenwald, Glenn. *No Place to Hide: Edward Snowden, the NSA and the Surveillance State*. London: Hamish Hamilton, 2014.

Griffith, Samuel B. *Sun Tzu: The Art of War*. New York: Oxford University Press, 1971.

Guthrie, Charles, and Michael Quinlan. *Just War: The Just War Tradition: Ethics in Modern Warfare*. London: Bloomsbury, 2007.

Hampson, Fen Osler, and Eric Jardine. *Look Who's Watching: Surveillance, Treachery and Trust Online*. Ottawa: Centre for International Governance Innovation, 2016.

Harding, Luke. *The Snowden Files: The Inside Story of the World's Most Wanted Man*. London: Guardian Books / Faber and Faber, 2014.

Hare, R. M. *Moral Thinking: Its Levels, Method and Point*. Oxford: Oxford University Press, 1981.

Hayden, Michael V. *Playing to the Edge: American Intelligence in the Age of Terror*. New York: Penguin Press, 2016.

Hennessy, Peter., ed. *The New Protective State: Government, Intelligence and Terrorism*. London: Continuum, 2007.

Herman, Michael. "11 September: Legitimizing Intelligence?" *International Relations* 16, no. 2 (2002): 227–41.

———. "Ethics and Intelligence after September 2001." *Intelligence and National Security* 19, no. 2 (2004): 342–58.

Herodotus. *The Histories*. Translated by Robin Waterfield. Oxford: Oxford University Press, 1998.

Hinsley, F. H., E. E. Thomas, C. F. G. Ransom, and R. C. Knight. *British Intelligence in the Second World War*. Vol. 1, *Its Influence on Strategy and Operations*. London: Her Majesty's Stationery Office, 1979.

Howard, Michael. *British Intelligence in the Second World War*. Vol. 5, *Strategic Deception*. London: The Stationery Office, 1990.

Independent Surveillance Review. *A Democratic Licence to Operate*. London: Royal United Services Institute, 2015.

Ingram, Martin, and Greg Harkin. *Stakeknife: Britain's Secret Agents in Ireland*. Dublin: O'Brien Press, 2004.

Intelligence and Security Committee of Parliament. *Privacy and Security: A Modern and Transparent Legal Framework*. HC 1075. London: Her Majesty's Stationery Office, March 2015. https://rusi.org/sites/default/files/20150714_whr_2-15_a_democratic_licence_to_operate.pdf.

Jeffreys-Jones, Rhodri. *We Know All about You: The Story of Surveillance in Britain and America*. Oxford: Oxford University Press, 2017.

Johnson, Loch K. *National Security Intelligence*. Cambridge: Polity, 2012.

———. *Secret Agencies: US Intelligence in a Hostile World Order*. New Haven, CT: Yale University Press, 1996.

Kant, Immanuel. *Kant: Political Writings*. Edited by Hans Reiss. Translated by H. B. Nisbet. Cambridge: Cambridge University Press, 1970.

Kean, Thomas H., and Lee H. Hamilton. *9/11 Commission Report: Final Report of the National Commission on Terrorist Attacks upon the United States*. New York: W. W. Norton, 2004.

Lathrop, Charles E., ed. *The Literary Spy: The Ultimate Source for Quotations on Espionage and Intelligence*. New Haven, CT: Yale University Press, 2004.

Lewis, Paul, and Rob Evans. *Undercover: The True Story of Britain's Secret Police*. London: Guardian Books / Faber, 2014.

Lowenthal, Mark M. "Towards a Reasonable Standard for Analysis: How Right, How Often on Which Issues?" *Intelligence and National Security* 23, no. 3 (2008): 303–15.

McDonald, Jack. *Enemies Known and Unknown: Targeted Killings in America's Transnational Wars*. London: Hurst, 2017.

Mearsheimer, John J. *The Tragedy of Great Power Politics*. New York: W. W. Norton, 2001.

Melzer, Nils. Targeted Killing in International Law. Oxford: Oxford University Press, 2008.

Moyn, Samuel. *The Last Utopia: Human Rights in History*. Cambridge, MA: Belknap / Harvard University Press, 2010.

Omand, David. "Ethical Guidelines in Using Secret Intelligence for Public Security." *Cambridge Review of International Affairs* 19, no. 4 (2006): 613–28.

———. *Securing the State*. London: Hurst, 2010.

Omand, David, Jamie Bartlett, and Carl Miller. "Introducing Social Media Intelligence (SOCMINT)." *Intelligence and National Security* 27, no. 6 (2012): 801–23.

Omand, David, and Mark Phythian. "Ethics and Intelligence: A Debate." *International Journal of Intelligence and Counterintelligence* 26, no. 1 (2013): 38–63.

Panetta, Leon. *Worthy Fights: A Memoir of Leadership in War and Peace*. With Jim Newton. New York: Penguin Press, 2014.

Pekel, Kent. "Integrity, Ethics and the CIA." *Studies in Intelligence*, Spring 1998, 85–94. https://www.cia.gov/library/center-for-the-study-of-intelligence/kent-csi/vol41no5/html/v41i5a05p.htm.

Perina, Alexandra H. "Black Holes and Open Secrets: The Impact of Covert Action on International Law." *Columbia Journal of Transnational Law* 53, no. 3 (2015): 507–83.

Peritz, Aki, and Eric Rosenbach. *Find, Fix, Finish: Inside the Counterterrorism Campaigns That Killed Bin Laden and Devastated al-Qaeda*. New York: PublicAffairs, 2012.

Perry, David L. *Partly Cloudy: Ethics in War, Espionage, Covert Action, and Interrogation*. Lanham, MD: Scarecrow Press, 2009.

Quinlan, Michael. "Just Intelligence: Prolegomena to an Ethical Theory." *Intelligence and National Security* 22, no. 1 (2007): 1–13.

Reed, Charles, and David Ryall, eds. *The Price of Peace: Just War in the Twenty-First Century*. Cambridge: Cambridge University Press, 2007.

Retter, Lucia, Alexandra Hall, James Black, and Nathan Ryan. *The Moral Component of Cross-Domain Conflict*. Santa Monica, CA: Rand Corporation, 2016.

Rid, Thomas. *The Rise of the Machines: The Lost History of Cybernetics*. London: Scribe, 2016.

Rodriguez, Jose A., Jr. *Hard Measures: How Aggressive CIA Actions after 9/11 Saved American Lives*. With Bill Harlow. New York: Threshold Editions / Simon & Schuster, 2012.

Rosenau, James N. *Along the Domestic-Foreign Frontier: Exploring Governance in a Turbulent World*. Cambridge: Cambridge University Press, 1997.

Roubiczek, Paul. *Ethical Values in the Age of Science*. Cambridge: Cambridge University Press, 1969.

Saunders, Frances Stonor. *Who Paid the Piper? The CIA and the Cultural Cold War*. London: Granta Books, 1999.

Savage, Charlie. *Power Wars: Inside Obama's Post-9/11 Presidency*. New York: Little, Brown, 2015.

Schneier, Bruce. *Applied Cryptography: Protocols, Algorithms, and Source Code in C*. 2nd ed. New York: Wiley and Son, 1996.

Shane, Scott. *Objective Troy: A Terrorist, a President, and the Rise of the Drone*. New York: Tim Duggan Books, 2015.

Sisman, Adam. *John le Carré: The Biography*. London: Bloomsbury, 2015.

Snider, L. Britt. *The Agency and the Hill: CIA's Relationship with Congress, 1946–2004*. Washington, DC: Center for the Study of Intelligence, Central Intelligence Agency, 2008. https://www.cia.gov/library/center-for-the-study-of-intelligence /csi-publications/books-and-monographs/agency-and-the-hill/index.html.

Solis, Gary D. *The Law of Armed Conflict: International Humanitarian Law in War*. Cambridge: Cambridge University Press, 2010.

Strawser, Bradley Jay. "Moral Predators: The Duty to Employ Uninhabited Aerial Vehicles." *Journal of Military Ethics* 9, no. 4 (2010): 342–68.

Tenet, George. *At the Center of the Storm: My Years at the CIA*. With Bill Harlow. New York: HarperCollins, 2007.

Treverton, Gregory F. *Covert Action: The Limits of Intervention in the Postwar World*. New York: Basic Books, 1987.

Tuchman, Barbara. *The Zimmermann Telegram: America Enters the War, 1917–1918*. New York: Viking, 1958.

Turner, Stansfield. *Secrecy and Democracy: The CIA in Transition*. Boston: Houghton Mifflin, 1985.

United States Senate. *Final Report of the Select Committee to Study Governmental Operations with Respect to Intelligence Activities*. Washington, DC: Government Printing Office, 1976.

United States Senate Select Committee on Intelligence. *Committee Study of the Central Intelligence Agency's Detention and Interrogation Program*. Washington, DC: Government Printing Office, December 2014. http://fas.org/irp/congress/2014_rpt/ssci -rdi.pdf.

Walzer, Michael. *Arguing about War*. New Haven, CT: Yale University Press, 2004.

———. *Just and Unjust Wars: A Moral Argument with Historical Illustrations*. Harmondsworth: Penguin Books, 1980.

———. "On Fighting Terrorism Justly." *International Affairs* 21, no. 4 (2007): 480–84.

———. "The Triumph of Just War Theory (and the Dangers of Success)." *Social Research* 69, no. 4 (2002): 925–44.

Warner, Michael. "The Divine Skein: Sun Tzu on Intelligence." *Intelligence and National Security* 21, no. 4 (2006): 483–92.

———. *The Rise and Fall of Intelligence: An International Security History*. Washington, DC: Georgetown University Press, 2014.

Wolf, Markus. *Man without a Face: The Memoirs of a Spymaster*. With Anne McElvoy. London: Jonathan Cape, 1997.

INDEX

ABOUT THE AUTHORS

Sir David Omand, GCB, is a visiting professor in the Department of War Studies, King's College London, and a regular commentator and writer on intelligence matters. His previous appointments in UK government service include security and intelligence coordinator, permanent secretary of the UK Home Office, director of the Government Communications Headquarters (the United Kingdom's signals intelligence and cyber security agency), and deputy undersecretary of state in the Ministry of Defence. He served for seven years on the Joint Intelligence Committee.

Mark Phythian is professor of politics in the School of History, Politics, and International Relations at the University of Leicester. He is the author or editor of some dozen books on intelligence and security topics, including *Intelligence in an Insecure World* (with Peter Gill, second edition, Polity Press, 2012) and (as editor) *Understanding the Intelligence Cycle* (Routledge, 2013), as well as numerous journal articles and book chapters. He is coeditor of the leading intelligence journal *Intelligence and National Security* and a fellow of the UK Academy of Social Sciences.